] Inside Out [

GIDEON HAIGH

Writings on Cricket Culture

Aurum

First published in Great Britain
2009 by Aurum Press Ltd
7 Greenland Street
London NW1 0ND
www.aurumpress.co.uk

First published in Australia by Melbourne University Publishing Limited 2008

A catalogue record for this book is available from the British Library.

ISBN 978 1 84513 472 3

1 3 5 7 9 10 8 6 4 2
 2009 2011 2013 2012 2010

Text design by Alice Graphics
Typeset by Megan Ellis
Printed and bound in the UK by CPI Bookmarque, Croydon, CR0 4TD

In memory of Emyr Williams ('Em'), 1972–2008

Contents

3 Bradman Unlimited

4 Tactic, Technique and Technology

5 Reading the Game

Play for Today

Some people take cricket too seriously, others not quite seriously enough. In one of his essays, Montaigne noted that 'children at play are not playing about', and that 'their games should be seen as their most serious activity'. Since the rise of organised sport, and the prosperous industries that now cater for our leisure and relaxation, the same observation might apply where adults are concerned. And cricket, so far unrivalled in Australia as a national game, justifies more and better than the broad but shallow attention paid it.

Inside Out collects some writings I have grouped under the loose heading 'cricket culture', by which I mean those customs and dimensions that distinguish it from other games. Every sport defines itself in contradistinction to others, but these processes in cricket seem peculiarly sophisticated and evolved, being comingled with notions of class, race, nation, empire, past and future. Mind you, rather more of this book than most I have published is a response to my own experiences and affinities, cricket being a game that somehow inspires direct individual allegiance. It's hard to imagine anyone feeling about paintball or beach volleyball the way that many do of cricket, perhaps because it doesn't make itself accessible immediately to the browsing or channel-surfing sports consumer. You *learn* to love cricket, because, as rather too many girlfriends have made clear to me, it's not transparently obvious why you should.

It is not a bad time, in fact, to be contemplating those aspects of cricket that make it so, when there exists considerable confusion about what cricket actually *is*. Cricket's variants now range from five days to twelve overs, with one of these variants, Twenty20, being vastly more lucrative than the rest put together. This is certainly a dimension that cricket has to itself—golf doesn't have two-hole tournaments, nor tennis three-game matches—and it is frankly unsustainable. Rather than emerging organically, moreover, the Twenty20 variation of cricket has been calibrated by corporate interests, with the objective of making cricket less 'crickety'. George Bernard Shaw once said that while he liked neither cricket nor baseball, baseball had 'the considerable advantage of being shorter'; he would find it a great joke, I suspect, that cricket had been redesigned to his tastes.

The most thoroughgoing retrospective concerns the evolution of the Australian cap; the most recent ruction described is the interminable affair of Harbhajan Singh v Andrew Symonds. Nonetheless, this is a book in which players take mainly second place to the game—not a position familiar to them recently, but one that will do them no harm just once. The only personality discussed in detail is Sir Donald Bradman, being not so much a cricketer as a cultural phenomenon. The book's longest essay examines what might be ascertainable about the flesh and blood Bradman from his first four years in the limelight—a question on which biographers, dazzled by his accomplishments, have been strangely unenlightening.

The last section of *Inside Out* is devoted to writing and broadcasting, which has become a kind of career for me almost without my seeking to make it so. Cricket books have become like sixes in the Indian Premier League: a debauched currency. I describe here some of the rare meaningful ones, which if you're reading this may already be on your shelves, and if not would probably suit them. I owe a great debt of gratitude to the cricket critics and commentators described here, and it's a good feeling to partly discharge it.

I also owe thanks to those publishers and editors who commissioned works for *Inside Out*: Sambit Bal, Tim Blair, Peter Coster, Stephen Fay, Graem Sims, Susan Skelly, Rob Steen, John Stern, Tom Switzer and Sally Warhaft. Likewise, thanks are extended to Foong Ling Kong at Melbourne University Publishing, a splendid hand in an industry in which they do not abound, and her diligent offsider, Cinzia Cavallaro. *Inside Out* is dedicated to the memory of Emyr Williams, past president of South Yarra CC, clubman extraordinaire and friend to all, who was earlier this year drowned at Blairgowrie, aged just thirty-five—and another reason to be thankful for cricket, without which we would never have had the honour to call him friend.

Gideon Haigh
August 2008

1
Room at the Bottom

Confessions of a Cricket Tragic

I blame John Howard. After all, that's what he's there for. It was with Howard in mind that Mark Taylor divulged the Australian cricket team's pet name for their most fervent fans: 'tragics'. It has since attained an extraordinary popular currency. After all, there has seldom been much danger of the other neologisms of Australian cricketers catching on. Glenn McGrath's '@#$%^&!' didn't; likewise Shane Warne's '*&^%#^%$*@!!!' And, of course, there's nothing remotely tragic about liking cricket. As Richie Benaud is wont to remind fellow commentators, the sinking of the *Titanic* was 'tragic'; an unlucky lbw dismissal doesn't really cut it.

But I suppose I would say this, wouldn't I? Me, with a library of more than 3000 cricket books and periodicals. Me, who recommenced training for his club cricket season in April. Me, with a cat called Trumper. If not tragic, it is undeniably not your standard allocation of interests or energies. And while it's not completely uncommon to have a cricket bat in the house, I'm bound to say that not everyone has one in the kitchen, one in the living room, one in the bedroom and one in the outside lavatory.

How did this happen? It's easy enough to explain how I came to the game of cricket. What's not easy to understand is why the enthusiasm has failed to fade, and how, for me, the curiosity about and fun extracted have never been greater. Usually one grows up and out of youthful excitements, takes on adult responsibilities, and is diverted into procreation, renovation and superannuation. Somehow, at 41, I'm still unmarried, unsettled and unhurried about either. Rather, I'm thinking about whether my bat needs a new grip and if I'm squaring up in defence to left-arm quicks. It's the kind of addiction that should really be the subject of its own twelve-step programme—where it's impossible to look away from a television screen on which cricket is visible, where one can discern the lilt of cricket commentary from 100 metres, where one can't look at vehicle number plates and locker numbers without being reminded of one of Don Bradman's scores, and where all your PINs are variously associated with cricket statistics—circumstances that must be lived with, and can sometimes be turned to advantage.

Some years ago, for example, I de-cabbed at Sydney Airport. It was pre-dawn, long before my brain has normally achieved traction, but as I moved to the boot the cab's number registered with me as the number of runs scored by Walter Hammond during the 1928–29 Ashes series. I then watched this number dwindle in the distance as the taxi prematurely pulled away, with my luggage still in it.

'So you want us to get the guy on the radio and turn him around, right?' asked the disembodied cab company voice on the airport pay phone. 'I don't suppose you got the number did you?'

'905,' I said confidently. 'At 113.12.'

'Hang on,' the voice replied hurriedly. 'I got 905. But what's the last bit about?'

'Sorry,' I explained. 'I gave you Hammond's average from 1928–29 as well.'

When the driver returned, I dismissed his flustered apologies. It might have been a problem had his number been 904 or 906. But 905 was never going to be a challenge.

Some explanations for my perseverance in playing can be dismissed at once, such as that cricket somehow keeps you young. It does, bollocks. Nothing reminds you quite so reliably just how old you are, how your reflexes are deteriorating, how your reach is shrinking, how you're not as fit, fast, straight or strong as you used to be; how you were never any damn good anyway, so why on earth are you bothering? Want to feel young? Buy a sports car. Get Botox. Cricket? Have nothing to do with it.

Another myth is that cricket is relaxing. It's Friday. I'm thinking about tomorrow. Our game is evenly balanced. I'll have to bowl. Will I remember how? The not-out batsmen looked like they could play a bit. How am I going to get them out? The pitch is as flat as the world according to Thomas Friedman. How am I going to turn it on that? These days when I serve on the committee of my club, there's still more to factor in. Will there be petrol in the roller? Will there be beer in the fridge? Will there be change in the till? Or, given the way we usually organise ourselves, will the change be in the fridge, the till be full of petrol and the roller full of beer? And will there be dog shit in my run up like there was last week, damn it? Want to relax? Listen to whale noises. Chant 'Om'. Cricket? Forget it.

The fact is that there are an awful lot of people in on this lark—and if there's anything better than a joke, it's a joke shared. In a big country that's thinly populated, sport brings us together more reliably than any other institution. And no sport does it better than cricket: a long, leisurely game of broad appeal and abundant absurdities that has a level for every individual. I suspect it has also become my own form of luxury—of psychological affluence. Some people want the best car, the coolest clothes, the snazziest accessories. I can't drive, still wear twenty-year-old T-shirts and a $10 watch. My idea of frivolous and decadent indulgence is a day without care beyond cricket, and freely taking seriously something I know isn't.

Because, just quietly—and this is to go no further—cricket's really not *hugely* important. Say it soft, but it's *actually*, in lots of ways, kind of trivial. You can take cricket or leave it: I choose to take it, because I know I can leave it. The opposite—the idea of being a professional cricketer—holds no appeal whatsoever. To be paid for playing cricket, to depend on it for my livelihood, to need to succeed in order to prosper, to have my deeds in it define my identity now and in the future: why, the thought is simply horrifying—perhaps even tragic.

Qantas: The Australian Way, January 2008

Alive and Kicking

As the barbecue sizzled at a Thursday night training session of the Yarras a few weeks ago, the club secretary produced a bulging official envelope from Cricket Victoria. When no cheque fell out, we almost lost interest right away. But hang on: what was this? An expensive looking blue folder and CD-ROM announced themselves as the 'Club Development Program'—or, to those in the know, the CDP.

Hmmm. Cricket Victoria is a large and prosperous body; the Yarras the trifling, battling, permanently impecunious suburban club where I've played for thirteen years. In that time, their correspondence has been mostly in the form of ... well, forms. This folder struck a new and helpful note from the first: 'The CDP is structured around four (4) key areas'. Not four (5) key areas, or eight (4) key areas, you'll notice. Oh no, not in the new Club Support Network—also known as the CSN. We read on. 'I trust the enclosed kit lives up to your expectations,' the covering letter said—not a happy choice of words, really, given that our expectations were essentially zero (0).

Actually, the business of running a successful club under the CDP in the CSN was made to seem compellingly simple. First, you appointed a Club Liaison Officer (CLO). He/she/it then convened a Working Party (WP). The WP conducted a Club Audit (CA); the CA inspired the Ranking For Action (RFA); to the RFA was applied the

Strategy (S). Vision, implementation, Arbitrary capitalisation. Why hadn't we thought of this ourselves? That's why they're paid the big bucks, we concluded.

Yet in the same way as you can't quite help filling out one of those magazine surveys promising to reveal whether you're a sensitive new age guy or a responsible pet owner, the temptation to submit the Yarras to the CA was too great. For instance: 'Do we ensure that the cost or location of our activities makes them accessible to all people, particularly those people with disabilities?' Big tick there: inability to play cricket is no bar at the Yarras. 'Do we actively seek to make our club more appealing by promoting and enforcing policies that eliminate harassment and discrimination?' Sure: we seldom if ever harass opponents by the quality of our cricket, and our selections are usually completely indiscriminate.

The CDP didn't merely set questions, however; it teemed with suggestions. We could, for instance, 'organise a special family day such as at Christmas to cater for all family members with appropriate activities eg jumping castle'. Time to form an IFFTF (Inflatable Fun Fortification Task Force). We could 'incorporate a variety of culinary options at Club functions, offering food choices that reflect your Club's membership base' and 'set up a "Club Café" with outdoor tables and umbrellas serving for example cappuccino, hot chocolate, fruit cake, fruit juice and sports drinks'. After all, there's nothing like a bit of polenta and tapenade while you're putting your pads on. A personal favourite was:

> Educate players on the importance of doing the little things that make a volunteer feel welcome and valued such as making an effort to smile, say hello and say thank you. Praise volunteers when they are on the job acknowledging their achievements and efforts eg commenting that 'your scorebook is very neat'.

Probably preferable not to add: 'What a shame it does not add up.'

As time went on, it became clearer that the CDP wasn't telling us much we didn't know. 'Offer players of lesser ability an off-field responsibility within the Club to maintain their interest and involvement'? As one who has served variously as vice-president, chairman of selectors, newsletter editor, trivia night quizmaster, karaoke impresario and greyhound syndicate shareholder, I can attest that we hew to this policy pretty closely. As for encouraging us to cater for 'people from culturally and linguistically diverse (CLD) backgrounds, old adults and socially disadvantaged groups', the author was clearly a knowledge-based non-possessor (IDIOT).

For cricket clubs—in fact, most of the sporting clubs I've been involved with—do this without thinking. Players at the Yarras range from 13 to 63. Their children run around all over the place, our collapsible middle-order being as entertaining as any bouncy castle. Probably a third of our members were born overseas; another quarter come from the country. The last club wedding I went to was Greek Orthodox; the next is in Shepparton. Sure, opportunities to include ethnic dancing in karaoke night may have been overlooked. But in summertime, the mixing is disarmingly easy. As one group pored over the CDP round the bar, another were kicking a Sherrin back and forth out on the oval, with Pasquale, an Italian, inducting Zameel, an Indian, in the mysteries of the drop punt—as the light petered out, Zameel was taking pack marks and booting it as long as anyone.

I often puzzle, in fact, why sports clubs remain burdened by their reputation as bastions of the malign male monoculture of old Australia. In general, they are far more diverse and far less inward looking than political parties, the media and academe. And amazingly, people in them toil away without complaint, without reward, for the sake of others, and for years at a time, in an era when, it is drubbed into us almost daily, Australia is the most selfish and decadent society since the last days of Imperial Rome. But it would seem that even sports organising bodies have bought into the cliché: thus the managerial, multicultural mush of the CDP with its CSO and WP to look after the CLD in the CSN. Mind you, Cricket Victoria did get one thing right, advising near the conclusion: 'A blank template is provided for developing Action Plans to achieve desired outcomes.' No kidding. But we tend to find a way.

Monthly, April 2006

The Heat of the Moment

January 25 2003 was a day of Ethiopic heat in the city of Melbourne. Temperatures exceeded 45 degrees. There was the reek of smoke in the air from fires raging on the Mornington Peninsula. Birds fell dead from the sky. Cats and dogs cowered pitifully. And my captain, Macca, threw me the ball.

My club, the Yarras, were at Mentone. On arrival, the umpires had advised that the association was willing for games to be abandoned with the consent of opposing captains. Hey, we said, we're here to play. I'd actually been at the beach for the previous week and returned expressly for cricket. So Macca duly went out, lost the toss and returned to the dressing shed, his face a mixture of dread and amusement. 'We're bowling, boys,' he announced. For his wholly misplaced belief that 'tails never fails', he was pelted with caps, batting gloves, abdominal protectors, whatever came to hand.

And that is actually one of the last events I remember clearly. It wasn't a day of quips and quiddities. There were no memorable *mots* or whimsicalities. Communication through the 85-over grind was minimal: nods, grunts, glazed looks, occasional pats of encouragement, glances of stifled despair when something went wrong. I had always griped to Macca that, as the team's slow bowler, I only got a go when nobody else wanted to—and finally, he was content to agree, keeping me on for twenty consecutive overs either side of tea. 'Got another?' he'd say occasionally. 'I hate you,' I'd reply.

The heat was so airless, so pitiless, that you'd bowl two deliveries of an over, and stand at the end of your run-up straining desperately after sufficient breath for the third. I remember having a left-hander caught at slip, and being unable to articulate my satisfaction. When I put my arm in the air, nothing would come from my mouth: it was like an appeal by Humphrey B Bear. If you chased a ball, it felt as though you were inhaling the back draft of a jet engine; you'd spend the next five minutes staring ahead, zombie-like, as your body clawed back its equilibrium.

The last hour of the innings was the worst torture of all. We were smashed everywhere. Everyone was avoiding Macca's eye, afraid they'd be asked to bowl. The opposition had plenty left; we had nothing. All that kept us going, I suspect, was a sense of shared ridiculousness, that somehow this ordeal was, for God's sake, our preferred form of pleasure. Our opening bowler was called for overstepping a couple of times. Each time he looked quizzically at the umpire, glanced at the ground, shook his head and laughed. That'd be right. *Another* ball to bowl. *Today*. Why not just shoot me?

Afterwards, we lay around the dressing shed, in martyred silence but for the occasional curse and oath as someone dragged themselves to the shower. A couple of guys threw up. On the way back to our home ground, our all-rounder, who was driving the car, had to pull over hurriedly to deal with a sudden attack of cramps. That evening at the clubrooms, however, the mythologising began. We talked about other hot days we'd played on, agreed that this was the mother of them all, and agreed, too, that it was something to have survived. Ever since, the day has been a communal reference point. 'You might reckon it's hot today, but there was this other game ...' My girlfriend was upset, remonstrating: 'What's the point? Why do you do this to yourselves?' The answer only makes sense, perhaps, if you have: to see if you can.

CLUB CRICKET

Save Our Soil

No-one can be unaware how precious water has become in the life of this city. What may not be equally obvious is the scarcity of the resource of common sense at the City of Melbourne. Yesterday, Mayor John So announced that Melbourne's fountains will flow and bubble again, thanks to an alleviation of the crisis in our water supply. But there was no announcement last week when it emerged that the council would start ripping out pitches for turf cricket, ostensibly as a water conservation measure.

The hard-working volunteer officeholders of the 85-year-old Mercantile Cricket Association turned up to their regular pre-season pow-wow with the city's recreation services department manager Graham Porteous to be informed that three pitches would be ripped up immediately and replaced by hard wickets, and another three would be gone by next season: a third of the total. Cricket Victoria's CEO Tony Dodemaide asked if there had been any consultation with the clubs involved. '*This* is the consultation,' replied Porteous.

The cricket administrators were both disgruntled and unsurprised. The City of Melbourne's attitude to cricket, and community sport in general, is grudging. Cities are for culture, festivals and mayoral personality cults. Sport? That's for ... ugh ... suburbs and their teeming unwashed multitudes. For years, City of Melbourne has been winnowing away logistical support for cricket, stinting on services, passing on more costs. Twenty years ago, the picture-perfect common Fawkner Park used to be maintained by a half a dozen council staff, who knew every blade of grass. Now it is maintained by contractors, CityWide Service Solutions, whose fealty is mainly to the bottom line; its pitches are prepared by one man. Luckily, Alex Brown, formerly with the City of Melbourne, is a prince among curators. After him, who knows?

Cricketers soldiered uncomplainingly through last season, when outfields turned to dust and pitches crumbled. Water had dangled like a healthy carrot for the forthcoming season. Instead it is being wielded as a stick. Because Porteous's pious invocation of water fools nobody. The water saved by the proposed austerities is equivalent to the water from fifteen households. You could save more by not washing John So's car every day.

The push trades on the fact that most people, being strangers to cricket, find it hard to understand why digging up just that teeny bit in the middle of a ground changes everything. The amputation of just 0.5 per cent of your body doesn't sound much, does it? Well, it does if that 0.5 per cent is your nose.

Cricket is a game in harmony with its surroundings. It is, as explained by the greatest of its writers Sir Neville Cardus, a 'competition of bat and ball with the groundsman holding the ring'. When Tony Greig prods and probes the pitch before a Test is played, he is honouring a ritual known to all cricketers: that quasi-mystical pre-match musing on what angels or demons lurk beneath its surface. Cricket takes time. Games evolve. Light fluctuates. The ball ages. The players tire. And what's underfoot is constantly being altered by the interaction of environment and man. Hard wicket cricket, by contrast, is a batsman's game all day. Pretty simple. And, at least when you're accustomed to turf, pretty damn limited. Think of cricket on turf as chess, cricket on artificial surfaces as noughts and crosses.

The Mercantile is a terrific competition, exceptionally well run by a volunteer group who care about the community—so well run, in fact, that the number of participating clubs has doubled in the last fifteen years. These clubs are populated by the salt of the game: exactly the kind of people who, in an age of sloth and obesity, everything should be done to encourage.

I love playing on grounds like tree-fringed, bluestone-edged Herring Reserve, tucked into the Domain Road corner, neighbouring the Shrine of Remembrance, carrying the name of a distinguished Australian military commander and Victorian Chief Justice. Yet if the City of Melbourne gets its way, Herring is one of those grounds facing an appointment with a concrete mixer. It was grand to hear the mayor speak so solemnly yesterday of the importance of helping to 'preserve these important community assets'. But it was pretty galling to know that he was talking about fountains.

Herald Sun, September 2007

PONSFORD V PENGUINS

Big Scores, Little Scores

Few books, let alone cricket books, could present greater contrast than these: a brief life of the private and prolific Australian batsman Bill Ponsford, and a larkish memoir of amiable English ineptitude from the brief life of comic Harry Thompson.

In *Records Are Made to Be Broken*, John Leckey has researched Ponsford's life fastidiously, exhaustive even in his genealogical explorations, and accreting detail rather as his subject, the only batsman to exceed 400 twice in first-class cricket, gathered runs. The image is of a solemn, self-contained soul, who would hide behind newspapers while on public transport rather than attract attention, and whose career ended quietly when he took off his gear after a practice session at the MCG and said quietly: 'That it. I've had enough.'

Alas, this does not make for scintillating reading, and the detail lies rather dead on the page, while the book's thematic structure means, for instance, that Ponsford's entire post-cricket career as an employee of Melbourne Cricket Club is dealt with before he has retired. The idea that *Records Are Made to Be Broken*, too, is left unexplored, although the 1930s fascination with telephone number scores was a harbinger of our own era's statistical fetishism. Perhaps the most imaginative chapter concerns Ponsford's cast-iron concentration and poor vision (he was colour blind), where his relatively modest grade career is ingeniously explained by reference to the lack of sight screens. In general, though, Leckey plays rigidly straight: good counsel for batsmen, but limiting for writers and uninspiring for readers.

In Marcus Berkmann's delightful memoir of a lifetime's cricket failure, *Rain Men* (1995), Harry Thompson appeared as 'an all-rounder of little obvious ability but frightening determination'. The writing of *Penguins Stopped Play* attests to this: the creator of the BBC's *Have I Got News for You* and *Never Mind the Buzzcocks*, a non-smoker, died of inoperable lung cancer three days after signing off on the manuscript. So does its content, the story of how he and his motley band of village cricketers, Captain Scott's XI, set out to play a game on every continent.

Thompson's specialty is droll repartee, whether it's being reprieved by an umpire in Delhi ('I had never been hit on the leg and not given out lbw before. I felt quite light-headed'), routed by pace in Perth ('He had run through our upper order like a chicken through a bag of millet') or watched by whales in the Antarctic ('It was quite incredible. Never before had I seen this many spectators at an amateur cricket match'). The games are interspersed with acid observations of English cricket in 'the desperate years' ('Remember Waqar's strut and Wasim's swagger? Remember Curtly's icy stare? Now compare them to Mike Atherton's attempts to glare aggressively back down the wicket ... like a sullen schoolboy whose calculator has been stolen from his satchel by an unknown classmate') and some unorthodox travellers' tales. Devotees of Vanstonia will enjoy the story of Thompson's teammate whose application for an Australian visa was declined because he presented at the High Commission in a leather jacket.

Yet what really makes *Penguins Stopped Play* click is Thompson's utter dedication to doing everything properly. Memoirs of cricket incompetence can be formulaic and repetitive. The members of Scott's XI may be light-hearted, but their impresario is in deadly earnest. Likewise, while Bill Ponsford may have been the man with the inexhaustible appetite for runs and records, it was Thompson who was buried with a cricket bat in his hands.

A review of *Records Are Made to Be Broken: The Real Story of Bill Ponsford* by John Leckey (Australian Scholarly Publishing) and *Penguins Stopped Play: Eleven Village Cricketers Take on the World* by Harry Thompson (John Murray). Originally published in the *Bulletin*, October 2006.

2
The Australian Way

THE AUSTRALIAN TEST MATCH CAP

Baggy Green Dreaming

To solve the mystery of 'The Blue Carbuncle', Sherlock Holmes has a solitary clue: an old trilby hat recovered from an affray. He encourages Dr Watson to look upon it as an embodiment of the wearer. 'What can you gather from this battered old felt?' protests his friend. 'I can see nothing.' The great detective reassures him: 'On the contrary Watson, you can see everything. You fail, however, to reason from what you see.'

The old felt perched atop Steve Waugh's head on the cover of his autobiography *Out of My Comfort Zone* seems likewise pregnant with meanings. The baggy green cap is as battered and faded as the face is leathery and lined. With the wary eyes and weary stubble, it completes the mighty cricketer's image as a slouch hat completes an Anzac—or, perhaps, a bashed-in stetson completes Clint Eastwood in a spaghetti western. Nor is it there for effect. Waugh, the most taciturn of cricketers, becomes positively effusive where his cap is concerned: it is 'almost mythical', has 'almost a power to it', lends the Australian team 'an aura', makes players realise that 'it's always a special occasion when you represent your country', and positions them as heirs to 'the Anzac spirit' of 'fighting together and looking after your mates'.

Yet what you see with the baggy green—or, at least, what Steve Waugh sees—is not necessarily what you get. Many common

assumptions nurtured about the Australian cricket cap are errone-
ous. It is far from eternally unchanging, having been extensively
modified over time. It has not always been baggy or even green;
it does not feature the Australian coat of arms. Its presentation
to newly minted international players has only been ritualised in
the last decade; indeed, it used to be distributed quite liberally to
players on non–Test match occasions. Even the phrase 'baggy green
cap' is of relatively recent usage. What is paraded as fact, indeed,
is often arrant nonsense, and sometimes memory itself plays false.
When Waugh introduced the custom of the whole Australian team
taking the field together beneath their caps during the Gabba Test
of December 1996, he was lavishly praised by the venerable Neil
Harvey, a member of Sir Donald Bradman's Invincibles:

> It was a wonderful sight. I'm pleased to see Steve Waugh is
> an old traditionalist, although sometimes you wonder if he's
> the last of them. In my day the baggy green was much more
> publicised. The papers in England would make a fuss of it and
> any new player wearing it. I just hope they never change the
> shape of it. Baggy is exactly how it should stay.

Yet you will search in vain for a photograph of Harvey wearing
a baggy green cap on the cricket field, and his view that the brim
was distracting was embraced by a number of teammates: Richie
Benaud and Alan Davidson, for instance, usually played bare-
headed, while the most magnetic cricketer of his generation, Keith
Miller, was famous for a mane of hair that no cap ever tamed. 'In
my day they were just cricket caps and flung into our bags,' said the
last surviving pre-war Test cricket Bill Brown. 'They were just part
of the attire and not regarded much higher than your boots and
treated much the same. We didn't look after them.' In short, we are
moving in the realm of Hobsbawm's concept of 'invented tradition':
a set of practices that 'seek to inculcate certain values and norms of
behaviour by repetition, which automatically implies continuity with
the past'. And sorting fact from fancy where the baggy green cap is

concerned is what Holmes would classify a 'three-pipe problem', at least one pipe of which would need to involve an amalgamation of the surprisingly little known about the headgear's generation.

~

In the pioneering days of touring, agreement about uniform was chiefly a matter of aesthetics. Australia's first team abroad, the Aboriginal XI mustered by Charles Lawrence to tour England in 1868, took the field resplendent in a uniform of white trousers and maroon shirt with a cream sash. Dave Gregory's team a decade later kitted themselves in a blazer of white and azure blue stripes, topped with a similarly coloured brimless cap. A peaked cap had come into vogue by the time Billy Murdoch's team toured again in 1880, playing Australia's first Test in England, although the raiment had become magenta and black. When Australia won the Test that inaugurated the Ashes tradition at the Oval in August 1882, it bore the colours of the Sydney-based 96th Regiment: red, black and yellow.

If Australian cricket had a colour at all in the first quarter century of international competition, it was blue. Murdoch's 1884 Australian team wore a fetching navy blue jacket with gold piping. The team that toured two years later were blazered in blue, red and white: the colours of the Melbourne Cricket Club who were the tour's organisers and underwriters. In Australia, meanwhile, there was not even this level of cohesion. Teams played in the colours of the colonial association hosting the match, a reflection of the fact that the local body was also responsible for selecting, marshalling, accommodating and paying the team. In a way, too, this was a truer reflection of the nature of the teams themselves: uneasy coalitions sometimes riven by intercolonial jealousies. Captains after the re-spected Murdoch bore their burdens uneasily. Percy McDonnell survived a 'muffled mutiny' against his leadership in 1888 because of his overreliance on fellow New South Welshmen; Jack Blackham was weak, suggestible and felt to favour other Victorians; George

Giffen asserted South Australian primacy simply by bowling himself interminably.

Australia's 1893 tour of England was the first under the auspices of a national organising body, the fledgling Australasian Cricket Council, and the team's blue caps and blazer bore a shield-shaped patch enclosing the stars of the Southern Cross in a cross of St George, beneath which was the legend 'Advance Australia'—a sentiment at least forty years old and dating from the first goldfields experiments with ersatz Australian heraldry. It did not have the desired inspirational effect. 'It was impossible to keep some of them straight,' complained the team's manager, Victor Cohen. 'One of them was altogether useless because of his drinking propensities ... Some were in the habit of holding receptions in their rooms and would not go to bed until all hours.'

Green and gold's sudden primacy is mysterious. Initially it found no favour: at a meeting of the council in Adelaide in January 1895, the motion of John Portus from New South Wales that 'the Australian XI's colours be olive green with the Australian coat of arms worked into the cap and coat pocket' lapsed without a seconder; the team that toured England the following year did so again, at the players' instigation, in 'dark blue caps and gold binding'. A plausible hypothesis involves the council's dissolution. At one of the starveling body's last meetings, in January 1898, South Australian delegate Mostyn Evan suggested 'a very attractive arrangement of green and gold colours' for the forthcoming 1899 tour of England. By the time it came for the tour to be arranged, the council was in its death throes and the Melbourne Cricket Club moved in to provide financial support for the venture. But the club's shrewd and ambitious secretary, Major Ben Wardill, was sensitive to whispered criticisms that his institution was too rich and influential in the local game, and insufficiently representative of the country to perform the role it had taken on. It would have been with his approval that the team in London outfitted itself in blazers and caps of 'sage green and gold', and also hoisted a flag in those colours above their headquarters at Holborn's Inns of Court Hotel, as a means of reinforcing that the team represented Australia rather than the interests of a private club.

In hindsight, the circumstances of the 1899 tour were ideal for the establishment of a tradition. It was the first in England to span what became the traditional five Test matches; it provided also the first Australian victory over the course of an away series. Above all, the coincidence of the triumph with the country's last wranglings over the form of its Federation earned the cricketers favourable comparison with Australia's bickering politicians. Under circumstances of defeat or disunity, the green and gold might never have caught on; as it was, success against strong opposition with prestigious consequences on this and the next tour three years later lent the colours and cap a talismanic quality. Cricketers are superstitious: they stick to teams, routines and gear that they associate with success. Victor Trumper was the foremost batsman of his generation but a man of ingrained habits: the sight of a clergyman on game day, for instance, filled him with foreboding. So it was, noted a teammate, that he clung to the cap in which he first dazzled audiences:

> Trumper always wore an old Australian XI cap when batting. It was bottle green. He was wearing it when he made 135 not out at Lord's in 1899, and he continued wearing it until he retired from Test cricket in 1912. It was faded but he would not give it up for the many new ones he had. There was a row if one of the other humorists of the side took his cap and hid it.

If the colours were condoned as politically expedient, they deceived nobody. The state associations regathered their forces to originate the Australian Board of Control for International Cricket in May 1905, and within three years had not only usurped the Melbourne Cricket Club but also successfully hosted their first inbound tour by an English team. With this authority came control of uniform, and the new body ratified the suggestion of its antecedent body: at the Board meeting on 29 May 1908 the coat of arms with the 'Advance Australia' motif was confirmed, having just three weeks earlier become official on the grant of King Edward VII. It was resolved on the motion of Evan's South Australian colleague Harry Blinman that the colours for Australia be '"gum tree" green and gold'. Both gum tree and wattle had been embraced around the time of Federation for their symbolic power; the former celebrated in the startling bush watercolours that won Hans Heysen nine Wynne Prizes, the latter in the subtle still lifes and landscapes of Clara Southern.

There remained ambiguity about the entitlement to these colours: at the same meeting, Queenslander Joseph Allen asked that full caps be awarded to those who had played in a non-Test 'Australian XI' match in Brisbane a few months earlier. His plea was ignored, and Australian cricketers themselves would almost certainly have disapproved. A letter from Wardill to Frank Laver, manager of the 1909 Australian team, suggests an already marked degree of proprietorship about the XI's colours:

> A man I don't know called on me just now and wanted to know where he could get the Australian XI uniform and colours for a friend of his in Montevideo (South America). I told him he couldn't get them, he was not entitled to wear them. He has been in South America for 8 years, is not even a member of any Australasian club, and his friend thought he could wear them to show off his loyalty to Australia!!!

Another feature set in stone from the first where the cap is concerned was its bestowal on every team member, regardless of seniority or social status. Australian players had always looked askance at divisions between amateur and professional in English cricket, whereby 'gentlemen' and 'players' changed, travelled and were accommodated separately, and even emerged from different gates at the ground. They thought it savoured of class distinction, too, when amateurs affected the caps of their schools and clubs

(Percy Chapman wore the bright cap of the Quidnuncs CC when he led MCC in the Ashes of 1928–29, and Douglas Jardine the multicoloured cap of the Harlequins CC when he led MCC during the unruly Bodyline series four years later). That the Australian cap is worn alike by cricketers in their first Test and their hundredth is not a triviality.

But if this has not changed, much else has. For the 1909 Ashes tour, the cap was augmented by a telltale year beneath the coat of arms; the blazer pocket showed the kangaroo on the left and the emu on the right. For the 1921 Ashes tour, the previously tight-fitting cap became baggy, in deference to the fashion of the times, and the fauna was reversed, where it stayed. Somehow, too, it escaped the Board's attention that a new Commonwealth Coat of Arms had come into being on the grant of King George V on 19 September 1912, so the Australian cap continued to bear the symbol that had officially been retired. This hybrid antique character was reinforced in 1931–32 when the legend 'Advance Australia' was finally replaced by 'Australia'—the formation still in use.

Where the Australian uniform was concerned, the Board had periods of both great restrictiveness and uncharacteristic liberality. In September 1931, the Board agreed that blazers and caps 'only be given to those who had not previously represented Australia'. Yet if this prohibition was ever enforced, it cannot have been for long, as the evidence of memorabilia auctions is that players who played over extended periods usually acquired multiple caps and blazers, and sometimes swapped the ones they received for the better-fitting items of teammates.

When after the war Australia toured New Zealand for the first time there was disgruntlement among players about the arrangements. Ian Johnson recalled:

> Our thrill was great when we were measured for that first post-war trip. But our disappointment was greater when we received the blazers. For, although ours had been carefully described

as the Australian team, we were given on our pockets not the traditional coat of arms but a depressing looking monogram worked in an unattractive manner with the letters A.B.C. This presumably meant the Australian Board of Control but was at various times referred to as the Australian Broadcasting Commission or the Australian Bottle Company, as well as less complimentary things. That rankled, particularly with the older players who had represented Australia many times and were properly entitled to nothing less than the full Australian blazer, with the coat of arms as the emblem.

Yet on their 1948 trip to England, each Australian player received two caps, as well as an official blazer, sweater and tie. Bradman's caps from this his valedictory tour suggest that even he wasn't impervious to superstition: one, on loan to the Melbourne Cricket Club from the private collector who acquired it in June 2003, is extensively used; the other, in the State Library of South Australia, is in pristine collection. Interestingly, too, for Bradman a cap was chiefly functional. He ended his career having given all his baggy greens away, and his collected works contain no emotional tributes to what it signifies. It was a generation with which he had precious little in common that erected the baggy green idol, and fashioned it in its own image.

~

In the 1950s and 1960s, interest in the Australian cap was desultory. Richie Benaud kept none of his. As fast bowler Frank Misson told the authors of a recent history, *The Baggy Green*:

> It was referred to as the 'cap' and not the 'baggy green', and if anything there was more emphasis on the romance of the colours of green and gold. There was probably a feeling that the cap was a little unfashionable. Certainly ours was more flouncy. I think there was a thought it was a bit old-fashioned and the other countries looked a little more sartorial.

Perhaps it is not surprising that Australian cricket administrators took so long to intuit the value locked up in their national headgear. While the Board was loath to sully its own hands with matters commercial, it looked on without comment as players wore the cap freely in advertisements and in their books; nor did it concern itself when England's Derbyshire CCC in 1970 adopted a baggy green cap not unlike the Australian item.

By the early 1970s, in fact, the cap had acquired a low-level recognition worthy of remark—overseas at least. Englishman Alan Hewitt lauded the 'baggy green Australian caps' that 'appear to underline the formidable nature of those broad and tall young cricketers, who offer relentless challenge to English cricket'; England's captain Ray Illingworth admired Australia's 'baggy green caps'. 'Under their green caps, their forces have been harder to repel than the Spanish armada,' stated the Australian cricket writer Ray Robinson in his canonical text *On Top Down Under*; journalist Ian Brayshaw entitled his eulogy for Australian teams of the 1970s *Warriors in Baggy Green Caps*. Even Kerry Packer deferred to it, having the Australians who appeared in his breakaway World Series Cricket troupe between 1977 and 1979 play in tight-fitting yellow caps. When his general manager suggested the use of green headgear, Packer snapped: 'You've got to earn those, son.' Australians began to play one-day international cricket beneath a gold cap out of a similar sensitivity.

Yet in a period of cricket upheaval, the Australian cap more often seemed to embody cricket traditions under threat—from the enticements of commercialisation, the demands of television and the deterioration of on-field behaviour to private incursions like Packer's and political perplexities like the excommunication of South Africa. In *The Baggy Green*, the Australian fast bowler Len Pascoe recalls finding an unmarked cap in the Australian dressing room at the end of a day's play at Lord's in 1977: none of his teammates ever claimed it. In fact, the Board itself was in one of its none-too-fussy stages about the cap's distribution. In the 1980s it was handed out to players picked for Australia B teams, for the Prime Minister's XI and even Australian Under-19s. 'I'm not sure why we were given the real thing, but I couldn't believe I had that almost mythical possession in my hands,' noted one player. His name: Steve Waugh.

If any individual is responsible for the cap's latter-day iconic status—and twenty years ago its figurative significance would hardly have been worth noting in a book of this kind—it is Waugh. Quite why is almost worthy of psychoanalytical scrutiny, although at one level it is probably as simple as Trumper's attachment to *his* cap: he made runs and won games wearing it. Like Trumper, Waugh was a disarmingly superstitious cricketer, who never played without his lucky red rag and regarded ladybirds as a good omen; the cap, likewise, became part of his psychological armour. As he gradually made a public fetish of his growing millinery obsession, through the media and his successful series of tour diaries, he became Australian cricket's glass of fashion and mould of form. After Australia's victory in the Frank Worrell Trophy in May 1995, for example, Waugh noted the conspicuousness of the cap in the dressing-room celebrations:

> Lang [Justin Langer] retained that Australian flag draped over his shoulders all night while Heals [Ian Healy], Slats [Michael Slater], Lang and I kept the baggy green on until we were told the festivities were over … When the party finally ended and we all staggered off to our rooms, Heals walked over and gave me a nudge. 'Tugga,' he said quietly. 'I want to give you some advice.'
>
> 'And what's that?' I said.
>
> 'I reckon it'd be a good idea to take your spikes off before you go to bed.'

West Australian Langer, known as 'Mini-Tugga' in the Australian team for his almost slavish devotion to Waugh, featured in a similar anecdote following Australia's retention of the Ashes two years later:

They said it couldn't be done. Well, they didn't count on the love affair Lang has had with his cherished baggy green cap. To everyone's astonishment, some four days after the Southern Comfort had done the talking in our victorious dressing room celebrations at Trent Bridge, Lang is still proudly sporting his cap, a fact which wins him a bet neither Slats nor I could fulfil. But at least we didn't have an odour any skunk would have been proud of, or a permanent red ring around our melons from the elastic band inside the rim of the cap. This was another morale boosting effort from Lang, who always does these little things that help bond a side together.

Respect for the past became a motif of Waugh's captaincy when he assumed the role in February 1999. In Hugh de Selincourt's classic *The Cricket Match*, the Tillingfold secretary rejoices in his team's sky-blue caps: 'If we all wears 'em, lord bless my soul, it'll fair put the wind up those Raveley chaps. We'll have them beat before the coin's tossed.' Waugh regarded the baggy green in similar light, and insisted on all his players wearing it in the first session of a Test. He inaugurated the custom of Test debutants being presented with their caps by a distinguished ex-player; he introduced a system under which each player was allocated a Test match number representing the order in which they had achieved their honours; he commissioned replicas of the turn-of-the-century Australian cap to be worn in the Sydney Test of January 2000; he flaunted the cap in public, even wearing it at Wimbledon, and celebrated teammates who proved their allegiance to be more than skin deep, like Colin Miller, who had the image of a baggy green tattooed on his backside. Above all, he led the team on a pilgrimage to Gallipoli in May 2001 en route to England, inspired by a conversation with Lt Gen Peter Cosgrove in which they 'compared cricket and the army, especially things that are important in both endeavours—such as camaraderie, discipline, commitment and the importance of a plan'. On the visit explicit connections were drawn between representing Australia in war and in sport; the slouch-hatted cricketers even attempted to re-enact the famous cricket game played on Shell Green to cover the Anzac evacuation on 17 December 1915. There were conjectures that Waugh was trying to shore his team up from recent criticism of its on-field behaviour, and the views solicited from the players afterwards suggest fairly superficial and self-conscious experiences. Some were bemused, like Matthew Hayden ('Very confusing') and Adam Gilchrist ('Very emotional but not sure why'); some perceived straightforward confirmation of their own good fortune, like Andrew Symonds ('How lucky are we?'), Damien Martyn ('a wake-up call') and Ian Harvey ('Started to think about my own life, my complaining ... we've got it easy'); Steve Waugh's twin brother Mark even tried to extract a sporting lesson ('We underestimated the Turks ... Plan to know your opposition and what they do'). The captain himself, however, felt it had 'a profound effect on most of the squad', and Cosgrove himself probably reflected a fair proportion of public opinion when he paid the cricketers cheerful homage: 'They're our sporting Anzacs. We want that cricket team to embody all those marvellous Australian characteristics we prize; you know, fair play, good humour, toughness, success. They represent all Aussies, just as the Anzacs who fought in those trenches represented all Australians.'

In his endeavours, too, Waugh, a sportsman who knew the value of his reputation to the last decimal point, had conterminous objectives with his administrators: the baggy green was a brand name ripe for exploitation, precisely because it had been so relatively little exploited before. The Board had always received legal advice that the Australian Trade Marks Office would not consent to trademark protection for an item involving a coat of arms. But various annoyances—including an advertisement by the brewer Coopers Brewing Company in which baggy green caps were transfigured into the lids on stubbies—encouraged a direct approach to devoutly cricket-loving Prime Minister John Howard from chairman Denis Rogers. Thus did the baggy green become an asset beyond value in the Board balance sheet, advertised by the

launch of the official Australian cricket website, www.baggygreen
.com.au run by Channel Nine, and tapped by licensed merchandise,
like the *History of the Baggy Green*, the 'consummate Australian
cricket collectable, taking you through an authoritive [*sic*] journey
exploring the history, tradition and pride of the coveted baggy
green' and featuring 'an actual green flannel swatch as used ... in
the crafting of the baggy green'.

So while all manner of reasons can be advanced for the baggy
green exhibitionism of the nineties and noughties—a hankering for
continuity in a period of change, the recrudescence of Australian
conservatism, the desire for values transcending the shallow mate-
rialism of modern sport—one factor shouldn't be overlooked: there
was nobody it did not suit. Everyone could share in the pride, for
example, when Michael Clarke, two runs from a century in his
maiden Test innings in October 2004, sent for his baggy and went
to his milestone with moistened eyes: players building private esprit
de corps and public reputations; administrators striving to generate
brand value and to control intellectual property; broadcasters
trying to engender viewer loyalty and extend their reach to new
technologies; sponsors anxious to identify with a premium product;
politicians happy to partake of a popular cause; collectors and
auction houses, who saw the value of caps rise sharply; ground
authorities wanting symbols to enrich the visiting experience, like
the MCG, where the National Sports Museum in March 2008
features a dimly lit and atmospheric 'Baggy Green Room'; and fans
seeking symbolic embodiment of their allegiance.

The attachment of that last group, however, involves some
unexamined assumptions. It is commonly repeated—in the spirit of
the foregoing comment of Peter Cosgrove—that the baggy green
is essentially held in trust for the public of whom the Australian
team are representative. Waugh did not feel that way: 'The players
"own" the Australian team traditions and to be able to partake
of these rituals and traditions has meant you have been awarded
the highest honour in Australian cricket—you have been selected

to play for your country.' In other words, it was the current players who defined the baggy green rather than the other way around, and in 'owning' the baggy green they could by implication define right and wrong behaviour—as, for instance, did Adam Gilchrist when the methods of former Australian coach John Buchanan came in for criticism in December 2007:

> I guess one of the traits that we have a lot of pride in, in wearing the baggy green, is that we show a lot of respect. It seems some guys in retirement have lost that ... [The Australian team] is an elite club and we've always felt a major characteristic of being in that club is to show respect.

In an allegedly egalitarian country, this was a strangely inegalitarian remark: an assertion of caste and status, a claim to be outside or beyond everyday modes of behaviour. When players were tempted by the hearty cash incentives of the Indian Premier League, Cricket Australia's public affairs manager Peter Young stated buoyantly: 'The status of the baggy green is more powerful than cash for any red-blooded Australian and cricketers will tell you that themselves.' The inference of remarks by Andrew Symonds, however, was that loyalty had its price:

> For me, there's no question the baggy green cap is still the jewel in the crown of Australian cricket. But the way things are heading, loyalty is going to become a major issue, particularly when you can make more money in six or eight weeks than you can in a season.

And as Sherlock Holmes noted in 'Silver Blaze': 'One true inference invariably suggests others.'

Symbols of Australia, 2008

7

THE AUSTRALIAN TEST MATCH CAP

The Peak of the Cap?

When somebody at an auction bought the baggy green in which Clarrie Grimmett played the Bodyline series for $1200 twenty years ago, it probably seemed a lot of money. 'You spent what?' you can hear his wife saying. 'On a cap?' Pleas that it was an 'investment' would hardly have placated her—why, the damn thing wasn't even fashionable.

Twenty years later, one can only dip one's own metaphotical lid. The 121 caps sold at auction since have fetched an average $17 254, and selling that Grimmett green would knock a fair dint in any family's school fees. Particular windfalls have awaited custodians of Bradman baggies: five have fetched an average $160 000.

In Bowral last Friday night, the Bradman Museum hosted a function to celebrate that capital appreciation, and also to ponder its meanings. An audience of 200 heard Mark Taylor speak in honour of an excellent new book, *The Baggy Green*, a joint project of memorabilia entrepreneur Michael Fahey and veteran cricket writer Mike Coward, and a fascinating exhibition grouping twenty-eight caps, no two of which are alike. For a symbol so storied, the Australian cap has been subject to relatively little historical inquiry; this book and exhibition fill the gap both snugly and appealingly.

Taylor, who is shaping steadily and surely as a future chairman of Cricket Australia, introduced himself cheerfully as a 'cap tragic', sharing some samples from his collection of 100, including the distinctive headgear of the Lake Albert CC from Wagga Wagga and of the Riverina Secondary Schools Sports Association, to illustrate his point that a cap is a repository of memories, of games and places and people. He is well placed to testify, Fahey and Coward speculating that he is one of only two 100-Test veterans to have played their whole career in the one cap—Justin Langer, to whom the cap was as his blanket to Linus, is the other.

Two other Australian captains in Brian Booth and Ian Craig, and former Test men Gordon Rorke, Grahame Thomas and Greg Matthews, chimed in with their own reflections. Having consulted his diary of the journey, Booth was able to report that he was presented with his cap in the Launceston hotel room of Australian team manager Sydney Webb QC on 14 March 1961. 'It's a bit hard to remember back that far,' he commented. 'I did well to remember to come along tonight.'

In interviewing forty-five past and present Australian players, however, Coward has refreshed the memories of others. Ian Chappell, for instance, divulges the origin of his habit of removing his cap while on the way back to the pavilion: the experience of having his headgear snatched at Wanderers in February 1970 as he ascended the steps. A couple of years ago, he adds, he met the cap's current Zimbabwean owner. 'You're not the bastard who took it off my head?' Chappell asked. 'No,' came the reply. 'But I might have bought it from the bloke who did!' At current exchange rates, it is probably worth 500 billion Zimbabwean dollars.

The exhibition, meanwhile, is comfortably the most complete of its kind, gathering caps as antique as Victor Trumper's, as recent as Adam Gilchrist's and as ugly as Tony Dodemaide's from the Bicentennial Test twenty years ago—a white cap ribboned in green that looks better suited to a Dairy Queen dispensary. The exhibition, brainchild of the industrious cricket collector and publisher Ron Cardwell, gives the lie to the idea of the cap's precise historical continuity, while actually making it a richer historical artefact.

This is overdue. In his speech, Fahey described the baggy green, rather artfully, as 'an icon and a sacred cow'. For despite the fashion for lachrymose expressions of loyalty to it, the cap's past is a refurbished one, and *The Baggy Green* faithfully reports the evolution not just of the symbol but of the reverence inhering in it—to the extent where, under Steve Waugh, the cap became like the Round Table of Australian cricket's Camelot.

We learn not only of the rituals established by recent Australian XIs—the numbers, the tattoos, the corroborees—but those *not* indulged in by their forebears. 'In my day, they were just caps and flung into our bags,' Bill Brown muses; like his fellow Invincibles Sir Donald Bradman and Arthur Morris, he gave all his away. Neither Richie Benaud nor Ian Chappell owns a cap between them. 'I don't ever remember having one discussion about the cap during my playing days,' Chappell insists. His contemporary John Inverarity, in fact, recalls an apathy about the cap that occasionally shaded into hostility. When he donned a baggy for the traditional Duchess of Norfolk's XI game at Arundel, he found he was the only player wearing it. 'I felt a little self-conscious,' he recalls, 'but felt I wasn't in a position to share that thought for it was a little too earnest or conscientious.'

It's not as though the players' elders taught them much differently either. Ken Eastwood recounts how before his Test debut in February 1971 he was asked to try on caps by Australian Cricket Board secretary Alan Barnes. The first one didn't fit; the second did. He was allowed to keep both, thus obtaining the unique record of one Test for two caps. Similarly, veteran administrator Bob Merriman recalls Barnes scattering caps among the team on its way to tour India almost thirty years ago 'as though he was delivering newspapers from a moving vehicle'.

These brisk and practical reflections are seasoned with some regrets—Doug Walters laments not having worn his more often—and some surprising differences of opinion. Incongruously, Steve Waugh comes in for as much blame as praise, especially his consecration of a cap in what, had it been a fashion accessory, would have been described as 'distressed felt'. Waugh's former captain Geoff Lawson says it was 'disrespectful not respectful' for Waugh to wear his cap until it was so battered, and his erstwhile coach Bob Simpson that the cap should always 'be in pristine condition'. Keith Stackpole expresses bafflement: 'I can't understand why they mean that much when they don't bat in the things.'

Deliciously, the players are now having reflected back to them their own public avowals of unswerving allegiance. When the Australians wore a sponsor's blue practice caps into the field against a Jamaican Select XI last month in the pipe-opener to their Caribbean tour, it must have been one of the few occasions in sports marketing where a corporation has been embarrassed at their logo's visibility. In a typically trenchant column in the *Age*, Greg Baum saw CUB as muscling in where corporates should fear to tread: 'Plainly, they [the Australian team] were playing not for us, but for yet another franchise. This was a breathtaking contempt, not just morally, because of the campaign against binge-drinking, and not just aesthetically, because it made the Australian team look like a pack of Sunday afternoon pub players.' Tabloid headlines reverberated; talkback radio hummed for days. There might not have been the same fuss had the players turned up in identical rainbow tams.

Even by the eccentric standards of Australian cricket controversies, this was a most peculiar incident. Team protests that they were simply acting out of solidarity with Brad Haddin, not yet capped at Test level, cut no ice: you tamper at your peril even with the totems you help create. Yet nobody seemed much bothered by the publication in April of an Australian Cricket Association survey revealing that almost half of Australia's contracted players would consider retiring prematurely from international cricket in order to maximise their IPL earnings potential. No wonder players are confused if the substance of change no longer bothers Australians so much as its symbols.

Perhaps, then, we are at a historic hinge point. Hitherto, there has been a synergy between the outpourings of the baggy green cult and the rise of the players as commercial commodities. But is the time coming when the cap will be a brand in competition with the players' *own* brands, restricting their commercial freedom and scrambling their individual messages? A survey last week by polling company Sweeney Research reported that six of the ten most 'marketable' Australian sportsmen were cricketers: Ricky Ponting (1), Adam Gilchrist (2), Brett Lee (5), Glenn McGrath (6), Steve Waugh (9) and Andrew Symonds (10). How readily does a mainly backward-looking symbol of collective purpose reconcile with the essentially forward-looking promotion of stand-alone stars? That the baggy green exists outside fashion doesn't render it impervious to change.

Cricinfo, June 2008

8

AUSTRALIANS AND TEAMWORK

Life during Waugh Time

International sport is surely a wonderful vehicle for mutual misunderstanding. After seven consecutive Ashes series defeats, the English cricket community is still striving to decrypt the formula for Australian success, but without noticeable headway.

Such anxiety is understandable. Nowadays you have to be at least twenty years old to have a coherent memory of England in the act of actually winning the Ashes, and that counts in both countries. A generation is growing up that sees Australia as the natural overlord and England as the inevitable supplicant: it is like colonialism in reverse.

Yet in common with previous orgies of English masochism, this one seems off the track. Perhaps as an outcome of prolonged exposure to Clive James and Germaine Greer, the English harbour many quaint notions about Australians, not least the one about the AIS Cricket Academy being the fulcrum of its current Ashes leverage.

The English view of the average Australian player is this. He is suckled by dingoes, sent to the academy where Rod Marsh stuffs him with cricket lore like a Strasbourg goose, then sent into battle with a baggy green and the *Observer's Book of Pommie Bastards*. This perception—and it is worth saying this now, as England seek to build their own hothouse for the cultivation of cricketers—not only sells Steve Waugh's side short but is also based on lousy logic.

National teams are not a shop window on a country's cricket. One need only look at the West Indies, who perceived their long dominance of Test cricket as correlative to the strength of their domestic game. This was never so, and it is a lesson the region has learned to its cost. What national teams tell us about the country they represent is more limited. Rather like the light that one perceives from distant stars, they reflect a country's ability to discover and nurture talent long before those individual players reach the top level. Adam Gilchrist, Damien Martyn, Ricky Ponting and Glenn McGrath are fruits of the academy as it was almost ten years ago. It does not necessarily follow that because Australia is strong at international level today that the junior base of the cricket pyramid is robust: we will know that in a decade.

None of which means that an English version of the academy is altogether mistaken. It may help, but only up to a point, Lord McLaurin. The members of this Australian side have been reared not in some exotic cricket battery farm but in their own dressing room. The secret of this Australian side—and it is no real secret given that Steve Waugh discusses it cheerfully—is its robust and harmonious culture. It is a team that has played a great deal of cricket together, that has spent a lot of time in its own company, and that enjoys being itself.

Remember when you were a kid, looking up to and wanting to join the toughest gang in town? This Australian team is that gang. It has its own codes, creeds and customs. It assimilates newcomers, largely because they wish to be assimilated. And it speaks with one voice, that of its captain. As Stuart MacGill recently put it, the prime directive of this Australian XI is: 'When in Rome, do as Steve Waugh.'

Waugh, meanwhile, is also like the peasant who accompanied caesars on their triumphal processions through the streets of Rome whispering: 'Remember, you are dust.' During the Test in Hamilton last year, Waugh donned the cap he had worn during his first series against New Zealand, when Australia was soundly beaten: a warning against complacency. Likewise before the Nottingham Test, he gave a brief but heartfelt address about what it was like to lose an Ashes series, something only he can recall.

It is almost—but not quite—a personality cult. Not quite because the loyalty of Waugh's players reflects his loyalty to them. Not so long ago, the Australians' psychologist Sandy Gordon asked team members to complete a questionnaire that included identifying scenarios they found 'particularly mentally demanding'. Waugh replied: 'Selection meetings—having to leave out players.' There can scarcely have been a more difficult moment for Waugh on this tour than excluding his ardent disciple Justin Langer from the First Test.

Waugh's strength as a captain—which he has passed onto his team—is that he has a gimlet eye for others' weaknesses. He reads not only the game, but also individuals. At Nottingham four years ago, for instance, he noted Adam Hollioake's failure to wear an England cap in what was his debut Test. Didn't it mean anything to Hollioake to be playing for his country? Later he saw Andy Caddick and Dean Headley being interviewed on the boundary while Mike Atherton and Mark Butcher were going out to open. Why, he wondered, hadn't they been in their team's dressing room to wish their comrades luck?

These appear trifles, and it is not even as though Waugh was impugning Hollioake's patriotism or Caddick and Headley's team spirit. It is merely that both he and his team draw strength from seeing others do things they wouldn't. The critics who devoted so much time before Nottingham to studying the *Art of War* should instead have been considering this Art of Waugh.

The problem for England in trying to replicate the Australian formulae is twofold. Firstly, it came with success, rather prefiguring it. Secondly, it hinges on a kind of naive nationalism built on simple symbolism: baggy green cap, Bradman legend, Gallipoli sacrifice et al. The days when English birth conferred 'first prize in the lottery of life' now seem long ago. It also means that even if Steve Waugh's calf injury should fail to mend in time for the Fourth Test at Headingley, the gap he leaves may not be so significant. He will be there in spirit, and a powerful spirit it is.

Guardian, August 2001

9

CRICKET AND POLITICS

Mix Well

Among cricket's hoariest chestnuts, only 'catches win matches' can rank ahead of 'sport and politics should not mix'. Of course, they always have and always will—and that's not completely undesirable.

Arguably, cricket and politics began mixing the moment that teams began taking the field bearing the names of countries. When 'Australia' met 'England' in the first Test matches, nobody saw it as merely a game involving two XIs: they were embodiments, epitomes, the pick of their generations, and certainly in Australia a measure of national prowess and progress. The game was enriched by that understanding, and mattered more for it; had it not been so, cricket would hardly have taken root.

Cricket also became a force for fostering imperial unity. Prime Minister John Curtin is now best known for his 'look to America', but when he was made a Freeman of the City of London on May 10 1944, he specifically positioned Lord's at the heart of what Australians were fighting for:

> The stock from which Australia has come gives to it its fibre, its physical stamina, the endurance of its people in adversity, and that unconquerable spirit which refuses to acknowledge defeat. You have had some evidence of that at Lord's now and

again. Lord's is to Australia what it is to this country ... We are defending the City of London and those 22 yards of turf ... so that the Motherland and Australia can decide whether the six-ball over is better than the eight-ball over.

With other countries, whose tie with England was more tangled, the blessings were more leavened. Having been shaped by the contours of empire, global cricket remains heir to the tensions of post-colonialism. Precisely because sport is meant to be a competition of equals can inequalities, inconsistencies and perceptions of bias sometimes matter more than in the normal run of events; precisely because it offers prompt and explicit resolutions of superiority does it offer satisfactions disproportionate to their real significance.

Sporting relations are often an index of the state of political play. When countries wished to register their disapproval of South Africa's system of apartheid, it was by isolating them from international competition. 'Just because the Union is so good at sport, such isolation would shake its assurance very severely,' wrote the dissident cleric Trevor Huddleston. 'It might even make the English-speaking South African awake to the fact that you can't play with a straight bat if you have no opponents.' When America and China sought to narrow the gulf between them in the 1970s, by contrast, the first frontier forded was sport, in the period of so-called 'ping-pong diplomacy'. Interestingly, the business of sport is now exerting influence on its politics: the right to stage Euro 2008 turned traditional antagonists like Greece and Turkey and Bosnia and Croatia into commercial partners.

It does not always work. The Koreas are no closer for having marched together at the Olympics. But cricket has done much to normalise relations between India and Pakistan. When these arch cultural and religious rivals and nuclear neighbours take the field today, no-one mistakes their rivalry for a walk in the park. Pride won and offence given reverberate beyond the field of play. The symbolic import was huge when India's Prime Minister Atal Bihari

Vajpayee agreed to his country touring Pakistan in February 2004, two days before talks in Islamabad formalised the restoration of diplomatic ties. To paraphrase Winston Churchill, better four-four than war-war.

No-one is ever happy when the politics of cricket disrupt the normal round of fixtures and contractual arrangements, as last year when the Australian government interdicted to prevent Ricky Ponting's team from visiting Zimbabwe. But given the benefits Cricket Australia derives from the prestige of choosing a team to represent the country in sport, it was a bit rich to protest that the organisation was merely in the business of arranging cricket matches. If you revel in the honour, you can't abdicate the accompanying responsibility. In some respects, the episode suggested that a bit of politics in cricket occasionally does no harm: it prevents cricket sticking its head in the sand and pretending the rest of the world doesn't exist.

Australian Cricket Diary 2008

Life—But Not as We Know It

When it was mooted that an Australian team be selected from the soldiers and airmen in England to play a series of Victory Tests in 1945, some doubted they would have the big names needed for such a contest. Sir Pelham Warner knew his Australians better than that. 'They may not have many well-known names, but all Australians are natural cricketers,' he said. 'I could pick a good eleven on Bondi Beach.'

Australians would like to imagine that such a natural affinity still applies. But does it? In the summer of 2005–06, Cricket Australia's annual census noted a 13.6 per cent growth in participation numbers in the local game: a stirring of interest associated with the stimulus of losing the Ashes for the first time in fifteen years. Yet this followed several years of incremental growth at best, and population increase slowed to 3 per cent in the next survey. The Australian sports fan has never been so omnivorous. For a century and more, Australian cricket has mostly had summer to itself. But in 2006–07, soccer's new A-League drew hundreds of thousands of patrons, while next year will be overshadowed by Euro 2008 and the Olympics in Beijing. The world confronted by Cricket Australia's chief executive James Sutherland is very different from that of the Bradmans and Chappells of yesteryear—it's life, Jim, but not as we know it.

Around 560 000 Australians of all ages now play some form of cricket, from those at old-fashioned clubs or in new-fashioned reduced number junior programmes. The latter originated in 1984 with the inauguration of Kanga Cricket, the accent of which was on involvement rather than outright excellence. It is sometimes overlooked that a country must not merely generate players; it also needs a public with a sense of the game. They also serve who only stand and umpire, coach, score, attend, watch, listen to, read about, talk about, drive their sons and/or daughters to their weekend games, wash their whites and/or clean their shoes.

One abiding trend in the census is the apparent strength of cricket in non-metropolitan areas. About 70 per cent of Australians are city dwellers, yet only 53 per cent of cricket participants are likewise. A cursory glance at Test stars from rural Australia attests the game's continued strength where distractions and alternatives are often fewer: Mark Taylor, Michael Slater, Glenn McGrath, Adam Gilchrist, Ian Healy, Matt Hayden, Matt Elliott. The disparity is only partly explained by the hallowed traditions of country cricket. Sporting facilities are often the last component thought of in our new mushroom suburbs. In the Australia of yore, there was usually a cricket club around the corner. Now the nearest sporting infrastructure may be an indoor soccer centre or a gymnasium, in some respects better suited to an age of increased population density and time poverty. And in an era of scarce water and growing carbon consciousness, big ovals of green grass may one day begin to smack suspiciously of indulgence.

Another imponderable for cricket participation over the next decade or so will be employment patterns. More people work week-ends, and on casual and consultancy bases. More women work, and child-rearing responsibilities are increasingly shared. The Australian Council of Trade Unions might be staging a rearguard action against WorkChoices with an eye on stumps, but they face the government from one end and business from the other: further deregulation of the labour market and atomisation of the working week seem inevitable. Certainly, to set aside a Saturday is already a great deal more difficult than it was even ten years ago; to set aside consecutive Saturdays for the standard Australian two-day club game is sometimes like persuading planets to align or tides to reverse; volunteer organisers, traditionally one of Australian cricket's great strengths, have seldom been scarcer.

The aspect of national recreational habits that is attracting most comment, meanwhile, is their absence. In Australia, about two-thirds of adult men, more than half of adult women and about a quarter of our children are overweight. Inactivity, too, is self-reinforcing phenomenon. The less active we are, the less active we are inclined to be, the strain of exertion being that much greater and less pleasant. The chances are that you could still find eleven able cricketers by walking along Bondi Beach today, but that most of them would be too lazy and apathetic to last a full game.

Australian Cricket Diary 2008

The Dustbin of History

There are many things an Aussie will never understand about England. Why, for instance, can I buy a tuna baguette in my local newsagent, but not a pad or notebook? And when did your telephone boxes also become public conveniences?

Another puzzle must be why the Ashes urn, having remained in symbolic Australian custody for twelve years, remains physically ensconced at Lord's: a state of affairs analogous to Custer telling the Sioux to lay off his scalp after the Battle of Little Bighorn.

The issue arises regularly; as regularly, in fact, as Australia winning the Ashes. No sooner are Australian complaints aired—and they've come this summer even from Australia's monarchist Prime Minister John Howard—than they are loftily dismissed by the urn's Marylebone owners. The Ashes, Aussies are told, have a note from matron: they are too fragile to travel.

This seems odd. With the possible exception of fugitive Australian financiers, virtually anything can be moved round the world these days, from radioactive waste to Ronald Biggs. The difficulty arises because the trophy is twice incarnated, as the Ashes (Actual) and the Ashes (Symbol).

The Ashes (Actual) were inherited by MCC in 1927 from the estate of Lord Darnley, who as the Hon Ivo Bligh was presented with them sometime on his team's 1882–83 tour of Australia.

They were a colonial jest, a play on that pioneering example of English sporting masochism: the death notice for English cricket placed in the *Sporting Times* after Australia's win in the Oval Test a few months earlier—since reprised so many times, of late with the embellishment of root vegetables.

The Ashes (Symbol), meanwhile, are different. They *do* change hands—at least in imagination. A system has even evolved that the existing holder retains them when series are shared.

While one clearly can have a situation where the Ashes (Actual) and the Ashes (Symbol) lead independent existences, it's not hard to understand complaints that it is a sub-optimal arrangement. Imagine if Arthurian legend ended with Gawain telling Lancelot: 'I've quite a nice cup at home that would pass for a grail. Sod this quest—let's go jousting instead.' No Australian expects the Ashes to feature in an extravagant presentation ceremony, manhandled by horny-handed, Foster's-flourishing cricketers. They simply crave the custody of an object that, originating in Australia, is as much part of its history as England's.

This exchange of views over the Ashes's rightful residence, however, is perhaps less interesting than what it tells us about a crossover in the way the Australian and English teams relate to their past. The little history in Australia has to be spread a long way, but much of what's there springs from sport. One of Steve Waugh's chief characteristics as captain has been his invocation of the past, and faith in continuities. His players spend the first fielding session of every Test beneath their baggy greens. Their dressing room is open to past players, their minds to past influences; even a cricketer as self-consciously modern as Shane Warne is affected. In his new autobiography, Warne identifies his most treasured cricket moment as reading the welcome on Sydney's scoreboard during his Test debut: 'Congrats Shane Warne on becoming Australia's 350th Test cricketer.'

English cricketers seem to feel differently. England might be accused of luxuriating in the past—as it was by my colleague

Geoff Lawson yesterday—but its cricketers do the opposite. Mike Atherton's last column in the *Sunday Telegraph*, for instance, was devoted to interrogating the legend of Headingley 1981. He grumbled that England's victory had proven 'more of a curse' than a blessing. The country remained on a futile search for 'another Brearley', while 'Botham's success had been a terrible cross to bear for a generation of English all-rounders'. Even the game itself had become an incubus for subsequent generations: 'Whenever the English cricket team find themselves in a hopeless position, the ghost of Botham looms large, only to disappoint again and again.'

Such logic would to an Australian seem perverse. One cannot hear Steve Waugh complaining: 'It is a terrible cross to bear that Australia scored 404 in the fourth innings to beat England at Headingley in 1948. Every time we chase a big target, those old codgers start banging on about Bradman.' The old roles have reversed: where this Australian team find their history enriching and empowering, their opponents find theirs baffling and burdensome. Where Steve Waugh sees a 'legend', Mike Atherton senses a 'ghost'. All the more reason, perhaps, for exporting the Ashes to the antipodes. At least there they would bring pleasure. And on present indications, the urn's fragility need not be too great a concern: it may not need to make a return journey for some time.

Guardian, August 2001

THE WARNE–MURALITHARAN TROPHY

Marriage of Inconvenience

In modern cricket, everyone has won and all must have prizes. The idea of a contest without silverware for fondling and flourishing seems unthinkable. The newly minted symbol of supremacy in competition between Australia and Sri Lanka, however, will serve purposes other than mere post-match prop.

The inauguration of the Warne–Muralitharan Trophy is a little essay in equipoise, bringing together the takers of more than 1400 Test wickets in the hope of bridging the gap between two cricket countries with good reasons to maintain a distance. Because for some Australians the gesture will smack of sullying the sainted Warne name by association, and even of an act of appeasement to delicate Asian sensibilities.

Warne rises in national estimation almost by the day—there's nothing like retirement at the right time to burnish a reputation. But Muralitharan, just nine wickets from overhauling Warne's Test wicket record, is still to convince many in this country that he has ever dismissed a batsman fairly, with Prime Minister John Howard among his detractors. It is three years since Muralitharan declined to tour Australia after Howard, whose embrace of cricket is as wholehearted as Tony Blair's of Jackie Milburn, branded his doosra a throw.

Australia and Sri Lanka begin their First Test at the Gabba on Thursday and their Second at Hobart's Bellerive Oval the following Friday, thus avoiding the scenes of Muralitharan's worst misadventures here: his no-balling by Darrell Hair at the MCG on Boxing Day 1995, and by Ross Emerson at Adelaide Oval on Australia Day 1999. If it's unlikely any umpire would be game to proscribe Muralitharan today, it's almost certain there will be those in the crowd determined to mete out their own sort of justice. They were noisily present on Muralitharan's previous visit, for the VB Series in January last year; that Warne's record might fall is just the sort of possibility that, these days, inevitably touches off patriotic puerilism.

Cricket Australia, which last summer casually exhorted fans to 'Go Off in Green and Gold', is this summer all sober and straitlaced, even proposing plain clothes police patrols of crowd 'hot spots' to curb abuse, perhaps by persuading them to more traditional chants such as: 'All Pommies Are Poofters.' Australian players have also rallied round, Andrew Symonds insisting it would be 'rude, straight-out rude, if they [spectators] didn't sort of respect him [Muralitharan] and give him the pat on the back he deserves'. But his erstwhile colleague Jason Gillespie believes that the Sri Lankan probably expects it: 'With Murali coming out he always cops a gobful in Australia and he'll be expecting to cop that again. He might have to grin and bear it. You shouldn't have to but that's often the way it is, unfortunately.'

Australians are unpredictable where foreign dignitaries are concerned. LBJ was famously followed by nonstop egg barrage when he became the first American president to visit this country; trade unionists black-banned Sinatra for dismissing a pushy journalist as a 'two-bit hooker'; and Sydney's recent APEC conference, attended by George Bush, was enlivened by a comic prankster dressed as Osama bin Laden whose motorcade glided serenely through several security emplacements. In general, sportsmen have been treated more deferentially. Harold Larwood was even able to settle in Sydney, and received a stirring ovation when he appeared in the middle of the MCG during the Centenary Test thirty years ago with his partner in crime Bill Voce. Some unlikely figures have become great crowd favourites, from Freddie Brown and Tony Greig to Dilip Doshi and Qasim Omar.

Yet if Muralitharan is any guide, that warmth of welcome no longer applies. Since his first visit, he has run a gauntlet of umpires, spectators and opinion makers. Richard Hadlee earned a bonehead odium in the 1980s for being rather too good, but it was based on dread as much as dislike. Muralitharan has actually never done particularly well here, and certainly never threatened to give his team an unfair advantage. Indeed, perhaps it's Sri Lanka's poor record down under that has turned their star bowler into crowd bait: it is hard, for instance, to imagine local spectators similarly risking the ire of the West Indians of Clive Lloyd or Viv Richards.

Australians, of course, hardly monopolise unruly crowd behaviour these days. Last month, players had the novel experience in India of being the butt of it: abusive and apparently racist chants at Vadodara and Mumbai directed at Andrew Symonds. In Australia, there was public bemusement, racism being one of those subjects that makes liberal consciences quail. Yet strangely, nobody drew any connection between the Australians' experience in India and the abuse commonly meted out to visiting teams here—the possibility that Indian spectators felt they were giving the visitors a taste of their own bitter medicine.

Exhibition of the 'passion' of the crowd is a familiar trope of televised cricket in Australia. Nobody ever attracted a camera's attention by clapping politely; flag, face paint and fervency are de rigueur. No Australian batsman hits a boundary without a choreographed exultation from the serried ranks of green and gold. It's possible that just as international teams have become more verbally aggressive, believing this to be an important element of the success of the world's best team, so, too, have international crowds absorbed the perceived partisanship of Australian supporters, convinced it is an important adjunct of their team's strength at home. (The same Gillespie who advised Murali to grin and bear it in Australia was most put out to be abused by English spectators during the Ashes of 2005: 'Some of the crowd behaviour is appalling, the insulting things people say. People pay their money to come in and they think it is their right to question your parentage and have a crack at your mother.') If this is so, we may be seeing something like the phenomenon christened by the Reagan White House—that of 'blowback'.

It is true, whatever the case, that modern cricket spectators go to be seen as much as to see, and that broadcasters are increasingly dependent on their telegenic revels: where would Twenty20 be without its air of patriotic rally and nonstop street party? For these spectators, a target for communal indignation is part of their idea of fun; the game is entertainment, the players heroes and villains, and the trophy mere bric-a-brac.

Guardian, November 2007

That Seventies Show

It's fifteen years since I was involved in researching *The Cricket War*, at which time fifteen years had elapsed since the events it described. Yet the writing, and even the phenomenon of World Series Cricket, still seem disarmingly recent, perhaps because what felt so uncompromisingly and vividly new then has become its own form of tradition. The cult of personality that so willingly enfolded the players of 1977 is still with us. The television formula of imposing narrative on the game and applying state-of-the-art broadcasting technology to elucidate the action is little altered: even the narrator-in-chief, Richie Benaud, and his longest-serving lieutenant, Bill Lawry, remain.

Kerry Packer, of course, has gone to his reward—or, as he suspected, nowhere. But he wasn't easily replaced. His son James, who was learning cricket at the time in a household through which the world's most famous practitioners passed as a matter of course and right, has taken up the chairman's remote control. Yet his outsized reputation seems to keep the Nine Network a captive of the twentieth century, those unmistakeable features looming spectrally from Gerald Stone's recent book-length obituary *Who Killed Channel Nine?*

In cricket, meanwhile, his name has perhaps never been more often invoked. Administrators have kept their eyes on the skies ever since, anxious that another media entrepreneur with a yen for sport should not descend and make off with the best talent. The nearest equivalent was the 'rebel tours' of South Africa between 1982 and 1989, which plundered players from England, Australia, West Indies and Sri Lanka, although these offered no head-to-head competition with the established game on its own soil. While Rupert Murdoch cast a long shadow over Australian cricket in the aftermath of his formation of rugby's Super League, he was content merely to spook everyone within cooee. Now, through the agency of the Texan billionaire Allen Stanford and Subhash Chandra of Zee Telefilms, we are watching the formation of new professional tours. Even the reaction of the authorities is tempered by the lessons of World Series Cricket, Packer having proved that cricket is a premium media franchise. The churchmouse-poor West Indies Cricket Board feels it might gain from making space for a savvy businessman; the filthy-rich Board of Control for Cricket in India believes it has too much to lose from the division of its lucrative market.

Stanford and Chandra, moreover, have proceeded in unconscious emulation of Packer by basing their enterprises on the game's new Twenty20 variant, just as Packer thirty years ago homed in on 50-over cricket, hitherto underexploited, as the growth end of the market. The International Cricket Council has also learned its lesson. Where the establishment in 1977 stood back in consternation and let Packer make use of the limited-overs template they had pressed, the ICC has this time staked out its turf with the recent World Twenty20 Championship in South Africa. But we can expect more of the same, explained with airy invocations of Packer, who made the unthinkable thinkable: that men would play for money rather than merely national pride.

Sometimes it is argued that the establishment should have seen Packer coming; that World Series Cricket was inevitable. The statement is essentially weightless. The end of the world is inevitable. That does not mean we must begin planning for it. One's death is unavoidable. But from this it might be inferred that one should live for the present—and this is what cricket's authorities chiefly did. In the 1970s, world cricket was a group of autarkical city states whose overriding end was raising sufficient revenues to cover their operating costs, and whose honorary administrators were strangers to strategic planning. It was a system little changed in a hundred years, and systems enduring so long might as well carve their by-laws into clay tablets for all the likelihood of their voluntary revision. Since writing *The Cricket War*, I have been involved in writing the official history of Cricket Australia, previously the Australian Cricket Board. It is striking just how precisely the external impression of the organisation tallies with its internal workings: its ink-dense minutes are like reading those of a big cricket club, absorbed in minutiae, taking it one season at a time, assuming that there'd always be players, trusting there'd always be fans.

It's truer to say that World Series Cricket originated in an enduring tension. In its pioneering days, Australian cricket was a players' game. The original tours of England were entrepreneurial expeditions, players returning home laden with honours and financial spoils. The players, with the commercial and moral support of the powerful Melbourne Cricket Club, were mainly their own masters. That changed with the foundation of the Australian Board of Control for International Cricket in May 1905. The eighteen months of wrangling that ensued subdued the players and marginalised the club, capturing the proceeds of Ashes competition for the game—or, at least, the game as it was constituted by the state associations whose members composed the board. With the Big Six dispute of 1912, when Australian cricket's half-dozen leading exponents stood out of a tour of England because the Board had denied them their choice of manager, the players were permanently shut from the game's organisation. I well remember Ian Chappell's words when I was talking to him about *The Cricket War*: 'There's three events that matter in the history of Australian cricket: 1912,

Bodyline and World Series Cricket.' I would qualify that judgement only by remarking that 1912 was a final efflorescence of player power: the Board had really cornered their cricketers in 1906.

It adds some piquancy to the events of 1977 if you recall that the roles were reversed seventy-one years earlier. In 1906, the fourteen best cricketers in New South Wales quietly signed with the Melbourne Cricket Club to participate in a Test series against a visiting team from England. When this alliance was revealed, the new Board moved quickly to establish their authority: the NSW Cricket Association banned the players, the Victorian Cricket Association moved to destabilise the club's tenure at Jolimont, and the conversion of the South Australian Cricket Association to the cause of a national cricket government left the allies isolated. Packer turned the tables, exploiting the discontent of the players at the power and privileges of which the Board had stripped them all those decades before.

The time was also ripe socially: after Vietnam, after Whitlam, an era of trade union militancy and of high inflation eroding the value of slow-growing rewards. In the aftermath of the blood feuds surrounding the Board's foundation, the players had become an obedient, complaisant lot. But by the 1970s, they were developing a renewed taste for contestation, personified by Ian Chappell, while the members of his unshaven, unkempt XI had acquired an anti-authoritarian aura that extended beyond the cricket field. Bandido moustaches, salty repartee, snappy threads, winning ways: they were a far cry from the short-back-and-sides sportsmen of the 1960s, even though Chappell and Doug Walters had themselves emerged from that time. The enduring age and experience gap between Australian cricketers and their administrators widened so starkly in the 1970s that it could almost have been measured in parsecs.

Writing *The Cricket War* was an unusual personal experience, because I was constantly comparing my findings with my own juvenile recollections. In 1977, I was eleven years old, had played my first few junior seasons in Geelong and was uncompromisingly crazy for cricket. Suddenly not merely the players but the game itself and all it stood for were up for grabs. I had attended the Centenary Test, basked in the warm glow of that century of tradition; now, it seemed, these things had meant nothing to the players involved. I wasn't so militant as my erstwhile colleague Mark Ray, who returned from England that year with a T-shirt reading 'Death to the Circus'. But I was certainly affronted: no-one is so shockable as a youthful prude.

All the same, what I recall mainly is the excitement. I attended World Series games as well as Tests, watched both on television, saw David Hookes absorb his fearful blow from Andy Roberts, was stirred by Bob Simpson's Cincinnatus-like return to the colours, and fretted that Lillee and Thomson might never again bowl in harness. At an age where too much cricket was barely enough, I had a lot to thank Kerry Packer for. That spirit shaped *The Cricket War*. At the time of its research, there remained a good deal of residual antagonism towards the World Series *sans-culottes*, and I sensed that a reconsideration was overdue: a retelling of the story without the censorious tone of the contemporaneous accounts. The book became, I suspect, part of a generational reconsideration underway, which culminated perhaps on news of Packer's death on Boxing Day 2005, when the players in a Melbourne Test formed two solemn lines during a minute's silence, and tributes poured forth from all quarters. Where the senior administrators in Australia in 1977 had been incapable even of enunciating his name—preferring to call him simply 'the private promoter'—Cricket Australia chairman Creagh O'Connor extolled his Bradmanesque stature. 'That cricket is today taken for granted as a natural part of the Australian way of life is in no small measure due to his influence,' he said. 'The so-called "Packer Revolution" in the 1970s has left a lasting legacy in the way the game is played, administered and presented to the public via the influential Channel Nine telecast.' This legacy continues to yield unexpected dividends, and will be debated for some time to come. Meanwhile, this is how it happened, those thirty years ago.

Preface to the new edition of *The Cricket War*, 2007

Animal Spirits

From the late 1960s, the minutes of the Australian Cricket Board feature a recurrent phrase, always repeated with a mixtures of dread and disapproval. 'Private promoter' might sound innocent enough; at the time, the sight of one was like the distant flutter of the skull and crossbones.

The first of these merchant venturers, theatrical impresario Jack Neary, was allowed a trial of his World Cricket (Doubles) competition before being denied permission to restage it. Others didn't even make that amount of progress. The DJ Foynes Organisation suggested an 'Australia v the World' Test at the MCG, with cuts for Greg Chappell and Tony Greig as well as the Board: it got nowhere. William Hollins & Co, representing the Viyella (Shirt) Company, proposed a 'World Cricket XI' to play games against first-class opposition: it was dismissed. Even an annual invitation game at Drummoyne Oval for the benefit of the Spastic Centre of NSW caused discomfiture.

Flirtations, meanwhile, only ended in confusion. In August 1976, former Australian captain Bob Simpson mooted a revival of the Cavaliers XI concept, killed off in England by the rise of the John Player League. After a cordial reception, Simpson recalled, 'suddenly, out of the blue, the Australian Cricket Board withdrew their approval of the venture' and 'the whole concept was put in mothballs'.

So where the public saw Kerry Packer's first Supertest at VFL Park on 2 December 1977 as a bold innovation, cricket authorities regarded it as a nightmare made real—something *also* fit for mothballs, if they'd had any say in it. It's not hard to understand why. Cricket run on commercial lines showed just how uncommercial was cricket's reality, with a tiny international treasure chest funding a massive loss-making support structure. The Australian Cricket Board thirty years ago was acutely vulnerable to competition, deriving the bulk of its revenue from gate receipts on inbound Ashes tours and profit guarantees on outbound Ashes tours. Other international visits barely covered their costs; first-class, junior and club cricket ran at significant losses; broadcasting rights and sponsorship had yet to make a significant impact on the national cricket exchequer.

Kerry Packer, by contrast, owed no fealty to anyone—even the players were mainly a means to his end of securing exclusive broadcast rights for Australian international summers. At the height of the drama surrounding World Series Cricket, Packer vouchsafed in a press conference that cricketers had long been exploited by authorities, and that they deserved better pay and conditions because of the pleasure they gave to millions. A journalist took up this thread and wondered if the businessman was saying that his enterprise was 'half-philanthropic'. Packer's realism was too embedded for him to agree. 'Half-philanthropic?' he said. 'That makes me sound more generous than I am.'

The freedom to define his own sphere of operations became an especially obvious advantage in the second summer of World Series Cricket. In the first season, Packer tried to replicate the structure of a conventional summer by playing five-day and one-day cricket in each mainland capital. In the second, he stuck to the two most profitable centres, Sydney and Melbourne, with a few matches at the Gabba when it happened to become available. Where the ACB in 1978–79 lumbered itself with two Tests in Perth, forgettable and poorly attended, WSC was busy expanding the number of limited-overs fixtures, and pushing ever deeper into nights. The ACB was constituted by fourteen members representing their states in proportions virtually unchanged in three-quarters of a century; Packer was, of course, the proverbial committee of one. The ACB could theoretically have run its own cricket along Packer lines for a limited time, scheduling games only in the most populace centres, disbanding the Sheffield Shield, abandoning grassroots cricket to its own devices, relying on the existing players to provide a nonstop cycle of international attractions. But a generation in action without a generation in waiting was always a finite proposition.

The war ended in April 1979, but life was never quite the same. On the face of it, the structure of cricket was little changed. The hierarchy of international and interstate cricket remained essentially unaltered, and the governance conventions continued unchallenged. The authorities were gifted their game and players back in return for the rights Packer had always coveted. The transaction, however, came with strings attached. The not-so-secret ransom was the agreement that Packer should promote the game in Australia through his PBL Marketing subsidiary: an arrangement that cut the ACB out of perhaps the most important and fastest-changing function in cricket administration. The result can only be a matter of speculation, but it is interesting that the 1996 World Cup in India made the 1992 World Cup in Australia look so staid. In hindsight, it may be that India stole the march on Australia in the 1980s and 1990s where the selling of the game was involved. Where Australia carried on with a single sponsor, Benson & Hedges, and an external promoter interested primarily in its own bottom line rather than the game's, PBL, India under its energetic czar Jagmohan Dalmiya was on the move.

World Series Cricket isn't simply to be understood by what it accomplished; it should also be assessed for what it made possible. Before Packer, the idea of Australian cricket having a 'market value' would have been unthinkable. As Dr Greg Manning observed in *Wisden Australia*, Packer didn't spend $12 million buying the game; he spent $12 million turning it into something that could be bought. In theory, it could have been bought by others, and the organisers of the rebel tours were able to make off with key assets. In reality, Packer so skilfully barred and gated the way here that international cricket in his wake was a monopoly more strongly fortified than before.

Thirty years after the World Series burglary, authorities have ears cocked for the bump in the night of other 'private promoters'. If anything, players are more susceptible to inducements than they were when they were paid a pittance. Now that everything has a value, nothing is beyond price. And although that discovery would probably have been made anyway, Packer's nimble recruiting agents John Cornell and Austin Robertson made it a decidedly memorable one.

The drive among administrators now is to develop the game before someone else develops it for them—if anything a reverse of the attitude that prevailed thirty years ago—with Twenty20 the game's manifest destiny. The reason is that World Series Cricket also fundamentally changed expectations among cricketers—and that these have continued to rise. Australian cricket now has something it did not have fifteen years ago: after the false dawns of 1977 and 1988, the players finally cobbled together their own trade union, the Australian Cricketers' Association, in 1995. It places the players within the system, and provides infrastructural support and mechanisms to resolve disputes. As Lyndon Johnson said when he appointed Bobby Kennedy his attorney-general: 'Better inside pissing out, than outside pissing in.'

But it doesn't answer everything. The best players are not always the most marketable. Jacques Kallis is probably a more valuable cricketer to his team than Brett Lee, but whose services would an advertiser prefer? And individuals and countries are essentially selling into the same market, Brett Lee being every bit as much a media property as the Australian cricket team, and perhaps even superior to it. In a zero-sum game, does not the promotional success of one deprive, potentially even impoverish, the other? One question, too, is seldom asked because the idea seems fanciful, although it is anything but. The game has been blessed by success and public support; if this weakened, how would the burden of sacrifice be distributed? Like most professional sports, cricket has seen its commercial value do nothing but appreciate for the last thirty years. But no market rises indefinitely, and in a game that now provides for so many hungry mouths that is a disquieting thought.

Asked to comment on the consequences of the French Revolution, the Chinese premier Zhou Enlai famously replied that it was too early to tell. The same applies to the cricket revolution. It will be little consolation to them looking on from Valhalla, but those Australian cricket administrators of the 1970s were right: the private promoter leaves nothing unchanged.

Cricinfo, November 2007

The Biter Bit

A week or so ago the cricket world was in a funk about Test cricket, how the inevitable advance of Twenty20 would crush all in its path, how the game desperately needed a five-day game to die for. The Sydney Test was made to measure: five days of high drama and fluctuation with a grandstand finish in which all cricket's skills were on display—except, maybe, umpiring.

Yet somehow the match's only beneficiaries have been India's effigy suppliers, whose stocks of white-coated figures are going up in flames all over the subcontinent—and mainly because one cricketer allegedly called another a 'monkey'. The twist in the tale is that the sledger was an excitable Indian, the sledgee a muscular and aggressive Aussie and his co-accusers more of the same. Otherwise the incident attests to the power of sport to make people lose perspective, proportion and all rationality.

Racism is serious. Racism is about the denial of another person's essential humanity on the basis of their skin and their culture. Racism is about embedded prejudices, institutionalised discrimination, real economic and social deprivation. Racism is South Africa under apartheid—on which, say it soft, Australia was the last cricket country to lower the boom. Racism is Robert Mugabe—against whose country the Australian cricket team would seemingly have been happy to play had it not been for the federal government. To say, then, that one cricketer calling another a monkey on a cricket field is racism is to define the idea frivolously. Was Symonds belittled? Was he hurt? Was he disadvantaged?

Curiously, when a few score Indians made monkey noises directed at Symonds at Vadodara last October, he went out of his way to state that he had not made any complaint, and affected not to care. 'I'm not the most deadly serious bloke,' he said. 'Life goes on.' Yet somehow Harbhajan's emission is now the gravest of offences and befitting of the severest sanction. Regrettably, the Australian complaint smacks of cricketers who in the process of scaling great heights of excellence have sealed themselves off from reality.

It also smacks of Australian players just a bit peeved about always being seen as the bad guys, who want the world to know that they, poor things, get taunted too. There is a sort of wounded self-righteousness to captain Ricky Ponting's comments in the aftermath of the Sydney Test that recalls those mealy mouthed defences of Australian sledging of the recent past: other teams do it but they don't get criticised because we're more honest and they play the beastly trick of doing it in Hindi and Urdu ... which, yeah, are their languages ... but oh, *it's not fair*!

For decades Australian cricketers have been steadfast in maintaining the principle that what happens on the field stays on the field, and regarded as snitches those opponents, such as South Africa's Graeme Smith and Sri Lanka's Arjuna Ranatunga, who abrogated it. Which is fine. Even if you haven't always agreed with it as a philosophy, it has at least been understandable and unambiguous, and in that sense worthy of respect. The common sense of the principle, in fact, is verified by this incident. Because when you abandon it, as Ponting has, you incite others to take grievances beyond the boundary, as the Indians are doing by trumping up their tit-for-tat charge against Brad Hogg.

Perhaps it's worth considering why cricket has a code of conduct, not to mention a preamble in its laws about the game's proper spirit. These exist to deter players from poor sportsmanship.

They aren't there to be pushed as far as you can in quest of a short-term competitive advantage. There is a case that both Harbhajan and Symonds should have been punished. There was nothing passionate, committed or red-blooded about their confrontation, nor any of the other boilerplate excuses. It was another unnecessary and completely avoidable face-off between players who are paid pots of money to know better. What was said will be endlessly disputed; what we saw looked bad, boorish, ugly.

There is still a quaint idea that provocateur and respondent in these exchanges are distinguishable. But who knows where the animosity between Harbhajan and the Australians began? And who cares? As for the cartoonish arguments about whether 'monkey' is racist in one culture, or 'bastard' is illegitimacist in another, cricket should be worried first about its own standards—and standing. The Sydney Test should have enriched it; as it is, the game has metaphorically dropped a catch off a hat-trick ball and somehow deflected it for six.

Daily Telegraph, January 2008

Monkey Business

A couple of days after the Second Test between Australia and India ended at the Sydney Cricket Ground amid acrimony and indignation, I boarded the tram for an evening's practice at my cricket club with 15-year-old Bill. A bright boy, Bill. I knew him to be keen on his cricket, and was interested in how his career had progressed since last I'd seen him.

I found that Bill was no longer quite so keen on his cricket. In the nets he was still a tidy player who essayed a pretty cover drive and lobbed a passable leg break. But, Bill explained, he wasn't playing so much these days. He'd joined a club where the coaches had impressed on their charges how important it was to be as verbally aggressive as possible—to, as they say, 'sledge'. Why? Well, because everyone does it. And while his club wasn't very good, it had won a few more games than the players' talents justified because they were capable of putting opponents off by being 'in their faces', by appealing for everything that appeared remotely out, by carrying on a bit if they did not get their way. Bill, he thought that was a bit stupid. His parents weren't keen on it either.

I'm pretty inured to petulance and cynicism among international cricketers these days, of which Sydney was merely the worst episode since the last episode which was the worst, following the one before that. This conversation with Bill, however—*this* was dismaying. For it is this aspect of sledging and general malcontentment on the cricket field that has become most pernicious: not that it is ugly or offensive or dehumanising, but the sheer, mindless, rote-learned nature of it. Now and again, there is a flash of exasperation, frustration, anger, even humour. Otherwise, it is a part of the game that has become noisily, and annoyingly, automated.

The skirmish between Harbhajan Singh and Andrew Symonds owed nothing to the spur of the moment or the heat of the contest. Harbhajan *knew* he had a way of irking Symonds; they had even discussed it off the field. The Australians *knew* Harbhajan to be a provocateur; the Australians entered willingly into the confrontation, aware of exactly what was acceptable boorishness under Paragraph 3.3 of the International Cricket Council Code of Conduct and what was not. Thus did a relatively small objective, a short-term tactical edge on an opponent, masquerade as a very big issue.

The game's ugliest image was provided by neither Harbhajan nor Symonds, but by Australia's captain, Ricky Ponting: finger aloft, bent forward at the waist, daring the umpire to doubt his assertion that a snick to slip had carried, turning even his lip service to good manners—a pre-match agreement with India's Anil Kumble to rely upon the fielders' word where low catches were concerned—into an emblem of Australian aggression. The appeal for a catch at the wicket when Rahul Dravid missed a ball by nine inches, meanwhile, was a miracle of harmony to rival The Beach Boys.

As it usually does, the charge of racism immediately deprived everyone of rational thought, entailing the inevitable 'I said, you said' claim and counterclaim. And if Australia's cricketers are the world's biggest bullies on the field, India's administrators are easily their match off it. At once there were threats that the Indians would take their bat, their ball and, most importantly, their money, and go home. A tit-for-tat charge was laid against Brad Hogg for barking at Kumble and his partner, Mahendra Dhoni: 'I can't wait to go through you bastards.' And so it became a busy week for the average cricket hack. Peter Roebuck, in the *Age* and *Sydney*

Morning Herald, took India's part, not a little impetuously. The *Australian* reopened the culture wars on a new front, passing off hectares of partisan comment in support of star columnist Ponting as news. Kerry O'Keeffe laughed uproariously at his own jokes— so, no change there. I was interviewed by a reporter from a television current-affairs show who, apparently unable to raise Roebuck, solicited my view no fewer than six times on whether Ponting should be sacked. I also participated in a surreal radio debate with a Punjabi editor who insisted that racism in India, presumably like homosexuality in Iran, does not exist.

Between times, just to bring it all back home, I played my weekly club game. While opening the batting I was called a homosexual, a paedophile, a cheat for not walking when I missed a ball by two feet, and a loser merely for existing. While bowling we faced a batsman whose idea of fun was to goad each fielder in turn and who, when a comment was made that this was obviously how they played in Frankston, droned on for several overs about 'racial vilification'. Monkey see, monkey do.

For this is cricket circa 2008, a game still hugely rich and various in its skills yet massively alike in its behaviours, in which you do not merely play to win but to dull your opponents' love of the game, and thus their appetite for the contest. This has become a means, in fact, by which groups define and unite themselves. Brad Hogg wasn't questioning anyone's parentage in Sydney; he was, after more than a decade hankering for Test selection, clamouring for membership of the tough boys' group. And Australian captains have been such noisy apologists for verbal aggression, psychological dominance and 'mental disintegration' over the years that the route to self-exculpation at lower levels of the game is obvious: *The role model made me do it*!

On reflection, then, part of my conversation with Bill was quite hopeful. People, even 15-year-olds, have agency. They can make choices. They can reject recommended and prescribed behaviours. Alas, they might have to leave cricket behind in order to do so.

And here the fault is not in our superstars but in ourselves, in that we have colluded in turning a game with perhaps more scope for individual expression than any other into another means of instilling mass conformity.

Monthly, February 2008

17

SUNIL GAVASKAR V ICC

Indian Chief

The usual excuse for misbehaviour on the cricket field is that it was done on the spur of the moment, in an excess of competitiveness, under the pressure of the situation. It doesn't always render such incidents forgivable, but it sometimes makes them more understandable: after all, these are young men strung up to concert pitch fighting for their livelihoods and in the name of national honour.

What to make, though, of those who should know better, those with vast experience and great reputations, who commit sins of tact and taste? What to make of those who hold roles in the game gravid with responsibility yet who cannot help making mischief?

Step forward Sunil Gavaskar, who somehow manages to operate as the chairman of the ICC's cricket committee while also acting as peppery columnist and media rabble-rouser. The ICC finds itself in a tight corner, as ever, as it strains to arbitrate on the matter of Harbhajan Singh's verbal skirmishes with Andrew Symonds. You might expect all at the organisation to be pulling in the same direction towards an even-handed settlement that allows both teams to move on with honour. But, unless someone has presumed to write under the nom be plume 'Sunil Gavaskar' in a syndicated column in various Indian newspapers, you would expect wrong. Because here this ICC senior officer has launched an attack on an ICC referee that can do nothing but damage to the organisation, to the relations between countries, and to the game itself.

'Millions of Indians want to know if it was a "white man" taking the "white man's" word against that of the "brown man",' Gavaskar says. 'Quite simply, if there was no audio evidence, nor did the officials hear anything, then the charge did not stand.' Millions of Indians might want to know this—but it doesn't actually make them right. Does Gavaskar himself believe this to be true? If so, he should say it. And if he *does* believe it, then he should almost certainly resign, for if the ICC is a bastion of 'white man's justice' then Gavaskar bears some of the blame for having failed to change it.

On the other hand, maybe he hasn't been paying attention. After all, how many times has audio evidence ever been definitive in any case of on-field behaviour? The stump mikes didn't pick up Glenn McGrath's tirade at Ramnaresh Sarwan in 2003, nor did the umpires David Shepherd and Srinivas Venkataraghavan make any report, but that didn't stop the failure of the ICC referee to take action being an abysmally weak decision.

That referee, of course, was Mike Procter. He was also the referee at the Oval in 2006 when Inzamam ul-Haq had his Achilles-like sulk, and at Melbourne in 2007 when Yuvraj Singh had his Paris Hiltonesque pout. There are some good arguments that while he bowled magnificent inswinging yorkers off the wrong foot, Procter has been a serial failure in enforcing the ICC's code of conduct. But you'd be forgiven for wondering exactly who is helped by the following assessment of his work by Gavaskar: 'This is what has incensed the millions of Indians who are flabbergasted that the word of one of the greatest players in the history of the game, Sachin Tendulkar, was not accepted. In effect, Tendulkar has been branded a liar by the match referee.'

Again with the 'millions of Indians'! It's not me, folks—it's those 'millions of Indians'. In fact, this debating point is a much less impressive notion than it seems. India has a population of

1.13 billion. There's probably at least a few million who believe in flying saucers. Should we really pay them serious heed? It's also far from clear that Tendulkar has been branded anything at all, for we know precious little of what was said during the relevant proceedings. Perhaps Gavaskar knows more that he lets on; if he does, it is disingenuous of him not to explain how he knows it. Perhaps he knows as much as we all do; if so, he is hastening to a conclusion on little more than supposition.

Nobody can be happy that the Sydney Test, and cricket, was dragged into ignominy. No Australian can be gratified that the deportment of their national team contributed to it. But the free bandying about of the word 'racism', and the use of phrases like 'white man's justice', might just make a few people look like particularly obnoxious hypocrites.

Which brings us back to Gavaskar. Because all this 'monkey' talk can't help but remind the cricket bibliophile of the chapter in Gavaskar's autobiography *Sunny Days* in which he recounts the blood-spattered Kingston Test of 1976 where Bishan Bedi famously declared his innings closed rather than risk further injury for his batsmen from the West Indian pace enfilade. Here's a sample:

> To call the crowd a 'crowd' in Jamaica is a misnomer. It should be called a 'mob'. The way they shrieked and howled every time Holding bowled was positively horrible. They encouraged him with shouts of 'Kill him, Maaaan!', 'Hit him Maan!', 'Knock his head off Mike!' All this proved beyond a shadow of doubt that these people still belonged to the jungles and forests, instead of a civilised country. ...
>
> Their partisan attitude was even more evident when they did not applaud any shots we played. At one stage I even 'demanded' claps for a boundary shot off Daniel. All I got was laughter from the section, which certainly hadn't graduated from the trees where they belonged. ...
>
> They were stamping their legs, clapping and jumping with joy. The only word I can think of to describe the behaviour of

the crowd is 'barbarian'. Here was a man seriously injured, and these barbarians were thirsting for more blood, instead of expressing sympathy, as any civilised and sporting crowd would have done. ...

The whole thing was sickening. Never have I seen such cold-blooded and positively indifferent behaviour from cricket officials and the spectators, to put it mildly, were positively inhuman.

'To put it mildly'! The reader would wish the author to get off the fence and share what he really thought! In hindsight, these are unattractive passages. Hell, let's be frank—they were unattractive passages at the time. These weren't cross words exchanged on the field; they were crude lines penned in repose and with malice aforethought. Perhaps they should be seen as reassuring. If Gavaskar can have become such an important figure in the ICC after peddling such poison, Harbhajan could in time represent India at the United Nations.

The point is, of course, that Gavaskar should *not* be that important a figure at the ICC. Pelham Warner acted as chairman of selectors for England while working as the cricket correspondent of the *Morning Post*, but that was in the 1920s and 1930s, and he wrote such namby-pamby nonsense that it hardly mattered. Cricket today is constantly bemoaning the lack of professionalism shown by its administrative classes. Gavaskar's dual role as bomb-thrower and bomb-defuser has become a key exhibit in the case for change.

The Queensland politician and oaf Russ Hinze was famously asked about his conflict of interest in owning racehorses while acting as minister of racing. 'It's not a conflict of interests,' he replied. 'It's a convergence.' Gavaskar seems to share the same attitude. But it is strange that he should be so gravely concerned about the damage Procter has done to the ICC's authority, and so little aware of the damage he is doing himself.

3
Bradman Unlimited

18

SIR DONALD BRADMAN

This Is the ABC

The A–Z of Bradman? Why, it's so obvious: a concept that falls into the 'wish I'd thought of that' category of publishing ideas.

The A–Z is, of course, a well-worn genre, with the entrancing idea that a totality of knowledge can be captured, contained and classified—an idea, I might say, that seldom fails to suck me in. On my own bookshelves repose titles from *The Encyclopedia of AFL Footballers* (1994) to *The Encyclopedia Sherlockiana* (1977), from *The A–Z of Hitchcock* (2001) to *Elvis: His Life from A–Z* (1988), the last brimming with such priceless detail as the King's army serial number (53310761) and the licence plate of the hearse that conveyed him to his final resting place (1-C5652).

Then there's Bradman, whose record seems to encourage filing and ordering, with its relentlessly steady accumulation and sense of in-built constraint—not *quite* an average of 100, not *quite* 7000 Test runs, a duck as its denouement. Of how many cricketers, I wonder, would an A–Z be of interest or of use? Surely not many. The mingling of familiar reference points with information less well known seems to be a prerequisite of a successful A–Z: thus in Alan Eason's book citations for both '99.94', the talismanic average, *and* '96cm', the Don's chest measurement in 1930. And of even WG Grace it cannot be said there is quite enough knowledge in common circulation to make the task a rewarding one: the Old Man better suits the majestic sweep and minute detail of JR Webber's 1100-page *Chronicle of W. G.* (1998).

Nor does *The A–Z of Bradman* stop there, for it is replete with the statistics that no compilation concerning the great man can be without. 163? The average length of his Test innings in minutes. 164? His number of first-class hundred-run partnerships. 165? His slowest first-class fifty in minutes. Quaint? Dotty? Ah yes, but Bradman provides, to quote one former Australian treasurer, a 'beautiful set of numbers': it is like studying the track record of a great portfolio investor consistently beating the index, a Warren Buffett or a Peter Lynch, or perusing the specifications of a huge manmade structure, like the Hoover Dam or the Pyramids. The exercises undertaken by BJ Wakley in *Bradman the Great* (1959), which truly put the 'anal' in 'analysis', are almost unthinkable in the context of another player. Alan Eason notes helpfully that Wakley saw only nineteen of Bradman's 28 067 first-class runs: as part of 83 added while Bradman was at the crease, these were the smallest proportion of any contribution to a partnership of his career. Somehow, it seems, Bradman made history every time he batted.

Finally, *The A–Z of Bradman* is a capsule of references to a lost Australia: of Sykes bats, of McKeown boots, of the Empire Theatre, of Associated Newspapers, of *The Flying Doctor*, of 'Goldie', of the Listerine Face Mask and of 'Scone Theory'. They evoke a world as past as the Don's records were permanent. Bradman's life wasn't only cricket; it's arguable it wasn't even mainly cricket. He was a husband, father, grandfather, businessman, country boy, Adelaidean and Australian through decades in which the nature of all these roles changed a great deal—perhaps rather more than he did. It was possible for Bradman to write at the end of *Farewell to Cricket* (1950): 'Without doubt the laws of cricket and the conduct of the game are a great example to the world. We should all be proud of this heritage which I trust may forever stand as a beacon light guiding man's footsteps to happy and peaceful days.' The view of his old derogator-in-chief Jack Fingleton in *Brightly Fades the Don* (1949) has arguably withstood the passage of time rather better: 'The cricket world, surely, is as crazy and inconsistent as the outside one.'

It's interesting, nonetheless, that *The A–Z of Bradman* should aggregate such a very stable and mainly positive set of facts and ideas. The Bradman story has been so frequently and faithfully retold in essentially the same terms that it now has an incantatory quality. First-hand experience of Bradman is today the property of a dwindling number. Only nonagenarians can meaningfully recall him bursting onto the scene eighty years ago; the standard memory of Bradman is usually in the context of a received greatness, like one shared by Major-General Peter Cosgrove at the Bradman Oration in January 2008:

> I never met the Don. I reckon I saw him, though, when as a very young boy at a benefit game in Sydney, my Dad took me to see the great man. I think I remember the physical impression—a neat quick man about a quarter the size of my Dad, briskly walking to the wicket of the suburban oval which had apparently never entertained such a crowd. I vividly remember the reverence and the rapture his entrance invoked from my Dad and all others there. Dad said in a hushed tone that sons don't forget, 'Son, that's the Don. That's Sir Donald Bradman!'

That we continue to emulate Cosgrove's father in adopting a 'hushed tone' where Bradman is concerned may tell us something about our desire to simply lionise sportsmen rather than to thoroughly understand them, to cordon some areas of our history off from contestation, to pay homage to values now honoured more often in the breach; a stable Bradman, too, makes for the readiest commercial exploitation and leverage. Whatever the case, I suspect it is true to say that no Australian figure has exerted so much fascination and so little genuine curiosity; we would rather know of than know him; we are content for the deeds to stand in for the man; we might once have wanted to ask a question, but in the end we have been happy to settle for his autograph. Bradman's profile remained, as Peter Fitzsimons put it in the *Sydney Morning Herald* on the Don's 90th birthday, 'low enough that we Australians were able to visit upon him pretty much any kind of personality traits we like—to best suit whatever we think the most admirable—for the most part unfettered by the reality of what he is actually like'.

Still the best biography of Bradman by far is *Sir Donald Bradman* (1978), Irving Rosenwater's incomparably thorough res gestae, now thirty years old; Philip Lindsay's *Don Bradman* (1951) is a delight but a cameo. It seems astounding that nothing has appeared in a generation to contribute significantly to an appreciation of Bradman, especially in an age where telegenia and tell-all memoirs follow inevitably every five minutes of fame. With the honourable exception of Brett Hutchins's *Don Bradman: Challenging the Myth* (2002) and Alf James's *The 'Don' vs the Rest* (2006), neither of them biographies, the books inflicted on us have been of a lavish, flagrant and sometimes quite cynical badness. Alan Eason has given us *The A–Z of Bradman*, and a most delightful artefact it is too. What a shame that Australian writers on the subject of Bradman have taken us, to use the famous title of Andy Warhol's artistic musings, *From A to B and Back Again*.

Foreword to Alan Eason's *The A–Z of Bradman*, 2008

The Old Testament

Sir Donald Bradman's *Farewell to Cricket* would be a book of significance had the author misspelled his own name and credited himself with 333 at Headingley in 1930. It is what it is: the testament of batting's most effective practitioner, and cricket's foremost Australian. Yet it is surprisingly little perused today, having gone through only three editions, the last of them a tatty paperback almost fifteen years ago—surprisingly, because Bradman the writer is as precise, comprehensive and analytical as the batsman so revered.

One of its most intriguing features is the title. For Bradman was far from bidding cricket 'farewell' as he wrote it in 1949, at the encouragement of his literary agent David Higham: he was settling in as the guru of the Australian game, which he would remain for more than a quarter of a century. Yet he clearly regarded active participation as the key to involvement in cricket: no continuing to speak about his career in the present tense à la Geoff Boycott, or in the third person à la Viv Richards. Unlike Richards, and also Sobers, whose autobiographies proclaim their knighthoods, *Farewell to Cricket* is credited simply to 'Don Bradman'. I can't imagine that this is not considered: little about Bradman was not. Indeed, Bradman comments in the book: 'No man ever had less ambitions in that direction. I neither desired nor anticipated any recognition of my services.' The writer is intent on keeping his head when others all about are losing theirs: much is offered, even if little in the end is truly divulged.

All the same, a cricket life is usually a sum of its stories, and Bradman has some of the best in history—precisely because he made history so reliably, and was perforce there when it happened. Bradman's first-ball duck at the Melbourne Cricket Ground during the Bodyline series had been redescribed countless times, including rather well by the bowler Bill Bowes in *Express Deliveries* (1958). But Bradman's is the essential telling; likewise there is delight in the sequel.

> Before an enormous crowd, I listened to a most inspiring ovation as I walked to the wicket. Herbert Sutcliffe, whom I passed on the way, commented on this wonderful reception and I replied, 'Yes, but will it be so good when I am coming back?' In a matter of seconds I was returning in deathly silence. Bowes's first ball pitched short and well outside the off stump, but aided and abetted by a faulty pull shot, hit my leg stump.
>
> Fortunately, I was able to make amends in the second innings by scoring 103 not out in a total of 191. It was amusing in the second innings when our last batsman, Bert Ironmonger, came in with my score in the nineties. The story is told of someone telephoning the ground to speak to him. On being told that Bert could not come to the phone as he had just gone into bat, the enquirer said, 'Well, I'll wait.'
>
> I walked to meet Bert but he got in first with 'Don't worry, son, I won't let you down.' Hammond was bowling and never have I seen two balls go closer to any man's stumps. But Bert did not let me down.

Bradman brooks little sentiment in his cricket views. He asserts rather than speculates, rationalises rather than romanticises. The logic is brisk. 'Has cricket improved?' he asks, then answers in the next breath: 'Unless we believe that cricket has improved we do not believe in progress.' Bradman's faith in nature over nurture, superficially superstitious, is actually explained in terms of a rational process. Advised to interfere with his grip as a colt, Bradman followed his own lights:

> I experimented—worked out the pros and cons—and eventually decided not to change my natural grip. Throughout a long career my grip caused many arguments but I think it is sufficient to prove that any young player should be allowed to develop his own natural style providing he is not revealing an obvious error. A player is not necessarily wrong just because he is different.

One of the reasons he cites for giving the palm to Bill O'Reilly as the greatest bowler of all time is that the mighty leg spinner stuck similarly to his instincts: 'O'Reilly did not hold the ball in the fingers quite like the orthodox leg spinner. It was held more towards the palm of his hand. He was advised by certain "experts" to change his grip but fortunately refused to be advised.'

Cricket was not, however, solely an exercise of will and reason, even for Bradman. There are hints of the high-strung psychosomatic make-up behind the game's broadest bat, the nervous energy harnessed, the dread staved off. 'I always felt anxiety prior to the start of a big game,' he explains. 'Once action commenced I lost the earlier sensation. It was replaced by a sort of tense exhilaration which, at the conclusion of a match, often gave way to a severe reaction.' The solitary nature is explained by reference to that temperament: 'I always obtained best results by seeking quietness. Music is a tonic to jaded nerves.' Bradman acknowledges misgivings even on the eve of his greatest triumph, Australia's pageant of 1948: 'I had returned to cricket in 1946–47 against the advice of my doctors and now I was going to England against my own better judgement—risking personal failure and other possibilities.' Not only was Bradman's book a farewell, then, but it revealed a sense of some relief that his active day was done.

IRVING ROSENWATER'S *SIR DONALD BRADMAN: A BIOGRAPHY*

The Right Stuff

I was once working at a publishing company when it was on the receiving end of a letter of complaint from Irving Rosenwater. In three closely typed pages, it scaled such heights of indignation and vituperation as I have very seldom seen. The offence it protested was indeed an offence, even if the length and tone of the protest seemed to say rather more about the writer.

Rosenwater's *Sir Donald Bradman: A Biography* (1978) is not so irascible in tone, but there's a similar pedantic exactitude. And, to use an annoying phrase much in vogue, it's all good. The book is as superior to all other Bradman biographies as Bradman's average is to those of other batsmen—perhaps, paradoxically, because it is the one that had least direct input from the man himself. The books of Moyes, Page and Williams, and the book-shaped object of Perry, had 'access' and used it to mainly unenlightening and sometimes tedious effect. Rosenwater believed, like Carlyle, that 'genius is ever a secret to itself'. He brought to his book instead an encyclopaedic knowledge of cricket's growth and diffusion, assembled it with an exhaustive survey of secondary sources plus some tasty primary titbits, then rendered it in plain, elegant prose. You can try recreating Bradman's duck at Melbourne during the Bodyline series through Creative Writing 101, or you can have Rosenwater's crisp, delightful, digressive dissertation:

There is a pleasing story—a true one incidentally—how this duck by Bradman almost certainly saved the lives of three young children in Tasmania. Listening to the progress of the Test on the radio in a hotel in Launceston, a Mr P. Hancock stood up and walked out in disgust at Bradman's failure. His brief walk took him past a nearby river, on whose bank three children—the youngest only two and a half—were playing and accidentally fell in. Mr Hancock promptly dived in fully clothed to rescue them—and one would like to think that all three (and the gallant gentleman too) are still thriving healthily and fully cognisant of the miraculous powers of a Test match duck.

The whole drama of this immortal stroke is preserved for posterity on the newsreels of British Movietone News, who covered that Melbourne Test particularly well, and is held at the Rank Laboratories at Denham. Occasionally television producers make use of it to remind their viewers that Bradman was no robot. It never fails to strike awe into those both familiar with it and fresh to the view. It was the one indispensable piece of film that formed part of the story of England–Australia cricket put out by the BBC in London to mark the centenary of Test cricket in March 1977.

There is information in *Sir Donald Bradman* that remains still nowhere else, such as the assertion by the Lancashire League president that it was Bradman who approached Accrington about playing there in the early 1930s rather than vice versa, and the airy dismissal of his leadership prowess by the first-class captain first opposed to him, Leicestershire's AG Hazelrigg: 'In fact there was very little he did right as a captain in that match and we all commented how extremely inexperienced he seemed to be.' It is one thing to describe Bradman's 232 at the Oval in 1930; another to tell us, as Rosenwater does, that a girl, Dorothy Pickle, scoring the game in Bowral, swallowed the fountain pen when the great man's hundred was posted, awaking in hospital some hours later with the words: 'He's a great boy, isn't he!' And if only someone could find the footage of the Don's appearance on *What's My Line?* in 1953, where he was recognised by Gilbert Harding on the blindfolded panel.

Best known for his statistical and historiographic works, Rosenwater revels in Bradman's scoring feats; the figures are almost musical in his hands. His footnoted forensic examination of the scorebook for Bradman's highest Test score is a miniature masterpiece; his examination of scoring rates in Bodyline is full of insight; he imparts with delight such observations as the fact that Bradman *is the only batsman to reach 1000 runs in May without being bowled*. The lack of a Bradman voice means that the book cannot really he considered definitive: it is Bradman as Bradmachine, as it were. But if it is not the last word on the subject, *Sir Donald Bradman* should always be the first. Thank goodness for grumpy old men.

Cricinfo, February 2008

A Tactic of Its Time

Times change, and so do attitudes. Thirty years ago, Kerry Packer was the unacceptable face of sporting capitalism. These days, administrators laud him to the skies while entrepreneurs queue to emulate him.

Three-quarters of a century ago, Douglas Jardine was about to become the most reviled man in sport, detested by every right-thinking Australian, and disliked by not a few Englishmen. The accepted philosophy had been that shared sport could only build warmth of international relations; the Bodyline series showed that different approaches to shared sport could have an equal and opposite effect.

By the mid-1950s, some of the breaks had healed, and some of the bruises faded: Jardine's chief instrument in his campaign, Harold Larwood, had even settled in Sydney. When the man himself visited Australia, he appeared on a radio programme called *Guest of Honour*, and found the natives disarmingly hospitable. 'Though they may not hail me as Uncle Doug, I am no longer the bogeyman,' he commented. 'Just an old so-and-so who got away with it.'

Confirmation of his complete rehabilitation, at least in English eyes, was then perhaps confirmed by the February 2002 cover of *Wisden Cricket Monthly*, which acclaimed Nasser Hussain as showing 'Shades of Jardine' in his deployment of a leg-side attack to restrain India at Bangalore. The background to Hussain's image was indeed a shade of Jardine, loitering palely, like an apparition in one of those trick photographs favoured by Victorian spiritualists.

Within, Mike Brearley opined that Hussain had reinvented Bodyline, albeit on a less intensive and more limited basis: 'Jardine won the Ashes but nearly lost an Empire. Hussain saved a reputation and might have won a series.' Editor Stephen Fay wondered aloud if he would prove 'as ruthless as Jardine or better than Brearley'. Six months later, David Frith's magisterial revisitation of the 1932–33 Ashes series, *Bodyline Autopsy* (2002), concluded with an approving nod to a late-life reflection of Jack Fingleton: 'I think, looking back, the Australians perhaps made too much fuss about it.' At this rate, Michael Vaughan's reintroduction of the harlequin cap cannot be far away.

This mellowing reflects not merely the passage of time, but also the changing of fashion. Batsmen skewered by pace from four prongs in the 1970s and 1980s found it hard to imagine bowling any more hostile; and if they could take it, then could Bodyline *really* have been so bad? After all, only Larwood, abetted by Voce, had kept the leg cordons busy; only once in that series had England taken the field without a slow bowler, and Voce gave way to a second spinner in Brisbane.

International cricketers teethed in the 1990s and 2000s exhibit an aggression more calculated and cruel than anything dreamed of around the time of the Great Depression. The only on-field remark that Jardine is recorded to have made with the hint of a sledge was after rival Bill Woodfull absorbed his famous body blow at Adelaide in January 1933. 'Well bowled Harold,' the legend goes, was uttered for non-striker Bradman's edification. It's hardly: 'How's your wife and my kids?'

Jardine having been brought within the realm of the acceptable, it was then but a small step to turn him into an exemplar. Beating Australia with Bradman was obviously no trifling achievement. And from a modern standpoint, beating Australia at all seems the stuff of which dreams are made. Undefeated in home series for fifteen years, still never having dipped its green and gold colours to India, Pakistan or Sri Lanka in front of its own audiences, Australia is cricket's benchmark. Jardine's deeds, then, improve a little as each year of Australian dominance passes.

There is, however, a missing dimension to these calculations: the enigma of Woodfull. The captain who had regained the Ashes in 1930 gave them up 4-1 without ever attempting to parallel England's strategy: as unreactive as Jardine was active. In his classic text *Cricket Crisis* (1946), Jack Fingleton reflected:

> Australia certainly could have retaliated. It is a moot point whether retaliation would not have been the best and quickest way out of the mess, and whether it would not have quelled the jibes of squealing which assailed the Australians from many points at that time and in later years.

But where some on his own side, such as his vice-captain Victor Richardson, favoured an eye-for-an-eye response, the Methodist minister's son turned the other cheek.

We now have a rather better understanding of Woodfull's thinking. In the course of the research for a new history of Cricket Australia, *Inside Story*, a letter came to light from Woodfull that was apparently read aloud at the Australian Board of Control's meeting of 30 January 1933. Woodfull thought that while 'not infringing the laws of cricket', Jardine's team were 'lowering the prestige of the game':

> There is evidence and like to the effect that two prominent English bowlers constantly attack the batsmen without paying the slightest attention to the stumps. ... Bowling of this type had unsettled the Australian batsmen during this season and all batsmen have been compelled for the first time to wear not only hip pads but also a pad covering the heart. A more serious injury than has occurred to date is only a matter of time.

Woodfull's suggestion—never entertained—was a meeting between the Board, Jardine and the aqueous English manager Pelham Warner. His general attitude, however, was that he was powerless to do anything—interestingly not so much because of Jardine as because of the Englishman's senior professionals:

> To my mind we can hardly legislate on such a question but I would suggest a meeting of the Board with Messrs Jardine and Warner to see whether amicable relations could not be restored to some extent for the present. I am of the opinion that Mr Warner is against the theory ... but that the professional players are too strong in their influence and opinions.
>
> The cricket bodies of both countries could bring pressure to bear, if necessary, on the cricket captains of first-class teams. England I am certain will fall into line, especially if they have a real taste of this theory next season in County Cricket. However, it is really on the field that the remedy rests, and while a cricket captain who still has the backing of MCC persists in the practice, little can be done by way of improvement.
>
> Since entering Test cricket I have not been sure that it is for the good of the Empire and in times when England and Australia need to be pulling together, large sections of both countries are embittered. Consequently I think that the utmost must be done to find a way out. It appears unlikely that this would be discovered before the end of the present series, yet I think it imperative that the matches be continued for more harm than good would be done by cancellation than by carrying out of the programme.

This stoical acceptance of England's strategy for the sake of imperial harmony has a certain nobility, but it is also strangely lacking in imagination. It left Woodfull's comrades to their own devices, although he also disapproved of anything that smacked of innovation: thus the captain looked severely on Bradman's response of retreating to leg to exploit the depopulated off. Woodfull was a strong enough man and a respected enough leader to enforce his will on the team, but in doing so and limiting Australian response he made Bodyline an even more effective approach than it might have been.

It may seem fanciful to suggest that Jardine would have been deflected from his course: he was no more for turning than Margaret Thatcher. But we do know he was surprised that Larwood and Voce proved so penetrative, observing during *In Quest of the Ashes* (1933) that he was not in advance 'inclined to rate the possibilities of leg-theory very highly', because he harboured 'a very healthy respect for their [Australians'] play off the leg stump'. Never imagining that leg theory 'would stand such a test as would prove its effectiveness throughout the whole tour', he thought merely that it 'might occasionally prove a profitable variation when two batsmen were well set'. He could persist in part because there was never any threat of reciprocity, or even countermeasure.

Would Jardine make a great captain today? He certainly had the pertinacity and inflexibility of purpose to which a leader facing Ricky Ponting's Australians must aspire, although the cool insouciance in the face of the media might today be harder to achieve. 'I'm here to win the Ashes, not provide scoops for your ruddy newspapers,' he is alleged to have said; not even Hussain at his rudest ever tried that.

All the same, for Jardine to triumph he needed a rival like Woodfull, prepared to be run roughshod over for the sake of imperial relations. Today it is hard to imagine a captain, least of all in Ashes cricket, responding with such passivity to the unfolding plans of his opponent; if anything, the modern custom is to get one's retaliation in first. So while Jardine's captaincy might appear to have a modern edge, its effectiveness was very much of its time.

Cricinfo, October 2007

The Serious Australian

In 1980, the editor of the *Age*, an accomplished and cultured Englishman called Michael Davie, was introduced by a colleague to the record-breaking Australian batsman Bill Ponsford. Davie, biographer of LBJ and editor of Evelyn Waugh's diaries, was nonetheless as excited as could be: he loved cricket, wrote expertly about it, and Ponsford, as a teammate of Sir Donald Bradman, had sat, as it were, at God's right hand.

The interview went swimmingly. Ponsford needed little persuasion to discuss his career and contemporaries, Bradman included. Turning a page in one of his scrapbooks, in fact, Ponsford let something slip with reference to their former captain: 'Bill Woodfull never forgave him for a couple of things.' There was a pause. Davie awaited elaboration; Ponsford, perhaps, awaited further inquiry. Neither man spoke further. Conversation moved on.

Davie lived to rue his failure of nerve, describing it as one of the chief regrets of his editorship. Woodfull, generally thought one of Bradman's staunchest admirers, was already dead; the same is now true of Ponsford and Davie. And when 27 August marks the centenary of Bradman's birth, it will reference a permanent but essentially static exhibit in the museum of national memory, shored up by generations of just such deferential incuriosity.

Still the most compelling aspect of the legend is the average—perhaps it should almost be called The Average. One hundred is not the maximum possible arithmetic mean score in cricket, but 99.94, with its tincture of human fallibility, its hint of Oulipian constraint, could not have been more exquisitely contrived. To a generation addicted to measurement and saturated in numbers, The Average is monolithic, unassailable, totemic.

Yet by The Average, it would seem, are we largely to know him. Of the 'man' in Bradman, so to speak, views are surprisingly vague. There is a certain comfort in calling him 'great' and leaving it at that; there is a certain contrarian glee, too, in deeming him an old, dead guy, especially given his unwitting implication in the Howard ascendancy, and the unevolving *bien-pensant* snobbery about sport. If only he'd been less popular, one is left to conclude, Bradman might have occasioned deeper interest.

On one level, however, Bradman's story concerns not so much sport as success. He performed a particular task more effectively than any man before or since; more effectively, perhaps, than any other Australian has performed theirs. The task was, to be sure, narrow and highly specialised, yet Bradman sustained a gargantuan superiority over a period of twenty years. One of the most elegant appraisals of Bradman is in the memoirs of GH Hardy, the outstanding English mathematician of the first half of last century. Hardy ranked mathematical brains by reference to cricket; into 'the Bradman class' he admitted only Newton, Archimedes and Gauss. 'It is a tiny minority who can do anything really well and the number of men who can do two things well is negligible,' Hardy noted. 'If a man has any genuine talent, he should be ready to make almost any sacrifice in order to cultivate it to the full.' Hardy was unillusioned about cricket's significance, but also unmoved by it: 'Poetry is more valuable than cricket, but Bradman would be a fool if he sacrificed his cricket in order to write second-rate minor poetry.' Not to be intrigued by Bradman's attainments, then, is a species of philistinism.

The Bradman story is also about fame, for the young Australians shortly to be lionised for their Olympic accomplishments will experience a limelight diffuse and fleeting by comparison with the one that shone on the cricketer. Bradman spent his entire adult life yoked tightly by expectation, more broadly famous and for longer than any other Australian, while his posthumous fame will shortly be sold to us again in XL value packs of nostalgia. All the more reason, in fact, to return to the story of Bradman's becoming famous rather than being already so, in his formative years between 1930 and 1934, when he changed the course of sport utterly, and his own life irrevocably.

~

Many distinguished individuals bequeath literary and epistolary estates to collecting institutions. Bradman's paper monument, a five-year project that he oversaw at South Australia's Mortlock Library in the 1970s, are fifty-two superbly bound volumes of newspaper clippings, diary entries, correspondence and photographs that fill almost five metres of shelf space. It is a time capsule—albeit, of course, of a very particular kind, being compiled up to fifty years after the events described, and with the tenor of an authorised version.

One respect in which this is obviously so is the choice of start date. Bradman famously first represented Bowral in October 1920 as an emergency: usually scorer, the precocious 12-year-old scored 37 and 29 not out when the team found itself a man short. By his own account, he then reverted to scoring, and in his preliminary commentary for the scrapbooks states:

> Leaving school at the age of fourteen I gave up cricket and devoted a whole summer to tennis, largely due to the influence of a favoured uncle. At the end of the following season I was persuaded to play cricket again but only batted twice, making 0 and 66. My serious cricket career began in 1925–26 and this volume commences at that point.

Biographers have taken this at face value, preferring to dwell on the singular image of the boy Bradman learning to bat by the solitary discipline of stump and golf ball. But two years ago, the industrious statistician Alf James self-published a remarkable chronicle of Bradman's 'minor' cricket: his 350 club, invitation and practice matches. *The Don vs the Rest* shows that in the seasons from 1920–21 and 1924–25, Bradman actually represented Bowral thirty times, with utterly unremarkable results—only two half-centuries. Was Bradman sensitive about having been so ordinary, so human? Likelier is it an index of his attitude to the game: cricket counted only when it was 'serious'; thus did he wish only to be judged after having, as it were, put away childish things.

Once Bradman became *un homme serieux*, of course, his ascent was steep: he represented St George in 1926–27, New South Wales in 1927–28, Australia in 1928–29, and finally took England by storm in 1930, vaulting the perils and pitfalls said to await every fast-rising youth. And it is by his seriousness, I think, that Bradman is first to be understood. Sent off on his first Ashes tour by well-wishers at Bowral's Empire Theatre, he described cricket in terms not so much of recreation, or even of patriotic expression, but of moral education: 'First my parents taught me to be a cricketer off the field as well as on. It was not "did you win" but "did you play the game" that made the man.' To Bradman, cricket was a peerless builder of character: 'I have no doubt that it moulds in an individual the right type of character better than any other sport. If that can be substantiated, no other recommendation is required, because character must surely be one of the greatest assets any nation through its citizens can possess.'

Bradman never budged from this conviction. Addressing the 'Bradman: Insights at Lord's' conference seven years ago, the venerable English cricket administrator Doug Insole described Bradman as almost more English than the English: 'Right up to the end of his life he was determined to preserve the overall integrity of the game, its entertainment value and its sporting traditions in an *almost amateurly English public school way*, in many respects.' [My italics] Bradman confided in Insole that the honour he most valued was the offer of the presidency of Marylebone Cricket Club: the unashamedly elitist private members' club that occupies Lord's and has traditionally served as the game's lawgiver:

> In all seriousness I did on more than one occasion have the opportunity to be president of MCC, and gave it serious consideration because of the honour it would have conferred on Australian cricket. But in the end my personal inability to physically cope with the demands made me rule it out. As a compliment to my services to cricket, I thought it in many ways would have been a greater honour than my knighthood which I never sought or wanted.

Some will carp at the identification of Bradman with such inegalitarian and irrepublican interests as amateurism, the English public school and MCC, yet his attitudes faithfully reflect the deeply English roots of Australia's sporting culture, to which homage is still paid in the interminable debates about athletes behaving as 'role models' and notions of 'bringing the game into disrepute'. Belonging to an era in which these were more than mere parrot cries, Bradman tackled cricket with an earnestness as much moral as mechanical.

Yet there is equally no doubt that Bradman was a genuine people's champion—a phenomenon abetted by the mass communication miracles of talking pictures, wire photos and wireless. From 1930, Ashes Tests in England were covered ball-by-ball on Australian radio stations, reconstituted in the studio from cabled messages: an initiative of 2UW perfected by the ABC. With each of Bradman's scoring feats came bales of telegrams that now savour richly of an old Australia: 'Congratulations from a boy admirer of Bradman's for breaking world record score'; 'Congratulations to Don Bradman from a blind soldier at Kurnell'; 'Congrats breaking record marvellous keep it up Don', signed by 'the Girls, Hotel Windsor'; 'Give Don huge embrace unique performance behalf Taralga Girl Admirers'. Responding on 2FC after his world record 452 not out against Queensland in January 1930, Bradman enumerated the locations from which congratulations had arrived—place names that could be of no other country: Adelong, Arncliffe, Austinmer, Bombara, Brewarrina, Cobar, Collie, Coolah, Coonamble, Cootamundra, Corrimla, Crookwell, Dapto, Dunedoo, Epping, Ettrigal, Jamberoo, Junee, Killabakh, Mandemer, Rylstone, Salt Ash, Toorooka, Trungely Hall ...

Nor was this admiration merely about runs and records: generally, one could hardly have sought a more exemplary national representative. John Howard was far from the first to mingle praise of Bradman the cricketer with generous estimates of Bradman the individual. Commentators on his first Ashes series in 1928–29 were as enamoured of his character as his talent. 'Australia has unearthed a champion, self-taught, with natural ability,' stated former Australian captain Clem Hill. 'But most important of all, with his heart in the right place.' Australian selector Dick Jones gushed: 'It is good to watch him talking to an old player, listening attentively to everything that is said and then replying with a modest "thank you".'

This modesty was unfeigned. English journalist William Pollock, who came to know Bradman well, found him quaintly self-effacing: 'He is not at all swell-headed. On the contrary he has almost a horror of saying or doing anything that might lead people to say that he is conceited or putting on side. He is very nearly fastidiously sensitive in this matter.' Yet, as Pollock noted, this was not so much graceful self-deprecation as an almost preternatural self-control: 'He accepts the position he has achieved just as any sensible man who gets to the top of any particular tree should accept it. He is remarkably free from affectation ... He is a calm person, and one thing I have noticed is that he can sit still.' There is something of this affectless calm, for example, in the sentiments he expressed after he passed the world record 437 of Bill Ponsford—sentiments so nonchalant that one needs reminding they were uttered by a country boy of limited education barely old enough to vote.

On 434 ... I had a curious intuition. While [Queensland's Hugh] Thurlow was preparing to bowl, I seemed to sense that the ball would be a short-pitched one on the leg stump and I could almost feel myself getting ready to make my shot before the ball was delivered. Sure enough it pitched exactly where I had anticipated, and, hooking it to the square leg boundary, I established the only record upon which I had set my heart.

Many people have asked me to describe my feelings when I realized that I had accomplished this performance. The best description I can offer is that I felt as a man who had achieved a specific task which he had set himself to do, and having done it was satisfied. I was not excited, and I cannot say that I suffered any reaction. My feeling was one of complete satisfaction.

No wonder that some were already regarding Bradman as superhuman—and that others, in time, would find him a little less than human.

~

Bradman approached his first tour of England with characteristic meticulousness. His diary of the Australian team's progress through Europe is richly detailed, although it is a compilation of things rather than thoughts, facts rather than feelings, from the fifty-two columns and 6000 statues of Milan Cathedral to the one pig and ninety-five loaves carbonised in an oven in Pompeii. 'First impression of Rome is one of greatness,' Bradman notes in a rare qualitative judgement; otherwise greatness is intimated in quantities and dimensions. Vatican City was noted for its 700 priests, 2000 people and 4000 rooms, St Peters for its 350 years, 284 columns and four central columns of 284 feet each. At the Tomb of the Unknown Warrior, Bradman was captivated by the memorial to Victor Emmanuel: 'Statue of Emmanuel on horse in centre. 20 journalists had a dinner inside the belly of the horse on conclusion. Moustache 3 feet long. Sword 11 feet.' Nor did the custom change when Bradman arrived in England. One entry concerns a visit to a munitions factory owned by Vickers Ltd.

> Saw machinery juggling a big piece of red hot metal as we would a penny. From a piece 4' long and 12" square it turned out a piece 20' long and 3" square. Another machine cut 12" metal as though it was butter. 15" guns, 50' long ordered for Spain, 18 of them at £30 000 each. 1927 order not yet delivered.

Quantities concerning him chiefly by this stage, however, were runs, which poured torrentially from the first, without ever affecting his temperateness of expression. In his hotel room after the first day of the Leeds Test, for example, he noted simply: 'Archie [Jackson] out for 1. I followed and at stumps was 309 not out, breaking the previous highest score in Anglo-Australian Tests. Reached my 2000 runs for the season. To hotel in evening for dinner and wrote letters, thence to bed.' Bradman pursued off-field ends with something like the same calm-browed deliberation. His diary is packed with business appointments as well as social engagements, men of means at long-ago companies, from bat maker William Sykes, who hosted Bradman at length, to soap magnate Arthur Whitelaw, who settled £1000 on Bradman for his Leeds triumph, not to mention the ad men McGloin and Kahane of Imperial Advertising, who kept the young Australian amused and busy in London. English cricket writer RC Robertson-Glasgow left behind a delicious vignette of Bradman in the writing room of his Folkestone hotel methodically scaling a mountain of mail: 'He had made his name in cricket. He was fresh from triumphs against England at Lord's and at the Oval. And now, quiet and calculating, he was, he told me, trying to capitalize his success.'

Bradman's most time-consuming task was producing a book—a course in which he was probably inspired by the example of teammate Clarrie Grimmett, who had dashed off a short, cheap instructional text en route from Australia aboard the Orient liner *Orford*. Soon after arriving, Bradman agreed terms with literary agent David Cromb of Cotterrill & Cromb, the work to be overseen by former *Daily Telegraph* sports editor Ben Bennison. Bennison, whose memory stretched back to WG Grace, and who numbered Jim Corbett and Jack Dempsey among his friends, found his 21-year-old subject as assured and painstaking as any. 'A more serious young man, or one richer in power of concentration I have not met,' Bennison recalled in his memoir *Giants on Parade*. 'To the last ounce, he knew his value, not only as a cricketer but as a man.' Certainly Bradman's authentic voice can be heard in such remarks as: 'It is a trait in my make-up which it is quite impossible to explain that I am an almost total stranger to that species of nervousness common to most people whenever involved in an unusual happening.'

Perhaps Bradman's most poignant encounter was one that no biographer has noted. While the Australians were playing Hampshire at Brighton, they found themselves staying at the same hotel, the seafront Metropole, as Amy Johnson—perhaps the only non-Royal person more famous in the Empire than Bradman after her nineteen-day Gypsy Moth flight from London to Darwin four months earlier. Johnson was then on an exhausting tour of England under the direction of a bullying and manipulative publicist from her sponsor, the *Daily Mail*, and finding public life an exquisite torture. Her identity as 'Amy Johnson', she complained privately, had become 'a nightmare and an abomination' to her; she would shortly voluntarily admit herself to the care of a Harley Street surgeon, saying she was 'on the brink on insanity'.

The 27-year-old aviatrix was one of very few who left a personal impression on Bradman. 'Was introduced to Amy Johnson and during the course of a drink together I had quite a long chat to her,' he diarised. 'Charming, unaffected girl.' He noted her presence again at a dinner the following night. One wonders whether their conversation traversed the wages of fame, on which Johnson was already expert and Bradman would become so.

~

On 4 August 1930, London's *Star* commenced publishing advance extracts from *Don Bradman's Book*, which at that stage was actually still being written, and not scheduled to appear until the end of November. This was actually the initiative of Cromb to whom Bradman had, somewhat naively, sold serial rights for a lump sum. But to manager Bill Kelly, the serialisation represented a prima facie breach of Clause XI of the Australian team's tour contract, which forbade 'any work for, or in connection with, any newspaper' or 'any member, servant or agent thereof'. According to a confidential report to the Australian Board of Control for International Cricket, Kelly 'immediately interviewed Bradman' and advised that he 'did not approve of the article appearing', and by implication would disapprove of subsequent articles. Bradman replied merely that it was 'too late to prevent them'. Nor did he show any trace of annoyance with Cromb, gifting his agent the bat with which he scored his Ashes-winning 232 at the Oval.

Yet Bradman's return was awkward. From January 1930, Bradman had worked in the sporting goods outfitters Mick Simmons Ltd in Sydney's Haymarket, his advertised presence a promotional drawcard: 'His charming personality ... his happy smile and expert advice are entirely at your service.' Now their public relations man, former journalist Oscar Lawson, wished to lever the relationship further, enlisting General Motors in a homecoming pageant that ushered Bradman to Sydney through Perth, Adelaide, Melbourne and Goulburn: a pageant, in fact, similar to Amy Johnson's in Australia and England. Civic receptions were interspersed with appearances on the 'General Motors Family Party Hour' on 5AD, 3DB and 2UW, in recognition of which the cricketer was presented with a red 'Don Bradman Model Chevrolet'.

Biographers have noted hints that the spectacle did not endear Bradman to teammates, already inclined to view him as a man apart. To be fair, it also perturbed Bradman. The 'serious' young man always gave an impressive account of himself, but found public scrutiny as strenuous as Johnson—particularly when scrutiny turned critical.

This it became when the Board summoned him on 30 December to explain the serialisation of *Don Bradman's Book*. The Board, then as secretive and censorious as a conclave of cardinals, docked him £50: a third of the 'good conduct' bonus of his £600 tour fee.

Bradman seethed about this reprimand. 'Had I thought for one moment I was violating my contract with the Board I would not have written that book,' he stated publicly. 'At the time I did not think I was committing a breach. I am still of the same opinion.' He would brood on the episode, revisiting it at intervals, complaining in his autobiography *Farewell to Cricket* twenty years later that 'the Board had given consent for Clarrie Grimmett' to write a book, although as a Board member at the time he preferred to deplore press sensationalism than administrative intransigence: 'There was no need for any fuss but the incident was seized upon to try and magnify an alleged breach between the Board and myself.' Yet there was nothing 'alleged' about the breach, and the old hurt returned in October 1993 during an unpublished interview with his friend Bob Parish:

> There was no appeal against it but I was very distressed because it portrayed me as a person who broke a contract and I'm not the sort of person who would ever break a contract. It also distressed me because I understand that Clarrie Grimmett did exactly the same thing as I did, but he had written to the Board and asked for permission and they gave him permission. ... Surely to God I'm entitled to tell the press what happened when I went to school at Bowral when I was twelve years of age.

The clause was, of course, a pettifogging restriction; a body that had profited by £21 825 begrudging the overwhelming contributor to that windfall. It was also poorly worded, bringing 'matters connected with the tour' as a prohibited subject into a secondary clause. But it is fairly clear that the Board was right on the letter of the contract, and that Bradman's complaint about Grimmett was weightless. Grimmett's book, *Getting Wickets*, was published *before* the Tests in England; nor had anything prevented Bradman emulating Grimmett in seeking the same permission. (Grimmett was reassured in a hitherto-unpublished October 1932 letter from Board secretary Bill Jeanes that 'you acted perfectly within your rights in everything you did' and 'you did not commit any breach of your agreement'.)

This was another dimension to Bradman's seriousness: when the willpower he brought to cricket was applied in controversy, it could heat grievances to incandescence. Bradman admitted frankly that, although his Test average for the summer of 1930–31 was 74.50, 'my mind was most disturbed', 'my concentration ... fell away because of these extraneous matters' and 'my form was patchy'. And while Bradman professed himself a stranger to nerves, between his feats he was coming to need reasonable rest, preferably in seclusion. 'I always felt anxiety prior to the start of a big game,' he explained in an unconsciously revealing passage in *Farewell to Cricket*. 'Once action commenced I lost the earlier sensation. It was replaced by a sort of tense exhilaration which, at the conclusion of a match, often gave way to a severe reaction.' Where his recovery was compromised, then, his efforts levied a heavy tax. There is a direct connection, moreover, between this first of Bradman's brushes with the Board in 1930 and the second two years later.

The cause of the second was again Bradman's commercial entanglements. Between August and November 1931, a mutual public courting took place between Bradman and the Lancashire League club Accrington: the leagues were then the world's most lucrative professional circuit, and had attracted several Australian players. Through Bradman's 1930 tour contract stretched another visible tripwire: Clause VII forbade the signatory, on pain of disqualification, from playing in England within two years of touring with the national team. But Bradman, amid grave public forebodings, evinced considerable interest in Accrington's enticements. Ivan Sharpe of the *Manchester Evening Chronicle* was with Accrington's secretary, Gideon Holgate, when the terms were discussed with Bradman by telephone.

This latest offer made to Bradman impressed him. There is no doubt about that. This is not surprising. It is the biggest fee a cricketer has ever been offered ... No, Bradman is not 'kidding'. They are all fuming about it in Australia, but the voice at the Sydney end of the line was that of a cool, calculating young man who is out to hit the iron while it is hot.

Bradman's services were retained for Australia by a consortium offer from the sporting goods retailer FJ Palmer & Sons, Associated Newspapers and radio station 2UE. The moving force was almost certainly Kerry Packer's grandfather Clyde, newly installed as Associated's managing editor after his long career at *Smith's Weekly*, and determined to make over its dowdy morning tabloid *Sun*; Bradman was also to broadcast an eponymous 'Cricket Talk' twice weekly on 2UE's Uncle Lionel and the Listerine Serenaders, as well as being 'heard often on the piano'. The sums were considerable: in a later court case, 2UE's general manager CV Stevenson disclosed that Bradman's annual fee for broadcasting alone was £1000—about five times the basic wage. But if radio was so new that it had yet to attract the usual Board of Control prohibitions on anything that savoured of commercialisation, it was obvious always that Bradman's writing for a newspaper would again incur administrative disapproval. Bradman was evidently prepared to forbear that displeasure; perhaps, subconsciously, he even courted it.

For friction there was, and the tables were exquisitely turned. The Board's unambiguous position was that only those players whose 'sole occupation' was journalism could write for newspapers, and then only after obtaining permission and while avoiding specified subjects like selection. Thus Bradman, penalised for breaking a contract with the Board, faced Board exhortations to break a contract with Associated Newspapers. In September 1932, he signalled his intention of doing no such thing: 'I have signed a contract to write newspaper articles and I intend to carry it out.

I must earn my living, and if cricket interferes with my living then I must give up cricket.'

Breaking a contract now seems a relative triviality; three-quarters of a century ago it loomed rather larger. The austerity measures of the Premiers' Plan had been the subject of agonised debate, involving as they did an alteration of the terms of Australia's debt. Political and fiscal conservatives like the silver-tongued Victorian MLA Robert Menzies deplored this violation of 'the sanctity of contracts', without which there was 'no hope for our salvation'—sentiments he reprised again and again. Bradman repeated himself with like insistence, even obduracy, for no employer would have dared hold him to a contract that prevented his playing—it would have defeated the purpose of securing an association. He dug in to such an extent that he ignored the company's offer to waive its rights. 'I have made a contract with Associated Newspapers which I intend to honour,' he explained. 'I am sorry but I cannot accept your offer of release.' In other words, he was insisting on writing for a newspaper that didn't wish him to write. The inference must be that he was bent on proving wrong the Board's decision two years earlier by demonstrating that he was 'not the sort of person who would ever break a contract'.

For Bradman these were dark and hurrying days. While his future was weighed in a bureaucratic balance, he crossed the Nullarbor with state teammates Stan McCabe and Jack Fingleton to play in a tour match in Perth against the newly arrived English cricket team; Bradman was trailed, Fingleton recalled, by oppressive expectations.

> Piping little voices traveled the length of the train calling 'Bradman, Bradman, Bradman' when infrequent stops were made along that desolate, dreary line. At Quorn, a sleep little hamlet drowsing in the hot sun, the Mayor came down to accord us a civic reception in the shade of peppercorn trees. Kalgoorlie, with its famous, bearded 6ft 6in Mayor Leslie,

wearing a sombrero hat, gave us another reception. Further down the line at Coolgardie hundreds of enthusiastic miners flocked to the station calling for Bradman. His patience was worn thin by this time. He locked himself in his cabin, but the miners were determined to get a glimpse of him. They began to ransack the train, several windows were broken and the conductor thought it time he moved out of Coolgardie.

Out twice in a day for the only time in his career, Bradman left the record crowd desolate. Local leg-spinner Teddy Martin recalled him as pensive: a 'very quiet' teammate who 'did little but sit in the corner and keep to himself'. Perhaps Bradman was mulling over the inducements coming his way as a result of his stand-off with the Board, like the Australian company offering to buy the Associated contract out so he could play, and the English newspaper dangling £3000 so he could write. In the event, according to Bradman's close friend Johnnie Moyes, it took Clyde Packer's personal entreaties to ensure Bradman's availability:

'You must play, Don,' said the chief.

'You can force me to write but there is nothing in the contract which allows you to force me to play,' returned Bradman.

'Well, Don, we are asking you forget writing for the time being.'

'If you put it that way, I will accept and play,' said Bradman. 'But I want it understood that at any time I am prepared to give up playing and honour my contract with you.'

Even then, Bradman was anxious to emphasise that he had not repudiated the contract. The statement announcing his availability for the series deplored 'that the Board of Control continues to prevent me from earning an honourable and permanent living from the occupation of journalism', while his retrospective summary in *Farewell to Cricket* was little less withering:

> My disagreement with the Board of Control developed into a public wrangle. This was due to no fault of mine ... All these things disturbed me tremendously when in fact I only wanted to do my duty. Finally the newspaper requested me to play cricket and forgo my writings during that summer. Thus the decision was taken out of my hands.

The dramatic use of the word 'duty' in the context of a straight-forward commercial agreement is perhaps his own homage to the Menzian faith in the 'sanctity of contracts'.

A larger drama was now in the offing, for the next match of the English team's tour involved the first fast, short-pitched sallies of what their captain Douglas Jardine would implement as 'Bodyline' bowling. Bradman, unsettled, skittish, was dismissed cheaply again, and shortly sent word to the selectors he would prefer to bat lower in the order during the Tests. The request became moot when, on the eve of the series, Bradman was examined at the Board's behest by Drs Archie Aspinall and Allan Holmes a Court, partners in a practice at 135 Macquarie Street. They declared him unfit to play— 'organically sound' but 'seriously run down'.

What this meant has never been explained. The most original hypothesis has been advanced in *Quadrant* by Frank Devine, who interviewed Bradman at length fifteen years ago for an unpublished biography; like Davie, alas, Devine confessed regret at his own tact.

> His [Bradman's] neglected teeth were giving him hell at the start of the Bodyline season and distracting pain may have contributed to a series of low scores against Jardine's team in preliminary matches. Don had only been to a dentist once in his life. At eighteen, intolerable pain forced him into the surgery of a dentist whose sign he had noticed on his way to and from Sydney's Central railway station. The dentist's treatment

consisted of extracting two teeth so roughly that Don, sitting alone in the lounge of the house where he was boarding, later fainted from loss of blood.

I have long suspected that Don had all his teeth extracted during the final day or two of the first Bodyline Test, which he missed through "illness", and that he spent the following week alone with his wife, Jessie, at a remote beach cottage, getting used to dentures. I regret that I didn't press Don harder on this in a series of interviews I had with him in 1993. He was evasive (conceivably not wanting to be thought a whinger or alibi-maker) and shushed Lady Bradman quite crossly when she attempted to contribute to the conversation.

Yet if Bradman was in general 'organically sound' on the Test's eve, the doctors must also have reached some conclusion regarding his psychosomatic condition. A Bradman presenting no physical indisposition and desperate to take the field would hardly have not; this suggests a deeper malaise, a man surfeited by cricket, with the hounding and now the hostility coming in its train. For Bradman certainly experienced presentiments about the summer, confiding in the Board member to whom he was closest, Frank Cush of New South Wales, that England's early tactics boded ill for the good conduct of the Tests.

When finally he did play, of course, Bradman's statistical effectiveness was essentially halved—his average of 56 in four Tests compared with 112 beforehand. His methods, moreover, forsaking his wicket in favour of fevered strokes from outside leg stump, spread dismay through his own ranks, while bolstering English morale. 'Don Bradman made some incredible shots,' wrote the English fast bowler Gubby Allen to his parents after the final Test. 'But he is a terrible little coward of fast bowling.' And such aspersions still cause squeamishness. When writer Brian Rendell was researching the Allen correspondence in the Mitchell Library from which the above quote comes, he was told initially that access to the letter in question was restricted on grounds that it contained 'references which would cause pain and embarrassment to a living person'.

Yet Bradman's response to the physical threat of Bodyline may be less interesting than his intellectual one. Remember: perhaps no great sportsman has been so invidiously placed. Without Bradman, there would have been no Bodyline; through no doing of his own he was the cause of a crisis endangering the reputation of the game he identified with all that was good in the Empire, and relations between countries to whom his loyalty was scrupulously even-handed. Perhaps this is why Bradman interpreted Bodyline from the first in emphatic terms. A key artefact is a letter he wrote the Lancashire League club Rochdale, then seeking his services, while the Second Test was underway.

> When my present contract expires ... I cannot say with any certainty that I shall receive any further offers to remain in Australia. In view of recent happenings, there is nothing definite as to the future of cricket.
>
> The Australian team [scheduled to tour England] in 1934 may not eventuate if conflicts continue or bodyline bowling may kill all cricket under MCC control unless they ban it.

Composed nearly three weeks before the outbreak of the notorious paper war between the Board of Control and MCC, these are exceptionally prescient lines. But unlike Jack Fingleton, who famously felt 'the crashing of an ideal' in his experiences at the brunt of Bodyline, Bradman essentially doubled his investment in the relevant institutions. He regarded the Board's cables to Lord's, which provocatively described Bodyline as 'unsportsmanlike', as an 'awful' miscalculation. His personal contribution to diplomatic relations—a two-page, typewritten letter proposing a change to the lbw law addressed to the secretary of MCC—lies unexamined in the Bradman Collection. Dated 30 January 1933, it is couched so humbly that the effect would be cloying were it not so obviously genuine:

Only after considerable thought have I dared to write this letter to the controlling body in cricket. In doing so I have but one thought in my mind which is 'the betterment of our glorious game of cricket'. I have taken the liberty of presuming my letter will be read to the members of MCC. Should my presumption be correct then it is quite possible that, after hearing the contents, the members will think it presumptuous of me to have the temerity to even dream of making a suggestion to them. Should they take this view no harm will be done. On the other hand if they are prepared to listen to my suggestion I would feel very honoured.

Bradman perceived Bodyline as the bowlers' attempt to redress the imbalance between bat and ball—for which he, Bradman, was, of course, partly responsible. Here he offered a careful exposition of how extending the lbw law to the off side might obviate the need for such extreme bowling countermeasures as those of Jardine's devising: 'Unquestionably teams would make less [sic] runs. To my mind it would be in the best interests of the game if this was so.' He concluded with another reference to his 24-year-old's station: 'Compared with the members of your club I am but an inexperienced youth but in a short space of time I have learned to love our grand game and if I have taken up your time with an impracticable idea I apologise.'

Not least is the letter fascinating because the recipient at the time was at loggerheads with the Board; the implied contrast is between Bradman's abiding contempt for Australian cricket's own governors and his serene faith in British good sense. He underestimated British tactlessness; MCC did not reply. But two years later Bradman had cause to renew his allegiance, for MCC changed the law broadly along the lines he had advocated. No evidence connects Bradman's recommendation with the reform, but none refutes it, which may account for his keeping faith with the ideal that Fingleton found 'crashed'. It may also explain why Bradman preferred in future to blame Bodyline on Jardine alone, while Fingleton, whose *Cricket Crisis* remains the essential inside story of events, was more broadly critical of an administrative class too hidebound to intervene.

~

Bradman's key relations were strained by the events of 1932–33. He had displeased administrators and alienated at least some comrades; the character so widely praised did not so naturally invite sympathy. Some in Sydney now thought him just a little too thrusting, a little too determined to have his way, a little lacking in metropolitan polish: Bradman himself would later assent that 'it was a handicap that my education had been of limited character', while proclaiming that it was 'no disgrace to come from humble parents of modest means in a small and somewhat parochial country village'. His story comes to involve intersecting strains of Australian snobbery: the Anglo disdain for the native, the urban for the provincial. Inclined to the former, Bradman incurred the latter.

Bradman, now married to his childhood sweetheart Jessie, was ever anxious about his financial security; he also had a taste for commercial life. 'The thing that most interests Don Bradman in life is work in business,' noted his friend Pollock. 'He is methodical, he has a mind for figures, he is keen on making money. He may never be a very rich man, but I feel sure he will never be a very poor one. His head is screwed on the right way. He is a clever little devil—and I mean that affectionately.' The trouble was that, in Sydney, the opportunities available almost always involved being even more public than appearing on the sporting field, like the partnership he forged with JT Smith, twenty years the general manager of FJ Palmer & Sons. Don Bradman Ltd, planning to 'carry on the business of tailors, mens and boys outfitters, and sporting goods dealers', issued a prospectus offering 35 000 £1 shares in September 1933. In return for its blessing, Bradman licensed Palmer 'the exclusive use of his name, photograph, likeness, signature and replica of same for the use by the company in New South Wales in connection with goods or merchandise which the company may offer for sale'. Bradman does not seem to have been devastated when not a quarter of the shares were subscribed, and the venture was abandoned.

Momentarily, however, Bradman was perplexed. As Johnnie Moyes recalled, he simply 'did not know what he would do'—a rare quandary for a man so organised and decisive. On behalf of the *Sun's* editor Delamore McCay, Moyes offered Bradman a job as a full-time journalist, but the cricketer had had his fill of writing, and the inevitable squabbles. Local cricket authorities also seemed disinclined to assist. When it was put to the secretary of the NSW Cricket Association that their star attraction was unsettled, Harry Heydon huffed that Bradman was morally bound to the people who had 'made him'. Bradman was thus uniquely susceptible to the inducements of South Australian Board member Harry Hodgetts while New South Wales was in Adelaide a week before Christmas. In return for relocating, Bradman became clearly Australia's best-paid junior sharebrokers' clerk: Hodgetts, whose eponymous firm was one of the city's most prestigious, offered Bradman a six-year contract, commencing 14 March 1934, paying £500 per annum during cricket engagements and £700 per annum at other times.

Publicly, the NSWCA blessed the move, on the grounds that perennially unsuccessful South Australia needed all the help it could get. Privately, they were wounded. Treasurer Ted Tyler wept openly at the news, as well he might have, for Sydney gate takings would next season be 55 per cent lower, while revenue from New South Wales's annual derby against Victoria would shrink 96 per cent in the next three years. And vice-president 'Doc' Evatt was so embittered even five years later that he weighed in unbidden when the committee of the Melbourne Cricket Club was considering Bradman, Heydon and Vernon Ransford for the club secretaryship. His unsolicited letter to the chairman of the ground's trustees, WA Watt, has not previously been published:

From the point of view of social charm and general prestige, Vernon Ransford clearly overshadows Bradman.

The latter, despite his genius as cricketer ... would be an utterly unsuitable successor to Hugh Trumble. He is intensely suspicious and has never quite outgrown his country boy complex. I have seen a great deal of him and yield to none in admiration for his many gifts. These gifts do not include those for which the MCC secretaryship has been renowned. Therefore I would say that either Heydon or Ransford has infinitely superior claims to Bradman.

Watt, perhaps surprised to receive advice from Evatt on matters of charm, replied coolly that 'some of the views you have seen to express in regard to individual candidates do not quite accord with my own', although the club committee would finally favour the local man, Ransford. And Bradman's move to Adelaide paid off: within the year, he would be deeply grateful for cultivating a life beyond cricket.

~

Bradman was named vice-captain to Bill Woodfull for Australia's diplomatically sensitive tour of England in 1934. In hindsight, the logic seems irrefutable, a step in Bradman's inevitable succession to leadership. At the time, more doubts attended. There was legitimate concern about the burden on Bradman's health and privacy. He skipped games en route in Hobart, Perth and Colombo on the advice of Sir Trent de Crespigny, University of Adelaide's renowned dean of medicine, that he was again 'run down'; he seldom roamed the deck of the *Orford*, dogged as he always was by well-wishing strangers. There was acute concern about the possibility that England, despite repeated assurances from MCC, would resume Bodyline, and Ray Robinson thought that this accounted for Bradman's 'comparatively feverish' batting in the tour's opening weeks. Bradman himself, anxious not to overtax himself, was irked when Woodfull pressured him into playing the tour's opening match: he made 206, but 'under considerable strain', after which he felt an acute 'drain on my resources'.

In fact, Bradman's promotion over the head of New South Wales's captain Alan Kippax and South Australia's captain Victor Richardson seems to have aggravated tense relations with Woodfull. Woodfull, a stoic in the face of Bodyline, had been displeased by Bradman's *sauve qui peut* methods; now he was unsympathetic to Bradman's complaints of weariness. Sir Douglas Shields, Australian surgeon to the rich and famous who numbered British Prime Minister Ramsay McDonald and Dame Nellie Melba among his patients, was guest at a dinner hosted by Sir James Barrie in the Australian team's honour on 15 May. He confided in team manager Harold Bushby that, from 'general observation', he felt Bradman would experience 'serious trouble before the tour was over'. Bushby's tour report, which came to light last year while the history of Cricket Australia was being written, graphically conveys the anxieties surrounding Bradman in England, and his uneasy status in the team.

> Dr Pope [team medical officer], Woodfull and I all discussed the matter with Sir Douglas Shields—Woodfull felt that if the vice-captaincy was worrying him [Bradman] the sooner he realised that he could not captain an Australian side the better. He was not inclined to think he was entitled to much consideration on account of his physical and mental condition. There was certainly a little feeling over his appointment as vice-captain.

Bradman was probably never quite so personally vulnerable as on this tour. Shields's suspicions proved well founded. After Bradman turned his indifferent tour around at Leeds with a resounding 304 and was sent to Shields to recover from a slight groin strain, he was learned to be suffering 'signs of duodenal ulceration', from which he convalesced at Shields's home on Farnham Common. Nor was this the Bradman to whom opportunities had surrendered themselves four years earlier, who had appeared on theatre stages and made gramophone records; this was a man in a kind of public hiding. Former teammate Arthur Mailey recalled seeing Bradman 'leave by the tradesman's entrance at the back of a seaside hotel and climb down a fire escape when running late for a match in order to avoid being bustled and delayed by a surging crowd at the front door'. In an era in which such words were not in free circulation, Bushby described Bradman's 'gloom and depression': 'He seemed very depressed at times and his condition in this direction was very far from satisfactory.'

Ironically, disaster struck just as Bradman's mood began improving after the Ashes's recapture: on 24 September he was rushed from Langham Hotel to Shields's private hospital at 17 Park Lane for an emergency appendectomy. The struggle to stave off peritonitis became a subject of imperial moment, King George V famously insisting: 'I want to know everything.' Health bulletins were issued hourly, then daily as anxiety eased. Jessie Bradman sped round the world—insofar as it was possible, for it took thirty-one days—to oversee his convalescence. Taking Shields's advice to rest entirely from cricket, the couple took a low-key tour of the British Isles, and from potential tragedy emerged some of the cricketer's happiest and most Anglophilial memories: 'Nothing in the world ever appealed to me more than England as nature made her, unchanged for centuries.' His sense of freedom—from care as well as pain—was palpable. In his autobiography *Men, Women and Things*, the Duke of Portland describes hosting the Bradmans at Welbeck Abbey:

> On the day after their arrival I heard the piano being played very beautifully for nearly an hour. When I went into the Gothic Hall there was Don Bradman playing, it seemed to me nearly as well as he batted. I complimented him on his skill and he replied: 'I enjoy playing the piano better than anything in

the world, and now thank goodness shall have plenty of time
for it for I have been forbidden to play cricket.'

~

It would be more than two years before Bradman took the field
again for Australia, this time as captain. But he had, in some senses,
already experienced every sensation cricket had to offer—the source
of his deepest satisfactions having steadily become an ordeal of
which it was exhilarating to be spared. And with the freedom to
review Bradman's life backwards, we regularly overlook that he lived
his life forwards, that deeds seemingly inevitable in retrospect were
achievements of flesh, blood and spirit. As a result, his legend has
begun to jade and fade, a Pindarian Ode recited a shade too often,
and too solemnly. While Bradman lived, there remained a sense of
wonder that this small, frail, softly spoken and self-contained man
could have cast such a long shadow. Now, as the Australia of which
Bradman was part recedes into antiquity, he is at risk of becoming
a straightforward statistical outlier. Succeeding generations have
found fresh and deeper meanings in Anzac Day; Bradman awaits
rediscovery.

Monthly, August 2008

Dead Don

'It is strange, but I think true,' wrote the English journalist Jack Ingham in August 1938, 'that all the time, day and night, somewhere in the world somebody is talking about Donald Bradman.' It is stranger, but hardly less true, that the same applies today. Stranger because, in an age when sports memory has become such a perishable commodity, it is sixty years since Bradman last represented Australia. Yet that eternal hubbub will be impossible to miss in this the month of the centenary of his birth.

Bradman was born on 27 August 1908 in Cootamundra, the youngest and smallest of five children to a farmer from nearby Yeo Yeo, and the fourth delivered by the redoubtable local midwife Erica 'Granny' Scholtz. 'Don was always a good boy and a bonny baby,' she said. 'He was a sturdy little chap.' So he stayed, chopping down cricket's giants with the cheek of beanstalk-climbing Jack, until the Bradman saga had acquired a genuine fairytale quality, passed down the generations and woven into national folklore.

Which is just as well. For these days, one must really be at least a septuagenarian to have a solid, independent recollection of Bradman in action. Even number-one fan John Howard never saw him in a Test; likewise the last two men to deliver the Bradman Oration, Alan Jones and Peter Cosgrove. And those with recall of the rise of Bradmania, as distinct from his established celebrity, may soon be as venerable as the last Anzacs.

It is not as though footage of Bradman abounds either. The most popular newsreel film is not even from a Test match: it is a snatch of Bradman cover-driving a boundary in the course of his hundredth first-class hundred for an Australian XI v the touring Indians in November 1947, a game the hosts actually lost by 47 runs. As for the fabled glimpse of Bradman being bowled at the Oval for the duck that deprived him of a three-figure Test average, it does not even show bowler Eric Hollies releasing the lethal googly. The giveaway, deserving of a pelting in the public stocks of *Media Watch*, is that Hollies is seen bowling round the wicket: evidently, it is a ball bowled later in his spell, crudely interposed for the sake of verisimilitude.

The name and reputation of Bradman, nonetheless, found ways of surviving not open to other cricketers, even famous ones. His praises were sung in songs: Jack O'Hagan's 'Our Don Bradman', Peggie Thorne's 'Mighty Don' and Edmund Luke's 'Take Your Hats Off to Bradman'. He was invited to play himself on stage (*It Ain't Cricket*; 1933) and on screen (*The Flying Doctor*; 1936). Inevitably, children were named for him, and not only in Australia: the head of the Colombo Port Police was so chuffed to obtain his autograph in October 1930 that he named his first-born Bradman Weerakoon. There was even a horse: 'Bradman' and also 'Larwood' were the names given to his draught horses by the great Australian industrialist Essington Lewis, when he used them to excavate a swimming pool on his estate, 'Landscape', near Tallarook in Victoria in the mid-1930s.

Bradman gave his name to a ship—albeit a small one. Launched in October 1936 as a fishing trawler, what became HMS *Bradman* when taken over by the Admiralty on the brink of World War II displaced just 452 tons and packed one four-inch gun. Evidently, it was hoped that it and other 'Cricketers' Class vessels—HMS *Larwood*, HMS *Hammond* and HMS *Jardine*—would intimidate

U-boats by reputation. Alas, German aircraft sank the *Bradman* off Norway on Anzac Day 1940, along with the *Hammond*—something of which any bowler would have been proud. More recently, the name Bradman took to the air, Austrian Airlines christening one of its B777s the *Donald Bradman* in a ceremony at Sydney International Airport in July 2002. It keeps even more exalted company than the ship, part of an air fleet also containing the *Ernest Hemingway*, *Pablo Picasso* and *Elvis Presley*.

Since the creation of the Bradman Foundation fifteen years ago and protection of 'Bradman' by legislation, there has been less latitude to put the name to work. The Foundation approved the propagation of the garnet-red Bradman Rose by family-owned flower breeders Meilland International. But it quashed Powers Brewing's Bradman Bitter Ale when an empty stubby was found at Bradman Oval during a game between a Bradman XI and South Africa—one-time temperance advocate Bradman hardly made an appropriate beer spruiker.

In the Federal Court, the foundation also sued a group of Sydney developers who had christened their venture Bradman Corporation. Settlement was reached two days before Bradman's death with the company agreeing to become Bradcorp, and to surrender the domain name 'bradman.com.au'. Papers filed in the action suggest that the Foundation cannot be accused of underestimating the great man's cachet: 'The Australian public ... regard Sir Donald Bradman as an Australian hero, icon and idol ... and they would regard the name Bradman appearing in relation to the supply of goods and services ... as having qualities of uniqueness, excellence and perfection which the public associates with Sir Donald Bradman.' The Foundation has so far ignored Bradman, the Melbourne-based wrestler, whose MySpace profile reverently lists him as 'Male, 100 years old', and offers as a motto: 'Life is fake, Wrestling is real!'

It isn't only Australians, of course, who have a stake in Bradman. For the English, 'Bradman' has implied the biggest obstacle. On the downfall of Mussolini in July 1943, for instance, a British MP rededicated his nation to Hitler's overthrow with the remark: 'We have got Ponsford out cheaply, but Bradman is still batting.' Writing on Bradman's retirement, the English cricket writer RC Robertson-Glasgow mused: 'So must ancient Italy have felt when she heard the death of Hannibal.' But then, from this can be inferred a shared regard, and a mutual understanding. Not for nothing was the long-awaited storming of the Monte Cassino monastery in March 1944 foreshadowed to soldiers from Britain and New Zealand with the signal: 'Bradman will be batting tomorrow.' No German, it was perceived, would understand the ominous portent of such a communiqué.

Today, 'Bradman' is the benchmark, the ultimate compliment. Nobody speaks of Tiger Woods being the Garry Sobers of golf, or Roger Federer as the Sunil Gavaskar of tennis. Indeed, it was ever thus: Walter Lindrum became 'the Bradman of billiards', George Moore 'the Bradman of racing' and Peter Brock 'the Bradman of Bathurst', while Richie Benaud keeps on keeping on, having been dubbed 'the Bradman of the microphone' by English journalist Tim deLisle. It is not a title lightly bestowed. Some believe that John Howard's premiership was doomed from the moment Workplace Relations Minister Joe Hockey called him 'the Don Bradman of Australian politics' last September, inevitably destined for an Eric Hollies moment. Nor does it cut both ways: nobody will ever want to be known as 'the John Howard of cricket'.

Qantas: The Australian Way, August 2008

The Gold Standard

Not so long ago I found myself at a trivia night when a round was announced with the designation 'Famous Faces': this involved a sheet of paper featuring the images of twenty allegedly famous persons. My table gathered to brainstorm and banter. After a pause, looks were exchanged. We reviewed the evidence again. Hmmm, nope—not one figure did any of us recognise: they were faces, it transpired, from reality television we'd never watched, pop music we'd never heard, sport we didn't care about. Few things today date you so reliably as that group of people you consider 'famous'.

What we honour today, on the centenary of the great cricketer's birth, is Sir Donald Bradman's defiance of that modern trend to a fame of instant perishability. There's the cricket, too—but that can be savoured any day, and has been, repeatedly, in the sixty years since Bradman's last Test innings. Centenaries are celebrations of continuity: they are tributes not just to the figure concerned but to ourselves, assertions of stability, recognitions of our abiding priorities.

If today's dinners and DVDs, speeches and specials are anything to go by, Bradman remains capable of remarkable feats. After all, how many cricketers have their centenaries marked in any significant way? It was WG Grace's bad luck that when his fell in 1948, all Englishmen could talk about was Bradman. By present trends, too, the legend survives on precious little. As a surgically enhanced Sachin Tendulkar emerges from his cryogenic deep-freeze in the multimedia megalopolis BCCI City on 10 November 2067, worshippers will probably be able to watch holograms of every ball of his career—a career, moreover, plied in every cricket country of the world as the champion of the most populous. Representing a nation in his time of only six million people, Bradman played cricket in two countries, and, bar the fragmentary footage that remains and the words he inspired, left behind traces only of his runs. Yet he is known to every cricket fan—and most of them know his batting average, too.

Bradman's feats, then, are only the half of it: a grasp of the phenomenon of fame enhances appreciation. In his pioneering study *The Image*, Daniel Boorstin explained fame as an outcome of technical innovation in the mass media: the telegraph, linking continents; the rotary press, allowing print on both sides of a newspaper; and the roll film, which made having your photo taken less like sitting for a portrait and more like giving your autograph. Studying content in popular newspapers and magazines in the United States, he found the most marked change around World War I: before it, three-quarters of the subjects of stories were from politics, business or the professions; after it, more than half came from entertainment, thanks to the explosion in the popularity of cinema, the dissemination of radio and the advent of the wire photo. There emerged a shadow form of fame, with the style rather than the substance. 'The hero' shared public space with 'the celebrity', who was 'well known for their well-knowness'.

The 1920s then saw the first frenzies of public acclamation, where the hero and the celebrity merged into one. The American aviator Charles Lindbergh went aloft in May 1927 a relative unknown, and landed across the Atlantic a divine. Scott Berg's classic biography describes a life turned inside out. Matrons in St Louis fought over a corn cob he had chewed. He could not cash or send a cheque, or send shirts to the laundry: neither would be returned. He had to marry in secret, leaving the ceremony hunched in the back of a friend's car, while a decoy led the press off to a false destination. Honeymooning on a yacht a week later, he and his bride were buzzed by a seaplane with a photographer dangling out the window. When their first son was kidnapped and killed, photographers stormed the morgue, ransacked the coffin and took pictures of the mangled corpse, then sold them as postcards on the streets of New Jersey for $5 each; later, photographers trailing a car taking their second son to nursery school forced it off the road.

And yet, *nothing* like this befell Bradman. To be sure, he was a source of enormous national pride and bore a crushing burden of sporting expectation. His public activities were somewhat restricted, and he was never comfortable with being an object of curiosity. But, especially once he moved to Adelaide, few famous persons can have lived, and also been permitted to live, so close to an ordinary life. He held ordinary jobs, as a seller of sporting goods and a dealer in stocks. He married once, to his childhood sweetheart, and raised children in the only house he bought.

It could have been otherwise. Nobody who wished it, for instance, could not find Bradman's address, and you knew you were guaranteed a response if you wrote to 2 Holden Street, Kensington Park. Bradman, too, scorned the template reply: he gave even his plainest letters a personal, humanising touch. But out of this developed a stable, sustainable, long-term, arms-length relationship between Bradman and his public; both sides, consciously and unconsciously, honouring their sides of the bargain. Thus was a pre-modern fame nurtured into a post-modern age; a compromise classically of Australia, a country that exalts the common man. Consequently, Bradman eluded some of the wages of fame. In his *What Price Fame?*, American economist Tyler Cowen presents detailed calculations suggesting that the famous tend to have far lower life expectancies than the non-famous, and to suffer disproportionately from heart disease, kidney failure, alcoholism and drug addiction. 'Fame tends to be bad for the famous,' he concludes. Not for Bradman. Perhaps it even kept him going: despite a relatively frail constitution, he lived to ninety-two.

~

England's embrace of Bradman was not foretold, nor was it immediate, but it was wholehearted. Richard Holt argues plausibly in the 2002 edition of *Wisden* that the summer of 1934 was 'the turning point in Bradman's relationship with the British'. Before his form came flooding back at Headingley, Bradman's batting was unexpectedly fallible that summer; his life or death struggle with peritonitis then kept the British public spellbound. The seriousness of Bradman's predicament sometimes eludes modern readers. It was fifty years since the first successful surgical removal of an appendix, but infection remained a deadly possibility in an age before antibiotics. In the most thorough study from the time—compiled in a Massachusetts hospital between 1929 and 1939—3 per cent of appendix patients died, the mortality rate rising to 13 per cent where perforation occurred. As Holt observes: 'The public suddenly saw this remarkable run-making machine in a new light, as a young man with a new bride, whose dash from Sydney to Perth to get the first boat caught the popular imagination.'

Four years later, like a good son of empire, Bradman apprehended the unfolding European crisis as an affair for Australians also, writing a friend from Naples: 'From the dock of our ship we counted 36 destroyers. Eight cruisers and seventy-two submarines. I guess they were not built to rust.' He was a popular, patriotic ambassador for his country, and would be more popular a decade later, when on his fabled final tour he was made an honorary life member of both Yorkshire and Lancashire. 'To the middle classes, Donald Bradman, batsman and stockbroker, stood for suburban virtue rewarded,' argues Holt. 'To the working man, his blend of virtuosity and grit struck a chord, especially in the North, where his professionalism was more appreciated than in the South.' If that's true, mind you, it can only be by an almost imperceptible margin. He was assuredly revered at Lord's, where he became on his fiftieth birthday the first honorary life member of Marylebone not a member of the royal family or to have held high political office. His appeal to toffs, of course, was in the way his rise validated social hierarchies, suggesting that the man of talent would always be recognised.

Bradman's influence is concentrated around cricket's Anglo-Australian axis, but not confined to it. In March 1976, for example, his image was used on a postage stamp issued in South Africa to mark the centenary of the Champion Bat Trophy, forerunner to the Currie Cup. Among the most famous Bradman stories of all, meanwhile, concerns Nelson Mandela, recently sprung from Robben Island, breaking the ice with former Australian Prime Minister Malcolm Fraser by asking: 'Tell me. Is Donald Bradman still alive?' On his visit to Australia in September 2000, Mandela vouchsafed: 'In the 30s and 40s, at least in our country, we regarded Sir Donald ... as one of the divinities, so great was he and such an impact he made.'

Then, of course, there is Bradman's reputation in Asia, with its many exhibits, from the schoolboys in Bombay in the mid-1930s who founded the 'Don Bradman Cricket Club' to the star-struck Ceylonese port policeman who had his newborn son christened Bradman Weerakoon after an encounter with the homeward-heading Australian. It is also a fame that has stood the test of time. More Indians than Australians watched Bradman's funeral service—in fact, more Indians watched (50 million) than *there are* Australians.

It's an exaggeration to report Bradman as feeling particular kinship with cricket in Asia. He made landfall on the subcontinent only in June 1953, on the way to reporting an Ashes series for the *Daily Mail*, stopping off in transit with BOAC at Calcutta then Karachi. Interestingly, his wife probably spent more time in India than he did, solicitously looked after by Vijay Merchant when she paused there on her 1934 mercy dash to England.

Otherwise, Bradman remained aboard the *Strathaird* when it docked at Bombay's Ballard Pier in 1948, and declined all the many subsequent invitations, including one from the Board of Control for Cricket in Pakistan to a series of one-day matches in November 1976 to mark the centenary of Mohammed Ali Jinnah (Keith Miller went instead and, twenty years after his retirement, was actually game to play.) Vasant Raji puts his claim that Indians regard Bradman as cricket deity rather elegantly, turning the absences into an argument for ineffability:

> God is perfect. In the eyes of the Indians Bradman is the perfect batsman. God is unseen. Indians have not seen Bradman play. God's ways are inscrutable. Indians cannot comprehend why, in spite of numerous pressing invitations, Bradman never came to India. Whatever happens is God's will. So if Bradman avoided India, it was Bradman's will. Disappointment but no ill-feeling or rancour.

Of course, Indian cricketers have partaken directly of the legend, forming the opposition when Bradman scored his hundredth first-class hundred, and his only brace of Test hundreds. But Bradman's role in Indian cricket seems to have been less that of an individual figure and more as a kind of yardstick or gold standard. He offered records to be aimed for, which at first seemed far-off: BB Nimbalkar came famously close with his undefeated 443 for Maharastra against Kathiawar in December 1948, within a boundary or two of surpassing Bradman's record first-class score. It was evidence of Indian cricket's maturity when Sunil Gavaskar made a few of the Don's records his own, surpassing Bradman's record number of Test centuries, and underwriting the successful pursuit of 406 in the fourth innings at Port-of-Spain to improve on the feat of Bradman's Australians at Leeds twenty-eight years earlier.

An idealised Bradman has also been a personification of good conduct. During his long-running wrangle with the BCCI's great Pooh-Bah Anthony de Mello, Lala Amarnath was strengthened by a description of him in Bradman's *Farewell to Cricket* as 'charming in every respect and a splendid ambassador'. 'De Mello has done me a lot of harm,' Amarnath told the *Times of India*. 'But my reputation has been fully vindicated by no less a celebrity than Bradman in his memoirs.' Bradman's acceptance of honorary life membership of the Cricket Club of India was front-page news; likewise his lofty praise for the methods of Sachin Tendulkar. More recently, he has been used to represent the lofty estate from which cricket has fallen. In November 2000, he made an improbable appearance in the Central Bureau of Investigations' report into cricket corruption: 'Cricket, as it is played at present, does not appear to be the same game played by Sir Don Bradman or Neville Cardus wrote about. The romanticism associated with the game has perhaps gone forever.'

That, in fact, is a possible next development of the Bradman legend: a symbol not of continuity but of dislocation, of what is bygone, of what the game has sacrificed. For it will be difficult to sustain a legend of the Don if the form of the game in which he excelled, Test cricket between countries, is destined for permanent eclipse—and were Francis Fukuyama an analyst of cricket rather than geopolitics he might at the moment be writing *The End of History and the Last Bradman*. History is surely full of ironies: India, which never saw Bradman, will be the country that chiefly shapes how he will be seen by future generations, whether he continues to provoke instant recognition or becomes one of those faces in a trivia quiz that you can't quite place.

Cricinfo, August 2008

CRICKET AND THE HONOURS SYSTEM

From Sir Donald to Sir Beefy

Knighthoods, and the pomp and circumstance of honours generally, seem ideally suited to cricket, a game long headquartered at a ground called Lord's. Yet until quite recently, there had been comparatively few. 'Lord' Ted Dexter was actually a mere CBE; only in the broadacres were 'Sir' Geoffrey Boycott and 'Sir' Fred Trueman known as such.

When England won the Ashes at home in 1985, cricket could claim only six practitioners knighted primarily for their on-field deeds. But by the time twenty years later they accomplished the feat again, earning themselves a sackful of OBEs and MBEs, a further nine had been so ennobled. Sir Ian Botham now makes a fitting addition to the pantheon. After all, he stomped out of an Aussie piss-take of the monarchy in Melbourne in February 1992; he also meets the apparently important qualification of having offended Pakistanis, somehow avoiding a fatwa twenty-three years ago for describing it as a country unsuitable even for mothers-in-law.

This says rather more about the honours system than about cricket, because much the same proliferation has been experienced in other sports, especially soccer. Until the 1990s, association football could muster just half a dozen knights, only one of them, Sir Stanley Mathews, a player of significance. Football Association president Sir Albert Millichip, recognised in much the same way as the Albert

Memorial—for longevity rather than achievement—was the first of eight to be recognised since (if the honorary honorific settled on Pele is included). In fact, the rise and rise of the athlete and also the entertainer in the ranks of the honoured is much as you'd expect since Sir John Major opened the system to direct nomination fifteen years ago.

The first of cricket's gonged belong to different time and habits. The original cricket knight was an administrator, Marylebone secretary Francis Lacey, dubbed eighty years ago. There is a hint of the award having a symbolic quality, a recognition of the administrative classes in general, because Football Association president Charles Clegg was honoured in the same year; likewise the knighthood settled on Yorkshire's secretary Frederick Toone a couple of years later.

The honours system at the time placed far greater accent on service than achievement, and was anything but demotic. WG Grace received no honour at all, despite his popularity—maybe even because of it. The only official communication Percy Chapman received while winning the Ashes in 1928–29 was an income tax demand; the playwright Ben Travers observed that England clearly expected each man to pay his duty. Important government telegrams abounded when Douglas Jardine retrieved the Ashes four years later, but none of them concerned his garlanding, and it was sixty years before Harold Larwood received his consolatory MBE. Not until Donald Bradman in January 1949, then four years later Jack Hobbs, were cricketers of the front rank honoured for their playing accomplishments alone.

Mind you, beating them both, for reasons partly of playing but mainly of sheer establishment cred, was Pelham Warner. To nobody can the knighthood have meant more: his autobiography *Long Innings* (1951) is exquisitely pedantic about ranks and titles of all sorts, with footnotes that rejoice in the likes of 'Admiral of the Fleet Sir Osmond de Beauvoir Brock GCB, KCMG, KCVO' and 'Lord Rugby, GCMG, KCB, KCVO, CSI, CIE'. Anyone puzzled by these abbreviations should consult Anthony Sampson's *The Anatomy of Britain* (1963), where the colloquial explanations for KCMG ('Kindly Call Me God') and GCMG ('God Calls Me God') were first famously provided.

Warner seems to have passed on a similar ambition to his protégé Gubby Allen, the lateness of whose recognition became a source of vexation in his circle. 'The question why the name of Allen does not figure among those who services to sport have been rewarded with a knighthood is often asked,' fumed EW Swanton in *Gubby Allen: Man of Cricket* (1985). 'The Honours system, naturally, is a closed book to those outside the corridors of Whitehall, and one can only note that the approaches on behalf of several within the cricket hierarchy have not, so far, borne fruit.' Perhaps the book wormed its way down one of those influential corridors, because Allen was honoured a year later. And frankly, an England captain without an honour is entitled to feel short changed: Lord Cowdrey and Lord Sheppard (albeit not only for his cricket) were elevated to the peerage; Sir Leonard Hutton and now Botham have been knighted; there have been CBEs for Brian Close, Ted Dexter, Ray Illingworth, Tony Lewis, George Mann and Peter May; OBEs for Mike Atherton, Geoff Boycott, Mike Brearley, Keith Fletcher, Mike Gatting, Graham Gooch, David Gower, Tom Graveney, Nasser Hussain, Mike Smith and Alec Stewart; and MBEs for Freddie Brown, John Edrich and Bob Willis. An association with Lord's, whether administrative or playing, has never been a disadvantage around New Year and the Queen's birthday: Denis Compton, Hubert Doggart, Billy Griffith, Doug Insole, Charles Palmer and Alan Smith have all been awarded CBEs.

Although Australian Labor governments ensured that Bradman would remain the country's only cricket knight by finally discontinuing imperial honours, its captains have also done well: Richie Benaud and Bill Woodfull were awarded OBEs, Ian Johnson a CBE, and Greg Chappell, Lindsay Hassett, Arthur Morris, Brian Booth and Neil Harvey all MBEs. MBEs have also been packed away by Dennis Lillee, Rod Marsh, Alan Davidson, Keith Miller, Doug Walters, Bert Oldfield, Jack Fingleton, Bill O'Reilly, Bill Ponsford and Ken Mackay.

The accent has since fallen on the local Order of Australia, inaugurated in 1975: Steve Waugh, for example, became an Officer in the Order of Australia (AO) four years ago, and Mark Waugh a Member (AM) two years ago. Perhaps the strangest award, and arguably the most masochistic, was the AO settled on Clive Lloyd in January 1985 'for service to the sport of cricket, particularly in relation to his outstanding and positive influence on the game in Australia'. Behind what seemed rather like the Roman senate sending Hannibal a certificate of appreciation was Prime Minister Bob Hawke, who had mooted Lloyd as a coach for the Australian team.

Lloyd also holds the CBE, and Caribbean nations have been among the most ambitious promoters of their own in honours calculations. Since 1995, Vivian Richards, Clyde Walcott, Everton Weekes and Conrad Hunte have joined Garfield Sobers and Frank Worrell as knights of the Caribbean court: alas, it has smacked of an effort to find a source of pride for West Indian cricket in the absence of any on the field. In some respects still the most accomplished of cricket's knights has been Learie Constantine, made Sir Learie in 1962, then Lord Constantine of Maraval and Nelson in 1969: the first life peer of African descent. Civil servant and lawyer in England, government minister and high commissioner for Trinidad, campaigner for Caribbean self-determination and against racial prejudice, he would have been a figure of stature had he never bowled a ball or lashed a boundary; his cricket, all the same, gave him entree to those circles he'd shake up. One shudders to imagine what he would make of the modern West Indies, let alone West Indian cricket.

How effectively has the honours system dealt with cricket? The increased profusion of awards has had an inflationary effect. As holder of an MBE, for instance, George Headley is equal in the eyes of the system to John Lever, and the inferior of Dermot Reeve OBE. There are some galling omissions: Walter Hammond's professional roots and Tony Greig's professional ambitions seem to have been held against them; Herbert Sutcliffe, whom Harold Wilson thought a hero 'to every Yorkshire boy of my generation', somehow failed to make the Lavender List; Ken Barrington, who according to Wally Grout trailed a Union Jack behind him as he came into bat, went likewise unrecognised. There are irritating inconsistencies: sometimes held up as the best keeper of all, and a man beyond reproach, Alan Knott holds no honour; Bob Taylor and John Murray, whom Knott kept out of the England team, both hold the MBE.

But to a surprising degree, the honours system seems to have recognised the right people: aside from the quaint figure of Sir Vijay Anand, the money-bags maharajah with a batting average of 8, there are no examples of egregiously undeserving recipients. While it is fashionable to criticise New Labour's honours lists for their luvvy-laden populism, would we really prefer an awards culture so impervious to public opinion that WG Grace rose no higher than country GP? As for Sir Ian Botham, it has an appealing ring. Night cricket might be passé, but knight cricket retains its novelty.

Wisden Cricketer, September 2007

4
Tactic, Technique and Technology

One Leg Good, Two Legs Bad

Doubtless with his American constituency in mind, Alistair Cooke once described cricket as a form of 'ceremonial coma'. He had a—kind of—point. It is a game engrained with rituals and archaisms that have become barely noticeable, that pass as fluidly as a waking dream. Yet their absence would strike one immediately as a breach of protocol, or even a lapse in taste.

Consider the act of taking guard. Every batsman from one to eleven goes through the pedantic, fussy formality of ascertaining where he is standing in relation to the stumps, holding the bat side-on and upright for the umpire's instruction. Over a match's course a crease will become fissured and grooved in the relevant reference points: middle, two legs, one leg. Yet one would no sooner rely on another cricketer's guard than share his socks: one must *always* take one's own bearings.

An apocryphal story concerns the tailender's tailender 'Bomber' Wells taking strike without seeking an umpire's advice, and deprecating the technicality: 'No thanks, I've played here before.' It relies for its humour on an awareness of the solecism, which only the likes of the waggish Wells could get away with: there is probably an HM Bateman cartoon showing a quivering bunch of fielders levitating in shock at 'The Batsman Who Didn't Want a Guard'. It is a custom, too, to which every batsman brings a certain individuality. Ian Chappell, a great bustler to the crease, always attended briskly to his markings, as though he couldn't wait to get to grips with the bowler. Graham Gooch would hold the bat erect with a single hand, full face showing, exuding solemn permanence. Nobody today makes a bigger deal of scoping his property out than Matthew Hayden, who wants GPS standards of exactitude, and digs a mark like the Marianas Trench.

'Guard', of course, began in cricket as a descriptive rather than a technical term, and dates back more than 250 years, James Love's epic poem of 1744 featuring the couplet: 'Now the two mightiest of the fainting Host ... With pow'rful Skill, their threat'ned Wickets guard.' The notion of orienting oneself at the crease then flowed from the phasing in of the third stump, an outcome of 'Lumpy' Stevens's famous torments at the Artillery Ground in 1775. The primo professional all-rounder of the early nineteenth century, William Lambert, was the first to advocate choosing a particular stump to protect. The Surrey man who hit 'what no man could meddle with' recommended in his exquisite little primer, *Instructions and rules for playing the noble game of cricket, as practised by the most eminent players* (1816):

> As guarding the wicket may be considered a very necessary part to be observed by the batsman, we shall remark that as the bat is only four and a half inches wide and the wicket seven inches, the striker cannot guard all the three stumps ... therefore we consider it necessary for a young beginner to guard the middle stump, or that which is most generally hit by the bowler, always guarding the weakest side.

The act of making a mark is referred to by Frederick Gale, a disciple of Fuller Pilch who would write voluminously as 'the Old Buffer' but then signed himself as 'A Wyhamist', in *Practical Hints on Cricket* (1843): 'Let the player first obtain guard ... for the middle stump, and then mark it carefully ... Draw a straight line from the guard to the crease.' In describing the 'off-cut half-volley' in *Felix on the Bat* (1845)—a 'stroke violent in its intentions' that 'produces a mighty stir in the field'—the polymath Nicholas Wanostrocht depicts the batsman's guard as his base of operations: 'To spring from your guard to adopt this most effective hit, the ball should pitch, say, four inches wide of off stump.'

First evidence of the umpire's involvement is found in the inaugural edition of *Fred Lillywhite's Guide to Cricketers* (1851), with a couple of variations on later practice. 'In taking the position at the wicket inquire from which side the bowler will deliver the ball,' Lillywhite counselled. 'Also ask the umpire from whence the ball is delivered to give you guard.' Now and again one still encounters a batsman who asks for guard from the bowler's position—conduct frowned on by commissars of correct technique ('That makes no sense at all,' says himself in *Geoff Boycott on Batting*). But it actually seems a vestige of the initial practice.

Lillywhite was also the first to fix a name to a particular guard: 'The best guard for the young cricketer to take is between the middle and leg stump, commonly called "two leg".' But he also recommended adjustment if the bowler changed direction: 'If the bowler should change his side you will require another guard, which, by asking the umpire, he will give you. Place your bat on the spot upright and make a mark on the ground so that you may know it again.'

How one referenced the guard was also left to the individual. Edward Ward, the first Australian round-arm bowler, took strike backside first—180 degrees to the way Peter Willey finished his career. And as late as the beginnings of Test cricket, the umpire's assistance was discretionary. The definition for 'Guard' in Charles Box's lexicon of the game in *The English Game of Cricket* (1877) explains: 'A batsman often applies to the umpire for guard, ie to know which stump or stumps his bat is defending.'

Guards have gone in and out of fashion, each having their advocates. Centre has always been a kind of golden mean, and became the default option in Australia. 'Custom and tradition,' noted Eric Barbour in *The Making of a Cricketer* (1926), 'lead us to obtain from the umpire the line of the centre stump, so that we may let the bat rest on it.' It is probably still used by nine in ten Australian club batsmen, and recommended by Warren Smith, coach to Michael Slater and Phil Jacques. 'I always reckon a young player should take centre because he or she will have good eyes,' Smith argues in *How I Taught Michael Slater to Play Cricket* (2006).

About a hundred years ago, the usual recommendation was 'one leg', advocated by such Golden Age ornaments as Ranjitisinhji, who thought that umpires were naturally 'more inclined to give decisions against batsmen who cover the stumps before the ball is bowled'. Jack Hobbs and Herbert Sutcliffe were also subscribers to 'one leg', Hobbs because it gave a 'truer sight of the direction of the ball' and put him 'in the best position to deal with all sorts of balls', Sutcliffe candidly because he felt a little vulnerable on the on side. 'Personally I find great difficulty in distinguishing between a ball pitching on the wicket and one pitching two or three inches outside,' he noted in *Batting* (1937). 'But I do feel certain the "one leg" guard helps considerably.'

Their contemporary Bill Woodfull argued for 'two legs', or middle and leg, for the reasons equal and opposite to those of Ranji, believing it important that 'the player does not show the bowler too much of the stumps, for if the attacker sees the way wide open it gives him added confidence'. Bradman took 'two legs', too, while it also seems to be the current vogue at the ECB National Academy, where assistant coach John Abrahams describes it as arising from an 'imaginary line drawn from the batsman's middle stump through the back of his head, coming out between the eyes and continuing down the pitch to the bowler's middle stump'. The effort of drawing these imaginary lines may explain the introversion into which English batting has recently sunk.

Yet Barry Richards, blessed with as naturally excellent technique as any batsman in history, deplored 'two legs'. A batsman, he thought, should either take 'one leg', as he did because it gave him 'plenty of room to hit my off-side shots', or centre, like his confederate Mike Procter, whose back foot tended not to go so far across. 'I am not an advocate of this guard [two legs] because I think it is neither one thing nor the other; it falls between two stools,' Richards said in *Attack to Win* (1973). 'If you have trouble outside the off stump, take centre; if you do not, take leg stump.' Nor is it uncommon for batsmen to alter a guard to deal with a particular bowler. In the West Indies in 1980–81, for example, Geoff Boycott acted on advice from Mike Gatting to bat on off stump to Colin Croft, whose peculiar angle from wide of the crease had the effect of drawing batsmen into playing at deliveries they should not. Latterly, Ricky Ponting among others has crept over to off stump when facing Muttiah Muralitharan, in order to keep his pads outside the line of the stumps.

The only wrong answer to the question of the right guard, then, is none of the above—the reason being that it is not merely a matter of technique. It is a key to the routine of preparing for the first ball, part of the act of stimulating and harnessing adrenaline: the unconscious familiarity of the actions helps calm nerves, gain time, proclaim resolution and direct thoughts. In the wonderful account of Derek Randall's marathon 150 at Sydney in January 1979 that forms part of Mike Brearley's *The Ashes Retained* (1979), Dudley Doust describes how the elementary business of marking his guard on coming in set the Englishman at once in a positive frame of mind.

> He scratched his right boot across the ground, loosening the hard-packed soil. Jabbing down his bat, he called to the umpire, Bailache, 'Two legs, please, Robin.' By chance it came right, spot on, the face of his bat square to the line between middle and leg stumps. Bailache signalled as much, and Randall was happy. A simple act had worked perfectly, first look and neat as a notch, and he found it remarkably comforting. Eagerly he knocked in his mark with the toe of his bat, deriving palpable pleasure from the feeling of it in the soil ...

Too much fiddle-faddle, meanwhile, can evince conglomerated thoughts. Marjorie Pollard became so frustrated with women cricketers taking guard seventy years ago that she reprimanded them in her book *Cricket for Women and Girls* (1934):

> There is no reason to plant the bat down somewhere on the crease and let the umpire signal or call several times before you get 'middle' or 'middle and leg', or whatever it is you want. Look at the wickets, make a rough calculation which is 'middle and leg' if that is what you want, and then put your bat there, hold it up straight and look at the umpire.
>
> She will move it, by word or sign, to the required position. If she says 'covering one' she means that your bat is covering the leg stump. 'Covering two', which is what most players want, means that you have got a position in which your bat is covering the leg and middle stumps. Having got your guard, make a mark. There is no need to dig yourself in—this thumping and excavating advertises nerves again.

Nor does cricket always stand comatose on ceremony. There is a story of a Sussex v Hampshire match in the early 1970s where John Snow was bowling to the Hants lower order and bumped into George Stephenson, whose homespun crouch bore an unfortunate resemblance to a batsman in the act of taking guard. Snow started his run, pulled up half way through, heaved a sigh and walked back. Then he turned, started again, and again pulled up, this time with an oath, and walked back once more. A third time he started, and again stopped himself, now more volubly—how long was this going to take? Advice that Stephenson was actually ready, legend has it, added 20 miles per hour to Snow's usual pace; whenever the counties met in future, the sight of Stephenson roused Snow to full fury. Alistair Cooke is famous for saying that the essence of his favourite game, golf, lay in its embarrassments—a pity he didn't know cricket well enough to see the parallels.

Fabian Batsmanship

The first ball of the Test in Chittagong from Mashrafe Mortaza was neither particularly fast nor especially demanding. It pitched just short of a length a shade outside off stump, and came in a touch—maybe even a smidgeon, but no more. Wasim Jaffer wasn't to be tempted. It was hot. It might be a long day. There was no need to expend energy prematurely, or go too hard too early. Best to look for the one on the hip, maybe; perhaps something on a driveable length. Oh …

Bowled without offering a shot. It's enough to ruin your day. It can even hold back your career. Strangled down the leg side; run out off the bowler's hand: these are meant to be the worst ways to get out. But at least these methods of dismissal savour of bad luck. To die in a strokeless ditch—well, it can't come any worse. Withal, such misadventures also remind us of a depth to cricket seldom explored. Many games involve hitting a ball. Only cricket also involves not hitting the ball to such a significant degree. True, the batter in baseball and the receiver in tennis are sometimes required to abjure a hit or stroke. Yet only in cricket is 'leaving' a skill in itself—albeit one curiously unacknowledged.

Check it out. Canonical texts on batting technique usually leap straight from stance and guard to the front foot defensive shot. If anything, the accent is on making contact as frequently as possible.

'I am a firm believer in attacking batsmanship,' insists Bradman in *The Art of Cricket* (1958). 'It is a batsman's duty to take the initiative and play shots.' But while it may be his duty, it isn't his only option. To play shots, one must first survive. And because cricket unfolds steadily, lasts a long time, and at least at first-class level need not be played to a conclusion, survival can be an end in itself. The skill is engrained even in popular imagination. In the excellent new Australian film *Noise* (2007), there is a sequence of the chief protagonist, a young police constable, going through a repertoire of fresh-air shots for his girlfriend. 'Square cut—straight drive—let it go,' he incants. 'Forward defensive—cover drive—let it goooooo.' The last is performed with particularly elaborate ceremony, as though it is the real badge of quality.

Call it Fabian batsmanship, for Fabius, the 'Shield of Rome' aka 'The Delayer', who thwarted Hannibal in the Second Punic War with his policies of 'masterly inactivity'. For sure, cricket is won by the team with the greatest number of runs; but to do so that team must also make optimum use of time. Take, for example, that glory game of Indian cricket, Adelaide 2003. Australia might have stormed to 400 on the first day, but their speed of scoring left scope for all conclusions; inattention to the tenets of masterly inactivity on the fourth day duly delivered victory to the visitors.

Leaving the ball—perhaps 'padding up' or 'shouldering arms' would be better, suggestive of volition and discrimination—is also arguably the subtlest of cricket acts, the exchange of an advantage so small as to be in most cases almost immeasurable. Is it a challenge quelled or a gauntlet avoided? Some batsmen are happy to leave. Some bowlers are happy to be left. But the world is not unaltered. Maybe the batsmen muses that the next ball in the same place should go, and squanders his wicket overeagerly; perhaps the bowler frets a little over wasting his energy and follows up with a straight ball that can be worked to the boundary. In the Cold War, détente was never inactive: it involved constant adjustment and readjustment; in the cricket war, détente likewise entails endless silent recalibrations and recalculations.

There are chiefly three reasons why a batsman might abjure a stroke. The first is that, perceiving a particular shot to be risky, he wishes to avoid error. In *The Game's the Thing* (1926), Monty Noble recalled reaching 92 for New South Wales against Victoria at the SCG in January 1899, then being baited by Hugh Trumble. The second new ball was taken, and Trumble knew Noble would be wary of its additional bounce, so sent his first ball wide:

> It was allowed to pass. The second or third were treated similarly, when there were cries from the crowd. 'Why don't you hit 'em?' The fourth was just the same and there was an increased deluge of advice from the Hill. When the fifth was treated in like manner, the barrackers rained down shrieks and howls indicative of a thunderous protest. The sixth and last ball of the over was bowled on the wicket and was played. When Trumble came into the slips at my end I said: 'Why didn't you bowl the last one out there, too, Hughie?' He only smiled, but there was a wealth of meaning behind his silence.

The circumspect batsman might also be looking for something. Walter Hammond went into bat for Gloucestershire against Yorkshire in July 1932 anxious about Bill Bowes's outswinger, and determined not to chase it as he had at Bristol a few weeks earlier. 'I contented myself for some time with watching the ball and getting the details of his delivery and timing into my head,' Hammond recalled. 'I marked a spot where I thought I could square cut.' In a passage in *Cricketers' School* (1950) that is a little classic, Hammond related how he finally summoned the nerve to hazard his cut: it went for four. He then tried to repeat the stroke: the edge flew to gully. Hammond was heading for the gate when a tumult alerted him to having been dropped. The attrition resumed, Bowes attacking the stumps to frustrate Hammond's surveillance, the great batsman scorning shots square of the wicket until he had passed his hundred. Then he got a few more away, but not for long: 'He watched me, tried an experiment or two, then, when I had 147, he cleverly disguised his slower ball. I played it a shade too soon—and there he was, grinning away, having got my wicket once more.'

A third objective is the purpose of tiring the bowler out, or otherwise neutralising them. Probably the most famous instance was fifty years ago, when Peter May and Colin Cowdrey set out to pad Sonny Ramadhin and Alf Valentine into submission at Edgbaston. Clyde Walcott lamented: 'We lost count of the number of times May and Cowdrey put their left foot down the pitch, bat tucked inside the pad, to let the deliveries from Ram and Val bounce away harmlessly.' Another fifteen years would elapse before the 'no genuine attempt to play the ball' augmentation of the lbw statutes that now composes Law 36.1 (d) (ii).

Likewise, when Australia hosted New Zealand twenty years ago, they set themselves to negating Richard Hadlee. David Boon drove Hadlee to distraction with a preternatural awareness of his stumps, compelling the mighty bowler to reorient his line:

> I made Hadlee bowl to me, rather than me trying to bat to him.
> I felt so comfortable about letting balls go, knowing where I
> was in relation to my off stump. Rather than dragging me
> wider and wider, a tactic of which Hadlee was a past master,
> I forced him to bowl into his pads, and it was from balls on
> this line that I scored plenty of runs.

In *MCC Masterclass* (1994), Geoff Boycott described the leave as a form of passive coercion: 'Wait. Have patience. Let him [the bowler] see you refusing to drive so that he is tempted to land the ball an extra foot closer to you. Then bang. Get on the front foot and drive the ball away.'

Mind you, such a self-denying ordinance requires a degree of willpower, for most batsman naturally prefer the feel of bat on ball to the sound of ball in keeping gauntlet. To say the least, Boycott was unusual, exhibiting the 'genius for inactivity' with which Walter

Lippman credited American president Coolidge: 'Nobody has ever worked harder at inactivity, with such force of character, with such unremitting attention to detail, with such conscientious devotion to the task.' When Boycott left the ball, it was almost a political statement—part passive resistance, part Yorkshire secessionism. There is a flavoursome Patrick Eagar photograph of Boycott at Headingley in July 1981, leaning back as a short ball seams past him at 'chin end'; the helmet is disarranged, but the wrists have dropped, the bat is safely out of harm's way and the gaze is bloody-mindedly fixed on the ball.

Other batsmen have also exhibited a distinctive personal style for leaving the ball unmolested. Greg Chappell let deliveries go later than almost anyone. The bat would sometimes be on the downswing before the stroke was aborted; it would then be daintily removed in an anti-clockwise rotation by the left hand alone. Only once did I ever see this *strokus interruptus* let him down, in a Supertest at Sydney Showground in January 1978, when Andy Roberts followed up a brutal first-ball bouncer with a ball that cannoned onto off stump from an inside edge. Chappell's great contemporary Doug Walters, meanwhile, contributed to the genre his distinctive 'periscope', leaving the bat pointing skyward as he went beneath a bouncer: a neglectful trait that cost him his wicket against John Snow, and caused RS Whitington to complain that his genuflections were 'more fitted for the aisle of a cathedral'.

Among the sweetest leavers of a ball was David Gower. Incapable of an ill-bred stroke, he brought a similar elegance to the non-stroke: it was like the ceremonial bow of a consummate courtier. Late in his career, it also indicated that his eye was failing him, for he developed a propensity for helping the ball on when reconsidering a shot. At Headingley twenty years ago, he was one of three batsman to fall in the first hour of a Test against Pakistan without a stroke between them.

For contrasting understatement, it was hard to surpass Mark Benson—these days an international umpire, but for Kent in the 1980s a phlegmatic and consistent opener. His trademark, emulated by several teammates, became known as 'the Kent leave': the bat was tugged just slightly to one side as the ball passed, so that there could be little to choose between a push-and-avoid and a play-and-miss. Marcus Trescothick's minimalist manoeuvre keeps the custom alive.

My countrymen in recent times have arrived at some eye-catching customs. Ricky Ponting has perfected a forward lunge towards the line of the ball with bat raised overhead, like a matador wafting his cape over a thrusting bull, while Justin Langer's two-handed flourish seems to be based on Luke Skywalker's style with a light sabre. Matthew Hayden's gestures at self-restraint used to look suspiciously studied, as though a resistance of instinct rather than an expression of it. He was bowled first ball, bat aloft, by Curtly Ambrose in the Boxing Day Test of 1996 against West Indies; a similar fate befell him six months later when, playing for Hampshire against the Australian side from which he had been dropped, he was castled by Jason Gillespie. These days he is lighter on his feet, and likelier to premeditate a stroke than a non-stroke, usually a calculatedly dismaying one.

For there's no doubt that players leave the ball less than of yore. The trend to faster, shorter bowling and the proliferation of one-day cricket in the 1970s encouraged batsmen to make more profitable use of width. Interviewed by Pat Murphy for *The Spinner's Turn* (1983) twenty-five years ago, Alan Knott noticed how his activity rate as a keeper had declined: 'Very few balls come to me behind the stumps now without the batsmen trying to play a shot. They're all looking to run it down to third man or trying to play the big drive.' The trend continues today, when most batsmen rely on the forward press to get them moving, and tend to go searching for the ball. In an era when few bowlers move the ball sideways reliably, furthermore, there is also less need for circumspection. Batsmen, Ponting observed recently, are cultivating a 'no-fear approach': bats are so powerful that their users know they can 'get away with hitting out when their eye and technique are in top working order', with the result that bowlers 'feel they have to bowl the perfect ball every ball or they are going to get belted'. Leaving the ball too much might relax the pressure on bowlers; the name of the game is intimidation. But, unique to cricket, it remains a challenging skill—arguably one of the more challenging because getting it wrong makes you look such a klutz. Just ask Wasim Jaffer.

Cricinfo Magazine, July 2007

? and the Mysterians

Watching Sri Lanka's Ajantha Mendis bowl is like trying to hold a conversation with a naturally quiet person in a noisy pub. What was that again, Ajantha? Didn't quite catch what you said—can you repeat it? Sorry pal—I thought you meant something else. Hey, can we go outside? Can't hear myself think in here.

Mendis's run-up is plain to the point of innocence, but his fingers are all subtlety, inscrutably resistant to sharing their secrets. The batsman is left groping, searching for cues and clues. Eh? Come again? What was that? Can you give me that once more? And finally: what happened?

His mixture of leg-breaks, off-breaks, doosras, googlies and top-spinners is a perplexity for statisticians, too. Cricinfo is calling him 'right-arm slow-medium' at the moment, but cricketers translate 'right-arm slow-medium' as 'bowls in the nets if he's lucky'. If he plays county cricket, *Playfair* will have to consider a designation like 'ROBLB' or 'RSM@#&%?!'

Others have already settled on the designation 'Mystery Spinner', the epithet conferred almost sixty years ago on the Australian Jack Iverson. They certainly seem to share prodigiously strong middle fingers. The ball settled into Iverson's grip like a marble for the squirting. Mendis, likewise, looks simply to caress the ball as he propels it, barely involving the palm of his hand at all, and holding one particular variation as delicately as an entomological specimen. Both bowlers possess the cardinal virtue of accuracy, and a liking for long spells.

Where they differ seems to be in variety and spin. Iverson spun his stock ball, a googly, massively, but his variations considerably less: batsmen finally figured on playing him as an off-break bowler, albeit one who looked like he was bowling leg-breaks. Mendis doesn't spin any of his options enormously; it is the combination of them, and the difficulty distinguishing one from the other, that makes him a handful.

There is always excitement when a bowler like Mendis appears. Batsmen scratch their heads. Captains and coaches confabulate. Cricket's *telephone arabe* buzzes. The original 'mystery ball', and still perhaps the most delicious, is the googly itself, the off-break delivered by the leg-break action conceived on his family billiard table before being hazarded on the sward at Lord's by BJT Bosanquet— and thus sometimes known as the 'bosie', and also as 'wrong 'un'. It's somehow fitting that such a double agent of a delivery should have multiple aliases.

At first the googly posed the more preposterous difficulties to its progenitor: the first to take a first-class wicket bounced four times. But it soon swept the world, the South African XI of a century ago including no fewer than four specialist purveyors, while the Australian team of 1910–11 featured perhaps the best exponent of all. Certainly it was the view of Johnnie Moyes, who saw all its antipodean advocates, Mailey, Grimmett and O'Reilly included, that no Australian mastered the googly more thoroughly than 'Ranji' Hordern.

> [Hordern] was without doubt an amazing bowler. He took
> a long run, brought his arm right over, was a length as well
> as a spin bowler, and of medium pace. He didn't seem to be
> flighting the ball, yet did so, as the batsman discovered when
> he tried to move down the pitch to him. That wasn't easy as

Hordern was slightly faster through the air, but the temptation was there, as I found to my cost in Victor Trumper's benefit game, only to hear Sammy Carter say 'Got you, son' ... Sometimes you could see the tip of the little finger sticking up skyward like a periscope of a submarine, but only if you were concentrating on it. If you did see it, you recognized the approaching 'bosie'.

The first googly in Australia bowled Victor Trumper; a googly was also the last ball to defeat Donald Bradman in a Test match. Simply by existing, it had an effect on cricket's ecosystem. 'If this sort of bowling becomes general I'm packing my bags,' threatened Archie MacLaren, before deciding he could live with it. It even enjoyed an oriental translation into the 'chinaman'. No other delivery, in fact, has had quite the same impact on cricket, and by never really being improved on it also caused cricket to revert to a batsman's game. In an incisive 1950 critique of Bradman's impact on cricket, the *Birmingham Post*'s cricket correspondent WE Hall observed:

In due course we shall come to see Bradman as an inevitable part of the evolution of the game. From Grace's integration of forward and back-play the art of batting advanced until, in Hobbs, a technique was perfected to master the 'new' bowling, as it has been called. It was the last of the qualitative changes in cricket, a fact realized by one writer who said that the game needed a new type of ball to do what the 'googly' once did. But there has been no new type of ball, and the only development left to batsmen between the wars was the quantitative one which followed, as surely as mass production followed the start of the Industrial Revolution.

Of course, mystery bowling is classically an individual pursuit, the result of lone experiment and lateral thought. Iverson is the archetype, his bowling having originated in a lifetime of nervous finger flicking with a table tennis ball; likewise were Iverson's protégé Johnny Gleeson, double-dealing Sonny Ramadhin and whizzbanging Bhagwat Chandrashekhar self-taught cricketers.

Ramadhin and Chandra made the most of their bowling's hidden depths. Delivering a stock ball that spun from the off, both buttoned their sleeves at the wrist, as though to deflect the curious glare. Ramadhin bowled his off-break with the middle finger down rather than across the seam, to sometimes startling effect. Ken Archer described playing with Ramadhin for a Commonwealth XI in September 1954 at seaside Hastings, when the bowler discovered that his quicker one seamed away with an ounce of extra effort; he could hardly bowl for his delighted laughter. Chandra's right arm was so withered from childhood polio that he could hardly hold a cup of tea to his lips. But with it he bowled googlies and leg-breaks that seemed to set his whole body whirring, like a child's spinning top. And like no other bowler, he haunted Viv Richards:

> It took me a long, long time to come to terms with Chandra.
> He was the most teasing bowler I ever had to face, and I never
> quite knew whether I was in charge or not. That was his
> greatness. His ability to lure opponents into a false sense of
> security was deadly. How is a batsman supposed to dominate
> such a man? How can he build his own confidence when he
> does not know whether the bowler is faking or not? ... To
> this day he probably remains the one bowler for whom I have
> most respect. He could do things with the ball that seemed
> supernatural.

In the last two decades, Muttiah Muralitharan has been perhaps the most mysterious of bowlers, and certainly the most paradoxical: a wrist-spinning off-break bowler. Indeed, to the interminable debate about Murali's action, a modest proposal might be worth making. One key exhibit in the case for Murali's legitimacy is footage of him, taken by Channel Four, bowling with his arm in a cast and spinning the ball every bit as far. What might be even more instructive would be were his wrist immobilised instead—I suspect it would draw much of his bowling's sting, and in doing so demonstrate the locus of his energy.

Curiously, too, the doosra—the ball the off-spinner has perfected to go the other way—might well predate him. Jack Potter went on Australia's 1964 Ashes tour as a right-handed batsman, but his part-time finger spin was just as impressive, for he varied his off-break with a ball going the other way without apparently changing action. 'If I had a ball like that,' Richie Benaud told Potter, 'I'd be practising at Lord's before breakfast.' As a batsman, Potter preferred to keep it as a party piece, to flummox county pros and amuse his keeper Wally Grout:

> You had no chance of detecting it from the hand and could only hope to pick the direction of the spin through the air, a dicey business particularly on the many English grounds with sightscreens ... [Gloucestershire's David] Allen muttered to me one day after Jack's wrong 'un had him swiping fresh air: 'What's this fellow doing?' and though equally fooled I did my best to convince David that the ball had hit something on the wicket. In later matches the appearance of Potter at the bowling crease prompted a conference among the batsmen, one I should have been allowed to join. I was as much in the dark about Jack's pet ball as they were.

Potter's chief contribution to the history of mystery would be as a teacher, for it was he who, at the AIS Cricket Academy, inducted Shane Warne in the enigma of the flipper, a back-spun leg-break that zaps from under the hand, and burrows straight ahead like a commuter running headlong for a departing train. This ball came in line of descent from Clarrie Grimmett through Bruce Dooland, who imparted it to Richie Benaud at Trent Bridge in May 1956. For a time when Warne bowled it, the flipper was so popular it seemed to be on the brink of getting its own talk show.

Yet Warne in time turned out to be the cricketer who best demonstrated that mystery is temporary, mastery permanent. Warne talked a good mystery ball, but in action he was quite the opposite, generous to the point of exhibitionism in the way he shared his art. Perhaps no bowler in cricket history has been replayed more often: the leg-break to dismiss Mike Gatting at Old Trafford in June 1993 has been viewed more than half a million times on YouTube alone. But study was no substitute for the experience of Warne's predatory presence.

For any modern bowling enigma quickly flushes out an army of Alan Turings: about *je ne sais quoi* they are soon saying *quelle barbe*. The googly of the last twenty years has been reverse swing, a decided advantage for Pakistan in the late 1980s and early 1990s but increasingly exoteric since then—to the extent, in fact, that Australia did not think it a skill worth mastering, and came a cropper against Simon Jones and Freddie Flintoff during the 2005 Ashes series.

The Australians are not usually so careless. Even when the doosra confounded them for one golden day at Bellerive Oval in November 1999, Saqlain Mushtaq taking six for 46, it was not through the lack of a plan so much as the forgetting of one. As Steve Waugh explained:

> Fair enough, this is a special ball delivered with the skill of an illusionist, but it's also one we have talked about in detail and always have a plan to. We believe that Saqlain hardly ever turns his off break, and that his stock ball is the mystery delivery that turns like a leg-break. To counter him, we believe that early on, until you've got accustomed to the difference in flight and bounce of this ball, you should play him as a leg-spinner and use your pad to neutralize the occasional off-break. However, for some reason we completely forgot about this strategy and paid the price, losing wicket after wicket to his 'freakish' skill.

Saqlain took four for 205 in the next three innings as the Australians, now on their mettle, swept the series clean. In other words, when mystery wears off, there must be a residue of skill and resilience. Indeed, many international cricket careers now unfold like whodunits solved in the first 30 pages; after that, the player is a quarry on the run, trying to stay a step ahead of his opponents.

The mysterious, or at least the unorthodox, can still have powerful short-term impacts; indeed, it is possible that the homogenising influences of television and top-level coaching have enhanced the value of the unusual cricketer. It was noticeable that the four most effective bowlers in last year's World Cup were all gifted with decidedly homespun methods. None of the spinners Murali and Brad Hogg or the pacemen Lasith Malinga and Shaun Tait obsessed about 'the channel' or 'getting it in the right areas'. They either spun the ball as much as they could, or slung it as fast as they were able.

None, however, has really prospered since, even Murali being below his exalted best in Australia and West Indies. Malinga hasn't lingered; Tait is gone temporarily, Hogg permanently. The acid test of Ajantha Mendis, then, is not what he is doing now, but how his game is standing up in two years' time, whether he's still breasting the bar or in the Last Chance Saloon.

Cricinfo, May 2008

Variety Show

Twenty20 seems so fated to take the world over that it cannot be long before batsmen start hitting four4s and six6s, and falling for duck0s. But the underlying idea of making cricket something faster, shorter, simpler and sillier is an old one. In fact, for a game whose commandments sometimes seem to have been handed down on clay tablets, cricket has throughout its history been interpreted with disarming freedom.

Nor should it be overlooked that the model of an eleven-a-side, two-innings game on which 'first-class' cricket converged was only one of a host of cricket variations in use two hundred years ago. Cricketers still took the field against one another as individuals in single-wicket competition, as threes, fours, fives and sixes in double-wicket competition, and against odds, often apparently overwhelming. When the first English team toured Australia from January 1862, it played eleven of its fourteen games as XIs against XXIIs, and not until 1946–47 did English cricketers undertake an Ashes tour in which every game was on equal terms.

Sometimes the concepts combined. In one of the most famous of duels, in 1810, the great all-rounder William Lambert took on Lord Frederick Beauclerk and TC Howard and won by 15 runs to claim a stake of £100. This Lambert did with wides, which did not then count against the bowler, and which, legend has it, drove the combustible Beauclerk crazy. There were concepts, too, that not even ECB marketers have dreamed up. Near Rickmansworth in May 1827, for example, 'two Middlesex gentlemen' were defeated by Harefield farmer Francis Trumper 'supported by his dog', providing a windfall for gamblers: an event of potential historical significance to Cricinfo, Coral and Krufts.

And while odds cricket hasn't survived, except when England want to fritter a couple of days away against an Australian state, the old-fashioned head-to-head contest has shown considerable durability. In the same year as the inaugural one-day domestic knockout was launched among the English countries, sponsored by Gillette, Scarborough hosted and Carling sponsored an international single-wicket competition featuring mainly county cricketers but also involving Chandu Borde and Joe Solomon. Relocated in July 1964 to Lord's, staked by the brewer Charrington and thrown open to a bigger field including Garry Sobers and Richie Benaud, it established a reputation for innovative cricket and surprising results. Over the next six years, the annual event attracted players of the calibre of Graeme Pollock, Rohan Kanhai, Wes Hall, Mushtaq Mohammed, Asif Iqbal, Saeed Ahmed, Bob Simpson, Bob Cowper, Keith Stackpole and David Holford, as well as almost all England's top players of the decade. The batsmen had a maximum eight overs to bat, amid nine fielders from the MCC ground staff backed up by quality keepers including John Murray and Bob Taylor.

A handicap was that, potentially, a game could last two balls. The shortest was at Lord's in August 1966, when Clive Radley danced out to and missed the first delivery from his county captain Fred Titmus, who then won by hitting a boundary. Games could also be fearfully one-sided. In the last final, in August 1969, Keith Boyce smashed 84 from 46 balls then had Brian Bolus caught second ball. The sponsor then lost interest when it was merged with Bass, Mitchell & Butlers.

The concept excited some imitation, with a National Single-Wicket Competition for Pakistan in August 1968, won by Mohammed

Siddique, and an antipodean double-wicket variation called World Cricket (Doubles) Pty Ltd staged in Australia on three consecutive weekends two months later, won by Garry Sobers and Wes Hall. But by this stage, limited-overs cricket had stolen the march on every other variation.

Again, limited-overs cricket was an old idea, perhaps the oldest of all: a game, and a result, in a day. And after the success of the inaugural Gillette Cup final, England's top sports columnist, Peter Wilson of the *Daily Mirror*, urged the spread of the short-form game as a matter of urgency:

> I am certain that if cricket as a whole ... is to have any serious
> spectator appeal, we must have more and more matches where
> a definite result can be expected and achieved within a single
> day ... When you come to consider it, it is as ridiculous for the
> man who can spare only one day at a three-day match to go
> there as it would be to expect him to watch only one act of a
> three-act play, or to read only a third of a whodunit.

Yet what's most conspicuous about one-day's development is not its pace but its slowness. The counties made no immediate effort to expand the Gillette Cup, to introduce new competitions or to take it offshore. The real initiative was shown by the International Cavaliers Cricket Club, an exhibition XI of rotating personnel devised by Denis Compton, Colin Ingleby-Mackenzie, Ted Dexter, Godfrey Evans, Les Ames and the sports agent Bagenal Harvey. The impetus, Dexter explained, was boredom, and the 'sense of frustration and futility of travelling 150 miles overnight to play county cricket in front of two men and a dog at some obscure outpost of cricket's over-expanded empire'; the rationale soon became rather more.

The Cavaliers played their first fixtures in 1963, offering their services as opponents in weekend benefit games. Then, in January 1965, their formula for 40-over-a-side Sunday afternoon matches, fitted into four hours and bankrolled by Rothmans, attracted an offer for broadcast rights from BBC2. Good crowds and better ratings followed, the paramountcy of the latter acknowledged by such gestures as restricted run-ups for bowlers so that games always finished on schedule. But virtue, as they say, is its own punishment. Enviously eyeing the Cavaliers's franchise, the counties decided to muscle in, winning BBC2's patronage with a 40-over-a-side county league sponsored by Rothmans's rival Imperial Tobacco: thus the John Player League, a part of the English season from 1969.

Nor did one-day cricket take root elsewhere until the Australian Board of Control took the tentative step towards its own domestic knock-out, staged over forty eight-ball overs a side, from 1969–1970. It made a faltering start: the sponsor, Vehicle & General Insurance, collapsed after two seasons, giving way to Coca-Cola, then to Gillette. But it did mean that the Australians had some slight fore-knowledge of one-day cricket before the inaugural international— when, thanks to the unseasonal rain that washed away a Melbourne Test, the game's short form was fought out first by the same opponents at the same venue as was the case in the long form.

Even then, nothing happened overnight. The subcommittee deputised by the International Cricket Conference in October 1971 to discuss a cricket 'World Cup' encountered resistance when it returned with the suggestion for a tournament of 'Gillette Cup-style' games. The term 'one-day international' was coined by Gubby Allen at the ICC meeting of 21 and 22 July 1972, even as he disdained the whole idea of them: a 'World Cup' of cricket, he felt, should be 'top-class games'. Ultimately, the Cup proceeded on a limited-overs basis because a full suite of three- and five-day games would simply have taken too long. In fact, that momentous first World Cup final proved that one day is sometimes hardly enough, not finishing until 8.43 p.m.

To squeeze cricket into less than a day has proven a greater challenge, at least without deskilling and trivialising the game. With only 10 overs a side, extra rewards for straight hitting and no lbw, the Cricket Max conceived by New Zealand's Martin Crowe was more like Cricket Min. With only eight players a side, and everyone but the keeper drafted for two overs, the Super Eights devised by Australian Cricket Board chief executive Graham Halbish resembled a play without quite enough cast members. Both were played domestically in the second half of the 1990s, then hazarded at international level, with a Super Eights tournament won by an Australia A VIII in Kuala Lumpur between 12 and 14 July 1996 and New Zealand beating England 2-1 in a Cricket Max head-to-head from 31 October to 2 November 1997. The brevity of these games was in a way their downfall: like most things conceived purely as 'entertainment' they left no trace on onlookers.

Australia and New Zealand pooled resources to create a hybrid version of their games: Cricket Super Max Eights. But you're in trouble when it takes longer to say your game than play it. Apathetic response to a tournament in Kuala Lumpur caused cancellation of similar plans in Hong Kong and Perth, and even the formal adoption of Cricket Super Max Eights as world cricket's 'official third generation game' at the ICC meeting of 23 and 24 June 1999 meant two-thirds of nought not out. The drive to popularise Cricket Super Max Eights also kyboshed the period's other cricket diversion, the annual five-over-a-side Hong Kong Sixes, which fell into desuetude after its sixth instalment on 27 and 28 September 1997, not resuming until 10 and 11 November 2001. Although Australians complained bitterly about the world not supporting their game, the same complaint could be made of them at the Sixes, to which they've never sent a representative team, losing as a result twice as many games as they have won and never improving on their second-place finish in 1994.

The quest for new variations on the game turned up some old ideas. There were several single-wicket contests, from the Courage Challenge Cup for batsmen at the Oval in September 1979 to the Silk Cut Challenge for all-rounders at Arundel in September 1985 and Hong Kong two years later, plus a few double-wicket tournaments, from the Brylcreem International at Wembley Arena in April 1978 to the Pepsi International at Gaddafi Stadium in April 2001. In some ways, even night cricket was a revival, given that electric light cricket had been promoted in South Australia from 1930 by the Returned Sailors and Soldiers Imperial League of Australia, albeit that this antique game featured underarm bowling with a tennis ball and fifteen-man teams.

Perhaps the most successful variation was the one on which authorities spent nothing. The first indoor cricket of significance occurred improbably in Germany: it was Husum CC, a club of minority Danes, who had the brainstorm of a tournament in a hall in Flensborg, South Slesvig, in the winter of 1968–69. Codified indoor cricket, with its dedicated courts and demarcated walls, then emerged in several varieties. In England, where it was originally a six-a-side game, it is considered the brainchild of former Worcestershire secretary Mike Vockins, who saw it as 'a way of keeping enthusiasts in touch with each other during the winter months'. The first league, in northwest Shropshire, was formed in September 1970; the first national competition, sponsored by Wrigleys and involving 400 clubs, culminated at the Sobell Centre in Islington in March 1976, with Durham City beating Entville in the final. By the championship of April 1979, more than 1000 clubs were involved, with Lord's Indoor Cricket School hosting the finals.

Indoor cricket in Australia has multiple parentage in the one city. During the upheavals of World Series Cricket, Dennis Lillee and a club cricket colleague Graham Monoghan invested in a cricket school in Perth with indoor nets where they coached schoolboys, adjourning outside to play fully fledged games. 'Then one day,' recalls Lillee in *Menace* (2003), 'the rain absolutely belted down, so we decided to pull the nets back and play the game indoors. The kids loved it, we enjoyed it and the penny dropped—maybe we should get some teams involved.'

Monoghan's involvement with Lillee in indoor cricket is not so well known as their other collaboration: the aluminium bat. And perhaps more ambitious were businessmen Paul Hannah and Mick Jones who around the same time began experimenting with an eight-a-side variation at their Subiaco Cricket Arena. Hannah and Jones later helped found the nationwide chain Indoor Cricket Arenas, and by the time the first national championships were held in 1984 there were an estimated 200000 participants in Australia.

Indoor cricket, like squash, is held back by its lack of telegenia. The game in Australia was also bedevilled by feuding between rival control bodies, then by overcapacity when its popularity plateaued. Nonetheless, Australians have dominated the confined game at international level since the first indoor World Cup was staged in Birmingham twelve years ago. Like their open-air countrymen in the Twenty20 World Championship that concludes in Johannesburg on 24 September, Troy Gurski's Australians are red-hot favourites to continue their global interior dominance in the Indoor Cricket World Cup that finishes in Bristol on 30 September.

That Twenty20 World Championship, meanwhile, is cricket's most considerable venture since the inaugural World Cup. The game itself pays cricket three important tributes, recognising that it is a team for XIs, in which freelance or far-flung fielders scarcely suffice; that equality of scoring opportunity in all 360 degrees is fundamental to its rich variety; and that batsmen should bat and bowlers bowl, overs of filth from specialist batsmen merely looking crude. Cricket's most successful variations, it seems, are those that actually look more like cricket rather than less. There may be something to be said for this quaint old game after all.

Cricinfo, September 2007

Too Good to Be True?

Nothing succeeds like success, says the proverb. For confirmation, look no further than the cricket grounds of South Africa. Test matches there usually struggle to attract a quorum. For the last ten days they have brimmed with life and noise for a world championship of the game's newest variant, Twenty20: a heady mixture of thrills, spills and mass marketing.

The conclusion, moreover, was close to ideal. Where the 50-over-a-side World Cup earlier this year was fatally undermined by the early exits of India and Pakistan, here those traditional antagonists reached the final, having earlier tied after 240 deliveries. As the subcontinent is now the hub of the game, India and Pakistan, and perforce the world, are about to go Twenty20 crazy.

Amid the excitement, Australians have been notable party poopers, and not merely because they went down to both finalists after earlier being tripped up by Zimbabwe. Trying to sound enthused about the crowds in Johannesburg, Adam Gilchrist let his ambivalence hang out: 'Er, yeah, yeah. It's um … well. The more I play it, I am starting to, not so much like it as a player, but love watching it.' Andrew Symonds came straight out and called Twenty20 'a frustrating game because you can be beaten by the lesser sides' who 'have to be good for a shorter period of time'. In this they echo their captain, Ricky Ponting, who last year confessed: 'I don't think I really like playing Twenty20 international cricket.'

Nobody else shows quite the same candour, perhaps because Twenty20 is looming as a means by which the much-resented Australian grip on international cricket might be loosened, and perhaps also because of its looming booty. An Indian Premier League has been mooted, with corporates bidding for the right to field franchise teams selected from a pool of internationals; likewise a Champions League along the lines of rugby's Super 14s involving teams from host India, Australia, England and South Africa.

For punters, Twenty20 has been a blast: a starburst of sixes, a welter of wickets and, not least, a farcical 'bowl-out' during the finalists' first meeting where trembling players proved embarrassingly incapable of hitting a set of stumps. Indeed, embarrassment is the essence of Twenty20. Players don't just fail; they are humiliated. A promising young bowler, Stuart Broad, was smashed for six sixes in an over; a brilliant young batsman, Michael Clarke, faced four balls for the entire tournament; Sri Lanka's able and stylish top order, which excelled in the World Cup, and whose variety of strokeplayers is one of the pleasures of the modern game, committed batting harakiri in ten overs. The fielding has been surprisingly ham-handed, with plenty of catches missed, and only three taken in the slips in the twenty-six games preceding the final. Twenty20, then, is in danger of turning a game of subtleties, intricacies and distant intimacies into a theatre of cruelty for television.

Cricket lovers underestimate this philosophical shift at their peril. Cricket has traditionally been a game for players, with everyone enjoying the scope and the time to show their own special skills. But this length, breadth and variety have made the game difficult to mass market.

When one-day cricket brought the spectators' understandable desire to see a result in a day into calculations, that balance was disturbed. 'In cricket, the players are the boss,' observed Peter

Roebuck. 'In one-day cricket, the game is the boss.' In Twenty20, that boss has an MBA and totes a BlackBerry, and his concern is chiefly ratings rather than runs or wickets. Indeed, the format originated on the marketing whiteboards at the England and Wales Cricket Board four years ago as a means of attracting cricket 'tolerators': sports watchers averse to the game who might consider going if it was shorter, sharper and noisier. A novel idea, this: to redesign a game to the specifications of those who don't like it—rather like creating art for consumers who prefer pornography, or composing music for listeners with a taste for cacophony. But the practitioners' acquiescence is obtained by an arrangement reminiscent of Alfred Hitchcock's principle for dealing with actors: 'Pay them heaps and treat them like cattle.'

So the administrators have a hit on their hands—a hit that will reverberate. We have already seen the best-case scenario: a successful tournament still tinged with novelty. Over time, however, it is likely that the main beneficiaries will be commercial intermediaries. Cricket will make a great deal of money in the short term, for which it has no obvious need and will mostly waste, and will be left a coarser, crueller, crasser game as a result. Now that the Twenty20 world championship is over, another proverb comes to mind: be careful what you wish for.

Australian, September 2007

The Game's Afoot

Friday was a big night for cricket. A large noisy gathering toasted the success of the happy band of international cricketers called … the Yarras.

Yes, it was presentation night at the club where I've been a member fifteen years, and have an apparently eternal commission as vice-president. A genuinely global affair it was, too. Harry, our Kiwi clubman extraordinaire, was extravagantly toasted—deservedly so. Knockbax, our Yorkie quick bowler, told us we were all 'roooobish'— deservedly so, too. Aravind, in receiving the award for most ducks, narrated in hilarious detail the only innings in which he scored a run last season. Nashad, having won the bat raffle, touchingly described arriving from Dhaka five years ago knowing nobody in Melbourne; now, he said, he regarded us as family.

Bangalore was mentioned quite a lot during the evening, although only because two of our boys, Zameel and Ranjit, have gone home there to get married, whereupon they should be boomeranging back to us. What else was happening in Bangalore that night … well, it seemed far away indeed. As Indian Premier League VIPs swanned around looking like they owned the universe, I sat on my couch carefully counting up the $583.50 in notes and coins we cleared on our event—an amount that wouldn't buy you the G-string of a Washington Redskins cheerleader. The only thing that reminded me of the Yarras thereafter was that no batsman bar Brendon McCullum could break 20 in perfect batting conditions.

Since then I've watched every ball of IPL. I mean, most anything with a bat and ball is to my taste: I'd watch a Danish Rounders Test match. Some of it's been okay. It's always cheering to see crowds at cricket. It's fun to see the nifty and inventive strokeplay, even if in Robin Uthappa's case it seems to have left him incapable of anything else, and when Rahul Dravid played an off-drive against the Mumbai Indians I was overcome by waves of nostalgia.

Shaun Pollock's craftiness, Muttiah Muralitharan's ebullience, Ishant Sharma's cutting edge—no cricket lover could not enjoy these, wherever they might be on show. The old-fashioned feeling of the Knight Riders v Deccan Chargers was also a delight. Batsmen having to earn their runs? How … twentieth century! India's chaotic contradictions, too, are always worth savouring. Lotus-eating celebrities watch multimillionaire athletes amid the splendour at Eden Gardens and … the lights go out. I can't recall whether it was while he was Kennedy's ambassador to India that John Kenneth Galbraith first considered the coexistence of 'private affluence and public squalor', but here was too perfect an example.

It's early days yet, of course, and nobody has the power of prophecy. 'Hopefully it will be a massive success,' Kevin Pietersen reckons. 'And I think it's going to be, because you have so much money being pumped into it, and you have the best players in the world, so there's no reason why it won't be.' But the ICC presented a similar argument ahead of 2005's Super Series, which became a bomb of Dam Buster proportions, and the assumptions that players and money are all it takes to manufacture box-office gold are … well, assumptions. Nobody knows whether we will see more Twenty20 as good as last September's World Championship final at New Wanderers, or more as pathetic as the fiasco in Melbourne ten weeks ago that couldn't last thirty overs.

Already, however, I'm struck by the fact that what I've enjoyed are those moments when Twenty20 has most closely resembled cricket *ordinaire*. And this is a problem, because there simply aren't enough of them. Twenty20 is envisaged as a concentrated form of cricket, without the pauses and longueurs that test the patience and understanding of the uninitiated. But it's less concentrated than crudely edited, and what is missing are those aspects of the game that make it linger in the mind, that impress on the imagination, that take time to understand, that need effort to appreciate. Twenty20 seems to require nothing of its audience but their attendance and their money. Apparently, the inaugural IPL game coincided with the first episode of Shah Rukh Khan's Indianised version of *Are You Smarter than a Fifth Grader?* Pardon me for thinking that Khan's two new presentations have a few things in common.

The game's skills, meanwhile, have been massively rationalised. What we see in the main is not so much batting as hitting, not so much bowling as conveying. The batsman is assessed by the change his strokes are leaving out of six; the bowler is like the fall guy in a comic routine stoically awaiting the inevitable custard pie. For sure, the players are stars, personalities, megabuck entertainers. But to be great under such circumstances is next to impossible—the game is neither big nor deep enough. No thespian has achieved greatness from a career of sketches; no old master won admiration for a skill at silhouettes. Cricket has traditionally made welcome a wonderful variety of capabilities and temperaments. The swashbuckler will have his day, but likewise the gritty opening batsman, the middle-order nurdler, the doughty tailender; likewise there are days that favour the merchants of outswing, googlies and subtle left-arm slows. From the combination of twenty overs a side, flat pitches, white balls and 70 metre boundaries, however, emerges what sort of cricketer? (In fact, you begin wondering which great past players would have found in Twenty20 a welcoming home? Kapil Dev, for sure. Maybe Gavaskar, when not in one of his obdurate moods. But can you see Chandrashekhar, Bedi, Prasanna? Given the choice, would you select Vishwanath and Manjrekar, or Patil and Pandit?)

The argument is advanced that this need not concern us: we are assured that Twenty20 will be only one of cricket's variants. There will still be Test cricket, first-class cricket and 50-over matches. Yet with the animal spirits of the market liberated, how realistic an expectation is this? Already players are falling over themselves to make IPL hay, egged on by managers taking a fair clip themselves. The likelihood is that the objective of the majority of cricketers worldwide will become not to play dowdy old domestic cricket that leads on to hoary old national honours: the longer forms of the game that prepare the most finished practitioners. The economically rational behaviour will be to adapt their methods to maximise their IPL employment opportunities. Consider just who is closer to the role model du jour: is it Rahul Dravid, the 'Wall' with his 10 000 Test runs, or Yuvraj Singh, who once hit six sixes in an over? Will a rising young cricketer earn more by emulating Dravid? If maximising individual income is what matters—and if any cricketer feels otherwise then he's keeping such a heresy to himself—then Yuvraj might well be the cookie-cutter cricketer of the next decade. Twenty20 has rightly been called a batsman's game, but it is a very particular kind of batsman—the type whose game is built on eye and strength. If a new Dravid were to begin emerging now, I suspect, he would face a career as a second-class cricket citizen.

Nor is it economically rational for franchise owners to rest content with enterprises that are inactive for 46 weeks of the year. You don't have to be Einstein ... hell, you don't have to be Napoleon Einstein to realise that if the IPL contains even a glimmer of promise, it won't be stopping there: pretty soon cricket's schedule will have more windows than the Sears Tower. What then? What might cricket look like after twenty years of Twenty20centricity? There may have been a few more Dhonis; probably a great many more Uthappas. But can you imagine another Sachin Tendulkar, with the discipline to budget for innings by the day, with a defence as monumental as his strokes are magnificent? And what price a new Anil Kumble—brave, patient, probing, untiring—in a world measuring out bowling in four-over spells?

Of course, it is too early to tell, and perhaps it will all sort itself out—but that, I fear, is what it will have to do, because you know that nobody involved in IPL gives a toss about any of the foregoing. For it is an enterprise concerned chiefly with the self-admiration of India's media and corporate elites, where nobody much cares what's happening on the field so long as Preity Zinta can be shown clapping her lovely hands, and the long-term interests of cricket are of no significance compared with how quickly the Kolkata Knight Riders can be reinforced by the Benares Baywatchers and the Mysore Melrose Placers. Short-term profit maximisation is the name of the game—and that goes for administrators, franchisees, players, managers, broadcasters and sponsors alike. The possible negative consequences for other countries or other forms of the game are of no account compared with the commercial and doubtless also political ambitions of the likes of Lalith Modi and Sharad Pawar. It is not even about 'giving the people what they want'; it is about giving the people what Modi and Pawar want them to want, and can then make a packet out of selling them.

Exactly why they deserve this is not abundantly clear. Perhaps it is an instance of what I once saw defined as the Golden Rule of Arts and Sciences: 'Whoever has the gold makes the rules.' But the contrast I noted earlier between the proceeds of my own humble cricket event and the IPL's was not merely a matter of quantum. All of the Yarras's hard-won $583.50 will go straight back into the game's beneficiation. Of what proportion of the billions raised by the IPL, I wonder, will that be true?

Cricinfo, April 2008

One Step Forward, Two Back

Albert Einstein famously never worried about the future—it arrived soon enough. A fast-arriving future, however, seems to be worrying cricket a great deal. Few weeks have shown cricket's divided consciousness about the promise of technology as clearly as the last.

First of all, Marylebone Cricket Club, in its capacity as holder of the worldwide copyright on the Laws of Cricket, rewrote Law 6 to curb experiments aimed at making already powerful bats more powerful yet. No sooner had this been digested than the International Cricket Council, in its capacity as holder of a worldwide reputation for being unable to organise a piss-up in a brewery with Oliver Reed and Keith Moon, foreshadowed an experiment under which captains will be permitted to refer three decisions per innings to a third umpire. Marylebone is probably right; the ICC is almost certainly wrong.

If you've been playing cricket in the last decade, even at low levels, you'll have noticed that bats are way more powerful than of yore. In fact, finding it psychically impossible to discard bats and having a veritable belfry of them at home, the comparison staggers me. The bat I switched to last season is so good it almost plays the shot for me—just as well, really. When the ball hits the middle, it emits a sound as euphonious as a violin concerto. If I hit a ball with the one I played with ten years ago, meanwhile, the noise is like that of fingernails on a blackboard.

That improvement, if it has not already gone too far, has certainly gone far enough, and the squeals of bat makers should be ignored. 'Tennis used to be played with wooden racquets and now it is much faster and more exciting,' complained Gray-Nicolls's marketing manager. Capacity for false analogy is probably why he is in marketing: the contest in cricket is between bat and ball, not racquet and racquet. Nor is it entirely true to claim that the transition from wooden to metal racquets was an unmitigated good; you'll find plenty of tennis traditionalists who lament the obsolescence of the touch player, who was blasted out of the game by weight of stroke. And not even in tennis does 'faster' translate automatically as 'more exciting', or every clay court would have been relaid with Rebound Ace.

Cricket is also a game with dense statistical records whose integrity it is obliged to take some measures to protect, and when more than a quarter of the runs in the Indian Premier League are being scored in sixes then the game's currency is being devalued by power hitting. In fact, this shows why it is not just prudent but desirable for the MCC to retain its position as the game's independent law giver. If the magnates and MBAs in power elsewhere had their druthers, bats would soon be as wide as gates and grounds the size of tennis courts. The MCC, for all its reputation for gin-soaked doddering, does at least have some coherent idea of cricket's greater good.

If only the same could be said of the ICC, presently without a CEO, CFO, in-house counsel and point, although its decision to aim for the half-pregnancy of three referrals per innings to the third umpire is risible even by its own debased standards. As Ian Chappell put it with characteristic pith: 'Following an occasionally spiteful Test series between Australia and India where much of the controversy arose due to the umpires having reduced control on the field, the solution proposed by the ICC is to further undermine the authority of the arbiters.' But given that to 'stand in the way of progress' nowadays invites being thought of as a luddite or obscurantist, it may be worth turning over some of the reasons why improving the precision of decisions by technology is thought worthwhile.

There is, for instance, the old chestnut that a cricketer's career could be cruelled by an umpire's mistake. Ahem—can you remember one? Arguably, if it should transpire that a player's whole future hinges on one decision, then he has only himself to blame should it go against him. And on the whole, cricketers are actually far more philosophical about the rub of the green than fans. Mike Atherton has put this most succinctly: 'Life is unfair. Why should cricket be any different?'

At the same time, it is confidently asserted that the introduction of technology will eliminate room for doubt. Yet this assumption that analysis leads at all events to greater clarity is not actually a given: sometimes further analysis introduces doubt previously absent. There was an interesting example of this during the Super Test that wasn't at the SCG in October 2005 where, if you recall, umpires were empowered to refer all decisions to an upstairs video jockey. The first such reference followed Matthew Hayden opting to pad up to the third ball after lunch on the first day, which pitched in line and carried on to hit the knee roll. A club umpire would have given Hayden out without hesitation; Hayden admitted later thinking he was 'absolutely dead'. Receiving the referral from Simon Taufel, however, Darrell Hair, brooded deeply on multiple replays, somehow located a scintilla of doubt, perhaps about the height, and allowed Hayden to carry on to a fat hundred. Asked after that game if the technology had improved the quality of the officiation, World XI captain Graeme Smith said simply: 'No.'

An attitude has insinuated itself into cricket that umpires exist purely and simply as part of the game's machinery—as necessary, but also as worthy of consideration, as the heavy roller or the Super Sopper. This is lamentable. Umpiring involves a knowledge base and set of skills every bit as demanding as playing—in the respect that they are never off duty, even more so. Why should their thankless task be made more thankless by the possibility of public humiliation because they are not possessed of supernatural powers, because the naked eye cannot magically capture what it has just seen and replay it at slow motion?

It is fascinating that such angst should attend the possibility of a mistaken decision in a game of cricket: a glimmer of human fallibility and we carry on like 9/11 Truthers. There was a time when we regarded cricket as a test of character; one of the challenges it posed being the manful acceptance of a decision not correct but made in good faith. At grassroots level, this remains the case. Which is why when Kumar Sangakarra accepted the error of Rudi Koertzen at Bellerive Oval last season, he grew in stature as a man as surely as his innings had enriched his standing as a player; which is why when Rahul Dravid swallowed his gall in Sydney a month later, he won many admirers. TS Eliot once wrote that 'it is impossible to design a system so perfect that no one needs to be good'. Yet this seems to be the ICC's aim: an arrangement under which there will never be any grounds for disappointment, so that nobody need ever cope with it.

Tellingly, the players who theoretically stand to benefit most directly from this new policy are ambivalent about it. Michael Kasprowicz, with rather more reason than most to complain of umpiring error after his misfortune at Edgbaston three years ago, commented: 'It's all a part of the game. Part of the beauty of cricket was that there was room for human error and sometimes it went your way, sometimes it didn't. It all evened out in the end.' Then he added, very shrewdly: 'Today, with all the money invested in cricket, the shareholders are going to demand the right decision all the time. You don't pay $800 million for a cricket team to let an umpire's error ruin it for you.'

Aye, Kasper, there's the rub. For this decision concerns not the welfare of cricketers at all, and certainly not the game. It is primarily about money. At some stage in the future, millions of dollars might ride on an appeal for lbw against the star batsman of the Mangalore Miami Vices where the ball might have pitched an inch or two outside leg stump. This, it has been resolved, cannot possibly be left to a mere human being. But when cricket is thought too important to be left to mere humans, it is in danger of mattering too much to be enjoyed at all.

Cricinfo, May 2008

Progress and Its Discontents

Cricket's Great Leap Forward began just over a month ago and already the world seems to have changed irrevocably—for some, entirely for the better, the stifling pall of tradition having been blown away by the cool zephyr of all-star entertainment and common-sense economics.

Listen to these people, in fact, and cricket beforehand must have been almost hell on earth. 'Typical traditionalist,' they complain if you suggest that perhaps not every development is to be welcomed. 'Hopeless romantic,' they huff if you speculate that the future is not entirely bright and shiny. Strangely, this injunction against romanticism is not thought to apply when Ravi Shastri gratuitously garlands Lalith Modi as 'the Moses of cricket'—nothing romantic about that, of course, just cool, dispassionate and financially disinterested analysis.

Even my esteemed colleague Peter Roebuck has been taking 'these stiff collars' to task. 'The trouble with traditionalists is that they present themselves as protectors of the game's values but are actually doomed romantics,' he argued a week or two ago. 'They lament the present state of affairs yet resist innovation.' He has a point, as ever, with one qualification. Cricket must indeed be wary of 'romanticising' that which has gone before; but cricket without 'romance' would be sterile indeed, and not worth buying and selling for millions of dollars either. The idea that there has been some sort of fuddy-duddy backlash against IPL, meanwhile, is a fantasy: on the contrary, it has been received with utmost cordiality. Those who've wished to have partaken, those unmoved have exercised their prerogative not to watch, and time will tell on its effects. What held up the rush to embrace Twenty20 cricket was not the dead hand of the game's jeremiahs, but the conservatism of the BCCI, loath to cannibalise the market exploited by its fifty-over money machine.

As for innovation, there is during accelerated phases of evolution as much danger of neophilia as in obstinate rejection of all change. Sketching an argument last week against the ICC's decision to allow three referrals to the video booth per innings at the captain's behest was actually worth it for some of the more incontinent responses. 'Stop being such a Victorian writer and come to reality'; 'It's the same old predictable traditionalist's reaction'; 'The trouble with historians is that they are romantics that live in the past and don't look ahead to the future.' Again with the T and the R words! For a few, medical attention seemed advisable: 'Some of these errors are so blatant that it makes the TV viewer want to puke.' And at the risk of even more emetic response from the Cricinfo commentariat, it might be worth here a slight further elaboration, with no thought of persuading anyone, but the intent of reflecting on what an attachment to the past is good for—and what, perhaps, it is not.

Argument against the ICC's recommendation only partly concerns technology in cricket. There's no doubt that use of the replay in line calls has been extremely efficacious, both in terms of justice done and skills rewarded. The dividends for a direct hit, an act of excellence, grew considerably; the potential cost of failing to judge a run correctly, a mistake, rose sharply.

The new ICC's system is of a different character. Undoubtedly it will prevent the occasional howler. But how many of these are there? And how great would the improvement *really* be? The usefulness of technology for caught behinds and lbws is unclear. The Snicko involves a retrospective marriage of sound to picture, and sound is in any case not an entirely faithful indicator of contact, while Hawk Eye parades beguilingly perfect parabolae while keeping from us its margin for error. What, furthermore, is the cost? For nothing, even the relentless march of logic, is without cost.

One of cricket's most important statutes is Law 3.7: 'The umpire is the sole judge of fair and unfair play.' It is no longer possible to argue this in an absolute sense. At home, where vastly more people consume cricket than in person, the umpire proposes but television disposes. On the field, however, the umpire is in charge, despite the concern expressed by one commenter last week: 'The argument that the umpires in the middle are the best people in position to make the right decision is not only generally flawed, but also borderline insane.' Obviously when insanity is congenital, it begins to seem like normal behaviour.

Under the ICC's proposal, that is no longer the case. The umpire's word is no longer final, and the way the game is moving one suspects it will become increasingly preliminary. As is widely known, the referral system trialled in England last season was an abject failure. But in the great tradition of Soviet science under Stalin, it is obviously intended that the experiment be repeated until the right result is achieved.

For the purpose of argument, nonetheless, let us say there is a problem with umpiring standards. And let us say that an innovative solution is required. Very well, then: let us ban appealing, which has reached operatic and obnoxious extremes that favour not the most honest players but the most calculatedly histrionic. I mean, have you tried doing your job with eleven belligerent men shouting at you, then cursing you under their breath?

Always accepting the debateability of the ICC's figures of 90 per cent accuracy in decision making—which suggest that the figure would improve to 110 per cent if they simply got shot of Rudi Koertzen—it is perhaps surprising that umpires get as much right as they do. And who can say that the chief reason for Steve Bucknor's awful gaffe involving Rahul Dravid at Sydney earlier this year was not the intimidating spontaneity of the Australian appeal? If the ball had passed Dravid's edge amid a cordon of pious mutes, what are the odds Bucknor would have given it out?

Everybody knows that players go up with razor-edged conviction for anything in the same postcode as out, then assume martyred postures, staring disconsolately into the middle distance, if and when they do not get their way; everyone knows, too, that the purpose of this is to seed doubt in the umpire's mind. Thus would a ban on appealing not just improve the working conditions for umpires but also reduce the ethical wriggle room that players have arrogated to themselves. Yes, logic demands it; hard-headed realism brooks no argument. But—hang on a moment—cricket has *always* had appealing. It is so *exciting*. It is so *dramatic*. It is *part of the romance of the game*. Damn these footling traditions! Damn these hopeless romantics standing in the way of progress!

It'll never happen, of course—fair enough, too. But one suspects that the reason it won't will have nothing to do with cricket; rather will it be because of cricket's increasing thrall to television's values. The referral system further entrenches the broadcast media's dominion over the game, while appealing is part of the colour and movement that makes cricket telegenic. What's the bet, in fact, that those dimensions of cricket best serving its home-viewing spectacle will be protected and nurtured in future, while those that do not will become vulnerable regardless of the potential cost? This bears watching at least as much as the IPL.

The opposition being set up between imagined progressives and malign reactionaries, then, is little better than name calling. Ideas are either mainly good or mainly bad, and the cry of 'innovation' is no more compelling than the invocation of 'tradition'—actually, sometimes less, when what is being replaced is flawed but essentially workable. Nor is the opposition all it sometimes seems. Consider two views of umpiring: the view that cricket is still a game, and that if the worst fate to befall you is your favourite player being given out incorrectly but in good faith by an official under extreme pressure then yours has been a blessedly sheltered life; and the view that umpiring mistakes are calamities of world-shaking proportions and flagrant offences to justice worth any price to prevent. Which of those is the romantic position, and which the realistic?

Cricinfo, May 2008

All Fall Down

Paul Collingwood has been rusticated to a county game with Durham this week for England's tardiness in bowling their overs at the Oval, but many see his punishment as morally condign. The two-player pile-up was one thing; extracting a one-wicket benefit quite another. Defeat was embraced with a relief perverse even for the English.

At such times, everyone vents their pet peeve, cricket's deteriorating politesse being seen as symptomatic of a deeper malaise—can WAGS and chavs be far behind? Perhaps Collingwood is lucky to only have been sent as far as Leeds; a couple of hundred years ago, he would probably have been sentenced to transportation. On the other hand, perhaps he'd fit right in down here. When Andrew Symonds knocked a spectator senseless last summer, one half expected a testimonial to be organised in his honour.

Some periodic fits of morality do cricket good, and this one might be the same—but not, perhaps, for the first reasons that come to mind. Concentrate first on the initial mishap, which it requires considerable rewinding of replays to absorb fully—an advantage, bear in mind, that Collingwood did not have.

New Zealand's Grant Elliott sets off, stops, restarts, then is inhibited from running wider by his on-rushing partner, and thus prevented from avoiding action. Ryan Sidebottom, formally the bowler but functionally the fielder, has eyes only for the ball. Cricket, of course, is full of such contraflows, usually negotiated by a protocol that the batsman has right of way. But nobody knows why or on whose authority—it's not in the Laws—and the protocol is subject to unconscious abuse. One of the reasons the run was viable in the first place was the assumption that Sidebottom would be diverted from fielding the ball by the need to yield Elliott space. 'Bugger that,' Sidebottom said to himself—and it's hard to blame him.

For, in cricket, the batsman can almost run where he damn well pleases. And it's hard to miss that, for years, batsmen have been abusing this privilege. You're stretching to make your ground; the ball's on its way—what do you do? If you're a 'smart cricketer'—and everyone wants to be one of those—you try to accidentally-on-purpose interpose yourself between the throw and the stumps. Do it successfully, in fact, and commentators will praise your sagacity.

Not surprisingly, this prerogative of the batsman has become increasingly irksome to fielding captains and bowlers. Fielding captains, most obviously Steve Waugh, started condoning, if not encouraging, searing returns sent within a micron or two of batsmen's heads. Bowlers, most conspicuously Glenn McGrath, started insisting on the right to hold the line of their follow through. The Australian order of battle for last year's World Cup, reveals John Buchanan in his new book *If Better Is Possible* (2007), specifically includes the instruction: 'Bowlers must position themselves in their follow through wherever possible to force batsmen to run around them.' Shaun Pollock and Kevin Pietersen going hip-for-hip at last year's Twenty20 World Championship was a harbinger of bigger and worse. Cricketers these days spend more time in gyms, putting on muscle, adding stature, and are naturally more confident of their ability to withstand a physical contact, especially under the influence of the head rush of adrenalin.

'The spirit of cricket'? Under these circumstances, it starts elasticising. In the incident at the Oval, Paul Collingwood took advantage of an inadvertent collision between wickets. But this came after a protracted period in which batsmen have taken advantage of the latitude for deliberate obstruction, and cricket's commentariat has winked knowingly at them doing so. Which of these is the more offensive violation? There was a time, furthermore, when umpires might have felt confident enough to impose on the action, to have promptly called 'dead ball', and been confident of the acceptance of the players and support of their administrators. But who today wants to be a 'brave' umpire?

So what does this episode say about cricket's perceived decadence? A bit; perhaps less than has been assumed. Because it's all about Geoff Boycott, the greatest living Yorkshireman immediately had recourse to the similar incident in his debut Test at Trent Bridge forty-four years ago when, with his partner Fred Titmus prone from a mid-pitch impact with hefty Neil Hawke, Australian keeper Wally Grout refrained from removing the bails: a noble act, to be sure. It seems almost a shame to add Hawke's recollection in his biography: 'From the covers came a startled cry, "I thought this was a bloody Test match".' There's always one, eh? Maybe, today, there are simply more.

What it might be truer to say is that modern cricketers think more like modern athletes, in straight lines, so that ambiguities are problematic. When their on-field deportment was under challenge five years ago, Steve Waugh's Australians didn't sit around reading Lord Cowdrey's lecture to one another: they drafted a document of their own headed 'The Spirit of Cricket' and signed it. A written 'spirit' seemed a bit daft at the time, and views will differ about how rigidly Waugh's countrymen have honoured its terms since, but it does say something about the preferences of modern professionals.

Thus the events of last week, because the pitch, where traffic has never been regulated, has been allowed to become a disputed zone, with batting and fielding sides asserting rights on the basis of expedience and strength. Perhaps 'right of way' needs statutory reinforcement; perhaps the batsmen's running area needs cordoning off. Whatever the case, the authorities have been slow to act, leaving players to improvise an ethical response; in some respects, it is surprising that what occurred last week was not sooner in coming.

Authorities slow to act: who knew? Sometimes, of course, they can be worse than slow. While Paul Collingwood is pelted in the public pillory, Indian cricket's potentates, in order that they might maintain their ICC gerrymander, lend credibility and shovel cash to the ramshackle, politically compromised, scandal-racked cricket administration of one of the world's ghastliest dictatorships. Why should players be expected to take the 'spirit of cricket' seriously when administrators behave with such cynical self-interest?

Cricinfo, July 2008

THE BCCI AND THE ICC

The Unipolar World

When the Cold War abruptly thawed almost twenty years ago, political strategists launched the expression 'unipolar world' to describe global Realpolitik in an era in which the United States was the solitary superpower. In the last five years, cricket has realigned to reflect a similar world order. Where it was once ritually complained that the International Cricket Council was weak, inconsistent, reactive and lacking in leadership, we now know exactly what that body will do on every issue before it: what India wishes. Sometimes not exactly; sometimes not without qualification. But, in the main, no significant motion can advance without India's patronage, and nothing to which India is resistant has a hope of progressing. On India's nod, the ICC can even change the result of Test matches. Hell, why play Test matches at all? Let's just decide them by vote at the ICC!

In one sense at least, a unipolar ICC is long overdue. India has always been the most populous, and arguably also the most passionate, of cricket nations. But their house has commonly been divided, and their stock abroad poor. In Australia in the 1980s and 1990s, we saw little of Indian teams—frustratingly little, for they were a purist's delight to watch. While the West Indies seemed to tour every other summer, Australians were denied a Tendulkar Test innings for almost eight years (from the start of 1992 to the end of 1999). The reason? India were not perceived as sufficiently bankable—and this is worth remembering lest it be imagined that the Board of Control for Cricket in India somehow introduced the evils of money to a cricket world of prelapsarian innocence.

The reasons for India's belated eminence are not far to seek either. Its democracy is stable, its economy vital, its political and media elite rich beyond the dreams of avarice; they covet the cultural clout due their wealth. I suspect it is no longer correct to talk about the 'globalisation' of cricket; rather is the game being 'Indianised', permeated by exported Indian cultural values and subordinated to Indian commercial agendas. And in a lot of ways, this is actually no big deal. There are worse cultural values to be pervaded by; and, well, most commercial agendas are alike no matter where they're from, India's commercial sector being no more rapacious and vulgar than any other. At its best, in fact, BCCI has shown an elan and imagination that other boards, and other sporting bodies, must eye enviously. At its worst, however, it exhibits the characteristics of a chip-on-the-shoulder superpower and insatiable monopoly capitalist.

Take, for example, the maintenance of Indian power at ICC level. In discussing the BCCI's shoulder-to-shoulder solidarity with Zimbabwe at the ICC, for example, one of my esteemed Cricinfo colleagues offered as explanation 'a deep-rooted suspicion about Western double standards', commenting with particular asperity on the involvement of Australian and British troops in the furtherance of US foreign policy in Iraq. It was hard not to savour the irony, for India's indulgence of Peter Chingoka is reminiscent of nothing so much as that famous US State Department MO of foreign dictatorship: 'He might be a sonofabitch but he's our sonofabitch.' It's also, of course, pure obfuscation to say that 'practically every cricket-playing country has blood on its hands': the difference in Zimbabwe is that its cricket has been degraded and exploited by the ruling junta, and that to continue allocating ICC monies raised to Zimbabwe Cricket is to collude in the vandalism of the country.

This 'double-standards' charge really needs picking over, because it is symptomatic of thinking as widespread as it is lazy, not just in cricket but generally. The accusation has become one of the bluntest, and also crudest, tools in the kit of argumentation. It is popular because it saves the labour of thought, because it can pass for debate when it is actually a substitute for it, and because it leaves a pleasing sensation of smugness. You believe in climate change ... but you drive a car! You speak of family values ... yet you once ogled a waitress! Smackdown! High-fives all round! Yet if a smoker tells you smoking is bad for you, he may appear a little conflicted, but he's not wrong. As George Orwell said: 'Some things are true even if they appear in the *Daily Telegraph*.' What the BCCI has wrought in preserving Zimbabwe's full member status at ICC is, in effect, a public bribe: BCCI will protect the flow of money to ZC in return for its vote. You have to admire the straight faces at BCCI as they piously proclaim that 'sport and politics must not mix' while striking such nakedly political arrangements: they have nothing to learn from 'Western double standards'.

As a matter of fact, the compromise at Dubai in the matter of Zimbabwe was not the worst that could have been reached. South Africa showed unanticipated fortitude, England was not obviously humiliated, Australia left fairly satisfied and Sharad Pawar got to pretend to be a statesman while defending the indefensible: by the ICC's abysmal standards, this almost merits a ticker-tape parade. And in cricket's unipolar world, this is how it will have to be—although that's not quite how it is yet.

If you're a student of political power, there are some parallels between cricket's geopolitical tectonics and diplomatic responses to Suez in 1956. After the lack of US support undermined Britain's hopeless mission, other powers were left with a choice: Britain cleaved to the US, hoping to exercise influence as 'Greece to their Rome'; France, still nourishing imperial fantasies, began leaning against the American hegemony. Cricket Australia has kept its relations with BCCI in good repair, believing this to be in its best interests. The England Cricket Board has reversed its country's post-Suez strategy by trying to becoming a countervailing force, seizing whatever support might be passing, clutching for Allen Stanford like the proverbial drunk for a lamppost.

Time will tell who has made the right call. Cricket Australia's strategy is essentially a rationalisation of weakness, as the country lacks the commercial heft to sustain its own Australian Premier League. Just as economically the country has become more or less a Chinese mine, so it faces a cricket future as essentially a mine of playing talent for mainly Indian consumption, especially if the IPL is expanded to three or four seasons in a year. The ECB, meanwhile, looks increasingly shambolic, its mercurial chairman running hard but gathering no real support, either nationally or internationally.

Will the rest of the world ever learn to love the BCCI? The United States has found that unipolar power is no guarantee of popularity—quite the opposite. And for a group arrogating so much power to itself, the BCCI is not always its own best advertisement, presenting a streamlined corporate image while maintaining standards of governance apparently patterned after Tammany Hall, with its immortal distinction between 'honest graft' and 'dishonest graft', and commitment to 'rewardin' the men that won the victory'.

Its CFO owns the franchise for the Chennai Super Kings. Its IPL administrators work as commentators. One of Lalith Modi's advantages in having baked such a big pie is the room for a few of his own fingers. If India's voting clout at ICC were not enough, new CEO Haroon Lorgat has the services of IS Bindra, the BCCI's grey eminence, as 'adviser'. Bindra is probably the most impressive of all Indian administrators—strong when he has to be, supple when he needs to be—but his position is a favour neither to Lorgat nor him, inviting doubts about ICC's transparency and eroding Lorgat's standing as an honest broker. David Morgan, meanwhile, will spend his presidency at ICC listening to Pawar, as vice-president, drumming his fingers waiting to take over. Actually, someone should tell Pawar that his Wikipedia entry introduces him thus: 'The MARATHA warrior Mr. Sharad Pawar is MOST DANGEROUS politician in Asia.' On second thoughts, perhaps they should tell Morgan first.

In the near term, evaluating cricket's future direction may become like a species of Kremlinology, studying who is taking the various salutes alongside Modi, Bindra, Pawar, and his successor as BCCI president, Shashank Manohar. Which could be quite fun. If ICC can vote on results of cricket matches, perhaps games could be used to decide votes at ICC: how about a tape-ball test in the office in Dubai to decide whether ICL receives official recognition? Power begetting responsibility, the sustainability of that model is another matter. The BCCI should understand that it is one thing to have earned the right to wield unipolar power, another to demonstrate deserving it.

Cricinfo, July 2008

5
Reading the Game

Larynx of State

'Try and make the game better for your having been in it.' Such was the advice the young Alan McGilvray received from his father when selected to play for New South Wales sixty-three years ago. He never forgot it. Over fifty years his commitment and devotion to cricket was unquestioned. Generations grew to know him as Australia's semi-official larynx of state.

During summer, McGilvray was the cynosure of all ears, calling Test matches with unvarying calm and tact. During winter when Australia toured, he was there each morning to sum up our fortunes abroad in cool measured tones. The solid Caledonian reliability of the name suited his mission: not for him the familiarity of 'Richie'; he was only ever 'McGilvray'.

The name stems from Dumfries, where McGilvray's father Thomas was born just before the family emigrated to Sydney in 1883. By the time Alan David McGilvray was born in Birchgrove on 6 December 1909 as one of four children, Thomas had become proprietor of a city shoe warehouse. Monty Noble's Australians had just retained the Ashes in England, and it was Noble who at Sydney Grammar School picked out McGilvray as an all-rounder of promise; he went on to captain the school First XI. While at school, McGilvray also attracted the help of an elocution teacher who cured a nervous schoolboy stammer and left him with a clear, well-modulated voice.

Alan worked alongside his brother Norman at Thomas McGilvray & Sons after leaving school, while striving to impress state selectors for Paddington then Waverley. Alan Kippax led a star-studded state side including Don Bradman and Bill O'Reilly, so the call did not come until December 1933: just days before his 24th birthday, McGilvray performed twelfth man duties at Adelaide Oval; days after, he had a walk-on part in Melbourne. He fared well enough to be mentioned in despatches concerning the composition of Bill Woodfull's 1934 Australian team to tour England, but another development associated with that trip was to have a greater bearing on his future.

It was the ABC's inaugural general manager Harold Parkyn Williams who in 1930 had conceived of the idea of broadcasts simulating cricket matches from England, with commentators expanding on coded cablegrams. But it was his successor Walter Tasman Conder who commissioned an ambitious subordinate, Charles Moses, to make the idea reality in time for the 1934 visit with the 'Synthetic Test' broadcasts. Moses himself led a commentary panel, featuring Noble, Clem Hill, Nip Pellew, Ted a'Beckett and Wendell Bill at the ABC's Market Street studio, which recreated the matches from cables composed by eyewitness Eric Sholl.

The team assembled at 7.30 p.m. every evening to pore over preliminary messages about the state of the ground, the weather forecast and the layout of the fielding positions, with which they embroidered their comments when the transmissions began an hour later. Gramophone discs provided crowd noises, while the sound of bat on ball was rendered by the rap of a pencil on a hollowed hemisphere of wood. The effect on a cricket-crazy nation as the broadcasts echoed through to 3.30 a.m. was powerful. Wireless sales leapt. Bars and cafes remained open round the clock so that customers could hang on every word. Families hosted all-night parties, where guests congregated round radio sets to catch every nuance of the play. Patronage at cinemas and theatres fell. Employers complained of workers arriving too fatigued to discharge their duties. Bizarrely, Australians enjoyed more comprehensive coverage of the series than Britons. The BBC carried only two ten-minute commentaries a day. Twelve thousand miles away the ABC filled the night with continuous ball-by-ball descriptions.

When Moses succeeded Conder as general manager, it was with a strong belief that the power of sport could be harnessed to popularise the young medium. Setting out to build his available cricket expertise, he approached McGilvray in November 1935 with a view to the cricketer delivering close-of-play summaries of NSW's forthcoming match against Queensland at the Gabba. McGilvray had by this time inherited the NSW captaincy, and was chary of doing anything to incur his association's ire. But he was persuaded by Moses's forceful advocacy and, after a faltering beginning, continued work until his omission from the state side in January 1937.

A word here of McGilvray's cricket capabilities is necessary. He batted left-handed in some style, bowled right-arm with some guile, caught well and analysed thoughtfully, his most memorable tactical coup being a trap he laid for Bradman (then playing for South Australia) at the SCG in January 1936. Deploying the inswing of left-armer Bob Hynes, he induced a leg-slip catch by Ray Little: one of Bradman's sixteen first-class noughts. Almost certainly, too, McGilvray was dispensed with prematurely: he was only twenty-seven, and would top the 1936–37 Sydney grade batting averages, having led the bowling averages the previous season. But he wasn't too fussed. Having just married Gwendolyn Griffiths, he reasoned that Thomas McGilvray & Sons needed his attention.

Moses, nonetheless, did not forget him, and McGilvray joined the ABC's 'Synthetic Test' broadcasts for 1938, a more ambitious scheme than four years earlier. McGilvray joined Noble, Hal Hooker and Vic Richardson in Sydney translating the cablegrams of Sholl and Chester Wilmot (the 27-year-old captain of the Melbourne University debating team, and son of the *Argus* correspondent RWE

Wilmot). After midnight, it was often possible for Sholl and Wilmot to be heard direct on shortwave from the UK.

McGilvray revelled in the experience. Moses dictated that his men participate fully in the experience. They ate 'lunch' at 10.30 p.m. as though in England, and referred throughout to pictures of the relevant Test match grounds so that they could describe their key features to listeners. McGilvray described it as 'broadcasting as an art form' and 'a pioneering adventure that left no doubt where my future lay'—although, piquantly, McGilvray did not actually see the country he had dedicated himself to describing for another decade.

Having accepted Bernard Kerr's invitation to call the 1946–47 Ashes series in Australia with Arthur Gilligan and Victor Richardson, McGilvray arranged a working trip to England in 1948, representing his family business, with time also to be the ABC's representative on the BBC. McGilvray's descriptions in the *ABC Cricket Book* of joining Gilligan for his first turn of the microphone remind us of the long-lost magic of long-distance broadcasts:

> Arthur joined me in the opening moments of the commentary and we spoke to Australia. What a thrill it was. I was really nervous. As I left the microphone after my first 20 minutes spell, that empty feeling returned, and I thought of all I had not done. Surely I spoke too quickly, forgot this and that, omitted to mention so-and-so. I anxiously awaited the cables that I knew my wife, family and friends would send me, giving their opinion of the reception. Strangely they were pleasing, so I gradually regained my confidence and felt a whole lot letter after the first day, and really settled to my task.

McGilvray was something of a novelty to English listeners accustomed to plummy voices and rounded vowels, and the BBC invited him to give a radio talk on the culture of his Australian audiences. 'I spoke of the nightly interest we people take in Test matches—of the homes and parties, and generally how people lived whilst a Test match is being played in England,' McGilvray reported. 'I generally found it difficult to convince the people of England that such things could happen.' The BBC's John Arlott also made use of McGilvray's antipodean intonation by casting him in a radio programme in July commemorating the centenary of the birth of Dr WG Grace. McGilvray put on his most nasal strine to recite the eulogies for Grace of former Test captain Billy Murdoch.

Curiously, considering they were to be bracketed as the best in their craft, McGilvray and Arlott were destined for a regard distant at best. Arlott deprecated McGilvray's unadorned fact-before-fancy technique; McGilvray thought Arlott and his partner Rex Alston were inattentive to the basic tenets of broadcasting with their long and picturesque descriptive ramblings. In David Rayvern Allen's biography of Arlott, McGilvray comments severely: 'He was a good commentator in his own way, but he didn't give the score or the card. I mentioned this to him and he said: "Who wants the score? I'm not interested in the score." You should give the score three times in every six-ball over.' Perhaps discord was inevitable between two men so confident of their respective styles. Arlott produced poetry in his other BBC guise and was an intimate of Dylan Thomas. McGilvray was a former player from an organisation happy enough with the breezy rapport of Gilligan and Richardson, but where Bernard Kerr once famously advised Michael Charlton: 'Just describe the game. Cut out the fancy bullshit.' McGilvray himself was advised by Charles Moses: 'Leave the jokes to Richardson. He has got a sense of humour.'

Yet McGilvray demonstrated that the 'straight' path in broadcasting need not be a narrow one. He invested with drama the simplest activity of a day's course, wringing from it every possible significance. For communicating the low-level drama of a tight Test match corner, he can hardly have been equalled. Think of a defensive shot. Now think of McGilvray circa 1948 describing it.

> Bedser to Morris, now, the bowler's long strides as he approaches
> umpire Chester. Bowls just short of a good length and Morris

eases part of the way back, pushing it to extra cover, where Compton skips to his left to field. Morris looks after the ball, as though it might have come off a little slower than he expected. And Bedser may have held that one back slightly for it struck low on the bat. He's a cunning bowler, this Englishman, and this has been a fine containing spell. The pitch has also been a little two-paced today. Morris would like to be driving those on the up by now, but the ball is fifty overs old, and the bounce is a little inconsistent.

Such description sometimes gilded the lily, but it involved the listener in every level of the struggle: batsman against bowler, player against himself, cricketer against conditions, captain against captain. The voice was usually low, sometimes sotto voce, almost entre nous. McGilvray's use of pauses—to whose potential he was wakened by Robert Menzies—was at its most telling when a wicket fell or a boundary was struck. He became wonderfully adept at enlisting the crowd in the instant of dismissal. 'And he's *caught* by Chappell!' would come the urgent report, followed by a break to allow audio of the public celebration, then a crisp vignette of the mode of dismissal. So subtle and nuanced was the McGilvray method that his style was actually very difficult to parody in the way that Billy Birmingham has made merry of Channel Nine's gallery of experts. There were certain elliptical phrasings peculiar to McGilvray ('As well as it was bowled, so was it played') but none that lent themselves readily to satire.

McGilvray's attention to detail made him the ideal foil for other broadcasters. During the 1950–51 Ashes series, he forged an outstanding partnership with the former sports editor of the Sydney *Sun*, Johnnie Moyes. Moyes had an encyclopedic knowledge of the game and a broad, laconic, unfaltering delivery. PL Williams—the legendary cricket coach of Geelong and Wesley Colleges—described Moyes as 'Cricket's Arch-Priest, the Prophet of Doom, the Fountain of All Knowledge, his cricket erudition matched only by a sort of satanic power'. Australia's captain that summer, Lindsay Hassett, was to become another great McGilvray sidekick after Moyes's death in 1963. Hassett was engaging and self-effacing, avowing always he would have hated to commentate on his own batting. And like an opening pair so familiar as to eschew calling, he and McGilvray seemed on a permanent wavelength. 'We had an affinity that meant we could get to the heart of any issue quickly,' said McGilvray. 'We knew each other's mind.'

~

McGilvray actually spent a good deal of the 1950s in commercial radio. When Bernard Kerr accompanied the Australian team to England in 1953, McGilvray anchored a studio show on the Tests for 2UW. When Michael Charlton accompanied the 1956 team, McGilvray was his competitor for 2UE. McGilvray was joined on that trip by his wife Gwen—one of the few occasions on which she was able to do so, for family considerations usually dictated otherwise. Son Ross (born in 1938) and daughter Carolyn (born in 1943) had an upbringing shaped by the cricket calendar. 'When he was overseas for three or four months at a time, my mother missed him terribly,' says Carolyn. 'He was a real "man of the house". I also remember the way we always used to have to finish our Christmas lunches early because my father would have to be on a plane for Melbourne this afternoon for the cricket on Boxing Day.' The daily diet of cricket talk at the McGilvray family home in Vaucluse was habit forming. 'We had cricket for breakfast, lunch and dinner when we were growing up,' Carolyn recalls. 'We thought that everyone did, because when you grow up with someone you don't know any differently.'

McGilvray returned to the ABC in time to call the high-rolling 1960–61 Australia v West Indies series, graphing its see-sawing fortunes with typical care. Yet he missed the season's crowning moment: the first tie in cricket history at the Gabba on 14 December

1960. Believing at lunch that the match was destined to dawdle to a draw, he decided to take an early flight home with Keith Miller, leaving the last rites to Charlton, Moyes and the ABC's local sporting supervisor, Clive Harburg. McGilvray rued his decision as 'the greatest error of judgement in my life'. Henceforward he never left a match early, draining each game to lees rather than risk missing a moment's drama; he also decided to dedicate himself to his craft full-time by selling Thomas McGilvray & Sons in 1961. On Moyes's death, too, the editorship of the *ABC Cricket Book* fell vacant, and McGilvray took over from journalist locums Eddie Kann and Ern Christensen, producing twenty-five numbers over thirty years. His pithy pen pictures and the statistics he compiled manually made it indispensable. As surely as *Wisden*'s yellow cover heralds the English season, so the ABC's hardy perennial foreshadows summer down under.

~

One of McGilvray's most notable characteristics was his quiet national pride; never partisan, he was nonetheless always patriotic. 'When Alan was commentating, you always felt he was with you,' says former Test vice-captain Keith Stackpole. 'Although he never let it get in the way of the fairness of his commentating, he was always an Australian: he was happy when you won, and he always suffered when you were beaten.' In the 1950s and 1960s, McGilvray could often be found around the Australian nets, watching and occasionally offering help. He helped Neil Hawke perfect a slower ball, talked captaincy with Ian Chappell and once cured Brian Booth of a technical flaw simply by his powers of observation. Booth recalls:

> I was having a bit of a run of outs and Alan came up to me one
> day and said: 'When you were batting well you always seemed
> to have a lot of time. Now you seem to be hurrying a bit. It

might be that you're picking your bat up a bit too late. Try and make an effort to start your back-lift as the bowler's letting go'. It was very good advice and it's something I try to pass on when I'm coaching kids now.

On a few occasions the advice was more personal. Queenslander Peter Burge was having a wretched run leading up to the Headingley Test of 1964, and admitted to McGilvray that he was anxious about his place in what shaped as the decisive match of the series. The evening before the game, McGilvray turned up at his hotel room door with a bottle of whisky. The pair steadily drained it as Burge poured out his sorrows, and the commentator left the bottle behind when he went to bed. A few days later, Burge wrested the initiative from England with a devastating 160: it won the match and tilted the rubber decisively Australia's way.

In distant climes, and before the age of fax and mobile phone, McGilvray was often the avenue of communication between players and loved ones. Bill Jacobs, who managed teams touring South Africa in 1966 and West Indies in 1973, recalls McGilvray arranging to advise Grahame Thomas of the birth of his first child while the Australians were playing at Kimberley. When Bill Lawry and Keith Stackpole suffered head wounds in Durban and Port-of-Spain respectively, McGilvray broadcast reassuring messages for anxious relatives at home. 'He was a top companion on tour, Mac, very good value,' says Jacobs. 'Two great things about him. One, he never invaded the dressing room; he could have but he didn't. Two, he always bought a drink. Some press guys'll turn up to functions and drink all your booze but never buy a round. Mac always did, or he'd invite you for a drink in his room.' There are legion stories of McGilvray's liberal out-of-hours hospitality, and also his cast-iron constitution. Alan Davidson recalls a morning before an Adelaide Oval Test match when he and co-selector Ray Lindwall accepted a McGilvray invitation to breakfast.

> Alan told us to come along to his hotel room at 7.30am. So
> Ray and I knocked on his door and Alan says: 'Don't worry.
> Breakfast's on the way.' Anyway it gets to 7.40am and there's
> no sign. And it gets to a quarter to eight and no-one's appeared.
> Then at ten to eight there's a knock on the door and in walks a
> waiter with a tray full of beers.

Yet if and when McGilvray thought something needed saying, he was quite capable of putting friendship to one side. Lindwall was a case in point. During the Fifth Test against the West Indies in January 1952, McGilvray expressed stern disapproval of Lindwall's short-pitched barrage at Everton Weekes. Normally the mildest of men, Lindwall was upset. 'You had no right to say those things,' he complained. 'I ought to punch you on the nose.' McGilvray replied: 'Hit me and I'll fall down. But I'll get up a gentleman.'

In the West Indies in 1965, McGilvray could easily have sided with the patriotic consensus that Charlie Griffith had thrown Australia to defeat. Contra Richie Benaud and Bob Simpson, McGilvray espoused the unpopular view that Griffith remained within the letter of the law. Heated responses from home had McGilvray fearing that he might be recalled, and he treasured the complimentary wire from Qantas chairman Sir Hudson Fysh: 'We are all proud of your excellent summary given tonight, upholding the best traditions of sportsmanship.' When the flak really flew, too, McGilvray was the coolest head in the room. In May 1978, it fell to him to describe the riot at Sabina Park that truncated the Fifth Test of a turbulent series. Fuzzy wire photos of the Australian team fleeing the arena under a barrage of bottles only hint at the day's disorder. McGilvray's electrifying broadcast—carried over the morning news bulletins with the sound of gunfire in the background—stuck fast in the collective memory. So forthright were McGilvray's descriptions that there were some fears about his safety: he was taken into Australian consular custody to be spirited home.

~

By this time McGilvray had come into his own, a still point in a moving cricket world being unsettled by professionalism and coarsened by mass marketing. Ironically he was to become a creature of marketing himself, the ABC exhorting the public to 'Watch the Tests on ABC Radio', and to admit that 'The Game Is Not the Same without McGilvray'. The campaign's climax came before play on the first day of the Third Test between Australia and England on 1 February 1980 when the MCG scoreboard was adjusted to read: 'McGilvray 100.' Saluting the achievement of covering a century of Ashes Tests, EW Swanton wrote in *Wisden*: 'For both quality and length of service, Alan McGilvray's career stands alone. To the listeners of every Test match-playing country he stands for generous-minded, unbiased, factual common sense. At any critical moment of an England–Australia Test, the ideal recipe, for me, is to turn on the television picture, turn off the sound, and listen to Alan.'

It was at around this time I had a little to do with McGilvray, after he selected for the *National Times* his all-time Australian XI based on the wisdom of more than four decades as a player and pundit—and with which I begged to differ on the basis of my 11-year-old's knowledge. *Surely* he should have preferred Victor Trumper to Bill Ponsford, a pushover against pace bowling; *surely* the attack needed a left-armer for the sake of variety, with Bill Johnston or Alan Davidson preferable to Dennis Lillee; and *of course* Monty Noble would make a better captain than Donald Bradman.

My mother warned me that I shouldn't really expect a reply; young but not entirely silly, I thought she was probably right. Little did either of us know that McGilvray was an assiduous correspondent. He once received a letter from an elderly woman who with unimpeachable logic calculated that he had uttered more than twenty million words in the course of his work at the BBC, finally concluding: 'And every one of them absolute rubbish.' He wrote to her anyway and they struck up a correspondence. So I was hardly a challenge. My reply arrived a week later and—judging from the typing errors and biro corrections on Commission notepaper—had been personally tapped out. It was also, of course, the perfect reply: detailed and balanced and never condescending. He could not judge Trumper, he pleaded, being 'old but not *that* old'. But he had utmost respect for Noble, and also for Johnston and Davidson, and thought my team 'hard to beat'; in any case, weren't such exercises fun? Happy the man still having fun in his seventies.

McGilvray gained so many new admirers in his later years that the fun may have been too prolonged. He was unsettled by the lack of continuity in ABC commentary ranks after Hassett's retirement in 1982, and in his last home summer, 1984–85, did not seem entirely comfortable. On his tenth trip to England a few months later, however, he seemed back to his best. Perhaps it was being away from the trappings of his own celebrity, perhaps the gravity-defying levity of the BBC's *Test Match Special*, but he sounded as poised as ever. After the Oval Test he launched the first of three books of memoirs written in cahoots with Norm Tasker, and made a successful and satisfying epilogue to his half century of broadcasting. His death severs a link to an age of grace when every ball was red, helmets were for miners and deep-sea divers, players drove Holdens and Fords, and one tried to leave the game better off for one's presence—as McGilvray assuredly did.

Alan McGilvray: The Voice of Cricket, 1996

Welcome to the House of Fun

We have here a gem of the first water. After reading only the first three chapters already I am deeply fascinated and enthralled by the incredible amount of absorbing detail which you have produced, obviously after long and diligent research. Your book should sell like Woolworths' pantyhose.

Thus Sir Donald Bradman to Ray Robinson after perusing an advance copy of *On Top Down Under*, just prior to its publication in 1975. And, first so often in matters cricket, Bradman was here first again: if ever a cricket book merited the designation 'classic' it is this one. It sweeps the reader along as though Australia's Test captains were characters in a great trans-generational family saga. The facts are rich, full of surprises; the phrases are painstakingly well turned. Bradman makes others' purple patches 'look like washed-out lilac'; Bob Simpson has a mind 'no easier to change than a 100-pound note'; Bill Lawry guards a wicket 'as inviolate as a detective's daughter'. Characters rise from the page as though coming to sign an autograph for you, not least Warwick Armstrong, aka 'the Big Ship': 'A simple switch of initials could have transformed WW Armstrong into *SS Armstrong*, a vessel more noted for tonnage than tact, and one not above a little gunboat diplomacy at times.'

Raymond John Robinson is a figure virtually unique in Australia. Our cricket writers have generally aimed low and even then often fallen short, swamped by the demands of deadlines drowned out by the pronouncements of ex-players. Among these past masters-turned-pundits only Jack Fingleton and Tom Horan have stood the test of time; Richie Benaud, Johnny Moyes and Dick Whitington follow; after that, the outlook is drear. 'Ray Robbie' was not a player of note; his reputation was built on what he said rather than the height from which he said it. And that reputation is entirely deserved.

Robinson was born in Melbourne on 8 July 1905 to Brighton butcher John Robinson and Clarice Isabel nee Drayton; brother Samuel Frank was born two years later, brother Andrew (Drew) in 1912. The family lived in Bay Street, near the railway station, and the Methodist Church that they attended. It was not an easy upbringing. In April 1908 John's father William was badly injured and deeply traumatised in the Sunshine railway disaster—Australia's worst. John had to fill the paternal role for his six brothers and three sisters, as well as his own three sons, and needed help when Clarice then fell ill. Ray Robinson attributed his fascination with sport to the months he was domiciled with his grandmother's family, the Dicks, a local football dynasty that included Alec (captain of Essendon in four consecutive flags in 1891–94) and Alec's son Bill (captain of Carlton in 1914–17). The boy Robinson eavesdropped eagerly on 'their conversation, their anecdotes of what was happening every Saturday'; it 'stirred my imagination'. His other great love as a child was Dickens, over whose work he pored endlessly and repeatedly. The influence is subtle but pervasive: no cricket writer has an eye for character more minute and loving. The first Australian captain he saw in the flesh was the gargantuan Armstrong, when older cousins took him to a Melbourne Test in December 1920. Robinson remembered Armstrong being 'subjected to barracking as heavy as his own tread': the crisp phrases were already coming to mind.

By then, Robinson had started work in a Flinders Lane warehouse, sickness having prevented him sitting a scholarship examination and his family's circumstances admitting no second chance. Journalism was actually not Robinson's first avocation. He liked to draw and at sixteen became an office boy at *Punch*. With staff like Will Dyson, Hugh McCrae, Len Reynolds, Alex Sass and Percival Leason, there was hardly a better place for an aspiring cartoonist. Robinson's uncle Ern Baillie, however, was chief-of-staff at Melbourne's afternoon daily, the *Herald*, and informed him of a vacancy for a copyboy: he took the higher pay, and excelled in the telephone room taking dictation from reporters in the field, using shorthand in which Baillie coached him. After being promoted to general cadet, Robinson became for two years a junior reporter at the *Herald*'s rural sister paper the *Weekly Times*. Although he abandoned his drawing, he retained an uncommon fondness for cartoons, using them throughout his books where they seemed more flavoursome than photographs.

Australian papers alone would not have made much of Robinson, and the first time his interest in writing and enthusiasm for sport converged the publisher was English. Sir Pelham Warner was still on the lookout for an Australian correspondent at his 4-year-old *Cricketer* magazine when he received a letter from 20-year-old Robinson, deploring its poor coverage of cricket down under. So began an association that would last fifty-four years. Scarcely an edition passed without some contribution from Robinson: news, match reports, profiles and obituaries, spreading his name throughout the world. His last contribution appeared alongside his own death notice.

Robinson quickly acquired a reputation for accuracy and tact. One of his closest friends was Bill Ponsford, who worked at the *Herald* in the print shop, and who for some years kept Robinson apprised of important events by numerical code. In fact, Robinson very nearly had the scoop of a lifetime while working as a sub-editor just before the First Test in November 1932 when he received a wire from Ponsford: 'Three declared unfit, signed Two.' Robinson's boss Syd Deamer, however, refused to believe that Bradman could be ill. 'The editor whom I was working for at the time hadn't been there long,' recalled Robinson. 'And, although a very good editor, he had his doubts about how authentic this could be, so the only thing that happened as a result of the message was that a guarded paragraph was put in the Stop Press.' Robinson had to be content with adding to cricket's lexicon soon after. Inspired by Jack Worrall's description of the bowling of England's Bill Voce in the *Australasian* in November 1932—'half-pitched slingers on the body line'—he coined 'body-line' as an adjective and 'bodyline' as a noun. The word was then pressed into common coinage by Robinson's colourful *Herald* colleague Hugh Buggy.

Editors nursed such a high opinion of Robinson as a sub-editor, however, that they were loath to let him loose on cricket. He found a champion in Jack Waters, who edited the *Star*, the afternoon tabloid cousin of the *Argus*, during its brief life from 1933 to 1936. But even when Waters induced the Australian Press Association to attach Robinson to their London bureau while Australia toured England in 1934, the young man found his path blocked. Geoffrey Tebbutt, who had followed the 1930 tour and written a book, pulled rank again and confined Robinson to a single weekly despatch; the visitor kicked his heels covering stories at Australia House.

All the same, the tour was an education for the 29-year-old, who studied English writers for the first time at close quarters. 'At the time of my first visit to England I had yet to learn that there was more to cricket writing than accuracy and clarity,' Robinson recalled. 'Working in London I had for the first time an opportunity to read Neville Cardus with his whimsical charm and the keener wit of RC Robertson-Glasgow.' Robinson and Cardus became close friends when they found themselves in Sydney during World War II, the former having accepting an invitation to become foreign editor of the *Sunday Telegraph*, the latter slumming it as *Sydney Morning Herald* music critic. Cardus gave Robinson a copy of his book of the 1936–37 Ashes tour, *Australian Summer*, and inscribed the flyleaf: 'To Ray, whose writings about cricket have moved me to gratitude—and sometimes to envy, from Neville Cardus.' The praise encouraged Robinson to persist in a book he was writing, which would finally take him four years. It was time well spent: Cardus was so enamoured of the manuscript that he wrote an effusive endorsement to the publisher Sir William Collins in London. 'It would be no great praise to describe this book as the best on cricket written by an Australian so far,' he argued.

The acclaim was echoed when the first edition of *Between Wickets* appeared in July 1946. 'A book to be read; every line of it,' said Robertson-Glasgow in the *Observer*. 'And not to be lent without an IOU.' James Agate in the *Daily Express* agreed: 'Open it anywhere and it is immensely exciting.' The *Evening News* paid perhaps the ultimate tribute: 'Ray Robinson's *Between Wickets* is as good among books about cricket as Don Bradman is among cricketers.' Such praise for Australian cricket writing in England was without precedent; it is still decidedly unusual. A second edition was needed by September, and a third the following month. On the proceeds of its eventual 55 000 sales over seven editions, Robinson was able to afford a house at 11 Wollombi Road, Northbridge, which he called 'Between Wickets'.

It isn't hard to see why Robinson's first book obtained such an instant fame in the aftermath of war. A cricket *tour d'horizon*, it builds a reassuring sense of continuity: the world has changed, is the message, but cricket abides. It begins with Bradman, the perfect Janus figure. It then profiles, with an ecumenical generosity, the Australians Stan McCabe, Bill O'Reilly, Bill Ponsford and Alan Kippax, the Englishmen Maurice Tate, Herbert Sutcliffe and Eddie Paynter, a gallery of fast bowlers, a succession of spinners, and includes a ripping burst of Bodyline. Later editions added appreciations of the first Indian tourists to Australia and Bradman's 1948 Australians.

Robinson's flair for phrasemaking, too, was at odds with Australian traditions of earnest, rather turgid reportage. Bradman on wet wickets was 'as ill-at-ease as a goldfish tipped from its bowl into a stormy sea'; Tate was superfluous to Bodyline because 'when the door could be battered down rapidly with an axe and crowbar, there was no call for the craftsman carpenter to unscrew its hinges without a splinter or a scratch'; O'Reilly's run could be 'performed perfectly to the first two bars of the *Song of the Volga Boatmen*'. In an era when cricket action took place far from its journalistic interpreters, Robinson brought you right up close. Bill Ponsford is described with the patience and understanding accessible to only a sensitive observer:

> The sturdy Victorian was so reserved that you had to know him for three years or the duration of a Test tour before his reticence relaxed. He was even camera-shy. Photographers who snapped him walking out to bat found that he usually hung his head so that his cap eclipsed most of his deep-tanned face. But in one picture he was oblivious of the camera, which caught him talking out the side of his mouth to Bradman. It transpired that he was saying: 'What are the beggars up to now?' He had scarcely passed through the gate before he noticed that a couple of English fielders were taking up positions a few yards (or feet) away from where they had been before the lunch interval.
>
> No player was more alert for an ambuscade. His concentration was so complete that he studied every sway of a bowler's body, every variation of arm and hand movement. He was remindful of the Solomon Island canoe sailors whose backs are so sensitive that they detect a two-point change in the wind … I always expected a chart of Bradman's strokes to be criss-crossed by jagged streaks, like a seismogram made by an earthquake recorder gone haywire, and a Ponsford chart to be like a net cast over bowlers and fielders, and tethered to the boundary by lines representing fours. While Don in his heyday seemed more to haul off and slash great chunks out of the bowling, Ponsford bored in on it, pounding and grinding it away.

Then there are the facts, polished like precious stones: McCabe's feet were small and of different sizes; Ted McDonald's finger tip to finger tip measurement was greater than Max Schmeling's, although they were the same height; Jack Gregory never took drinks on the field, no matter how hot; Lisle Nagel's career was curtailed by an injury sustained from cranking his car. Robinson was to become known as a walking encyclopedia of the game, and stories are legion of his elephantine memory—such as one related by English cricket historian Jim Coldham, concerning a correspondence he commenced with Robinson in 1970:

> In my letter I stated that, although he would not remember me, we had met many years before during an Australian tour of the UK. In his reply, almost by return of post, Ray insisted that he remembered meeting me on evening in 1948 at Geoffrey Copinger's house and that we had spent a small part of the evening at a local hostelry. Moreover he was able to recall in passing the district and name and whereabouts of the latter place. In conclusion he recalled that I had bade him farewell at a local railway station whose name he also knew.
>
> All this had happened one evening twenty-two years before in the life of a very busy, well-travelled journalist and, for me, it underlined strongly two of the essential ingredients in the outlook of anyone who wished to become a worthwhile journalist—a keen regard for people and a sharply retentive—indeed, photographic!—memory.

Nor has any journalist before or since been so utterly and universally popular among cricketers. Bradman would say that Robinson 'left behind not a single enemy', EW Swanton that Robinson 'enjoyed the confidence and respect of the players to a degree I have not known equalled by any other cricket writer'. Lindsay Hassett explained:

In common with many of my contemporaries, I regard Ray Robinson as a welcome visitor to any team's quarters. Players may speak as frankly in his company as when only teammates are present, assured that—unlike some they have met in their travels—he has never broken a confidence or rushed into print with anything that, in the interests of the team and the game, would have been better unpublished.

Robinson was not so lucky among his paymasters. At the time *Between Wickets* was published, Robinson was sub-editing at Sydney's *Sun*, in their 'Fact News Review' section. On the strength of the book, he was seconded to write about the first postwar Ashes series, and then followed Bradman's all-conquering Australians round England in 1948. Then, however, he found himself supplanted by the acerbic Dick Whitington. He kept his hand in as a cricket writer by working for *Cricketer*, as well as a range of foreign papers like the *Times of India*, sitting mainly in the company of Bill O'Reilly as he covered exercise books in his unintelligible ball-by-ball cipher. But he remained overshadowed in his own country by bigger names who were considerably lesser writers, something that baffled visitors. Chastising Australian cricket writers for their sameness and sensationalism in 1950–51, EW Swanton commented: 'One other thing for which I can scarcely forgive the Australian newspaper proprietors is that for all their space they do not allow an outstanding cricket writer like Mr Ray Robinson to write about the game at all.' A visitor during the next Ashes series here, John Arlott, thought Robinson 'surely the most underestimated of cricket writers'. Arlott said: 'His output was high; his work-rate fast; his reliability monumental; his patience inexhaustible; his good humour unfailing.'

These frustrations took their toll. In order to follow cricket, Robinson had to work more or less incessantly. His marriage fissured under the strain. He wed Ellen Jessie Gilbert, a farmer's daughter from Tasmania's New Norfolk, on 6 October 1928. When their son Brian was born in November 1930, Robinson was following

Bradman's triumphal progress across Australia; he learned of the birth of his daughter Audrey when the *SS Oronsay* carrying Bill Woodfull's Australians reached Naples en route to England in March 1934. Brian, later a radio astronomer at the CSIRO, noted: 'He was steeped in the traditions of mateship of the twentieth century. For men of his generation, mateship was preferable to the demands of parenting. He loved bowling to me, or donning black tie to take his daughter to the opera.' Robinson followed Australian teams in England in 1953, the West Indies in 1955 and South Africa in 1957–58. Between times were the books, including *From the Boundary* (1951) and *Green Sprigs* (1954). Family albums intersperse birthdays and Christmases with cricket events; holidays were impossibly scarce.

The toils also broke Robinson's health. Aged sixty, he suffered a detached retina that needed treatment in Boston. Such was the esteem he enjoyed in cricket circles that the New South Wales Cricket Association advanced him the fare he could not afford. But the American surgeons discovered that Robinson also had a hereditary colonic volvulus: a twisting of the bowel causing obstruction that often leads onto gangrene. As he trembled on the brink of death, Australian journalists in the United States donated fifteen pints of blood. He survived at the cost of the sight in his right eye, taking a job as a special writer for *People* to support himself, and contributing monthly to the new *Australian Cricket* magazine that commenced publishing in November 1968. His daughter had also died suddenly and, holed up in 'Between Wickets', subsisting on a diet of baby food, eggs and blackcurrant juice, he seemed lucky to be alive himself. In the winter of 1970, the volvulus became so bad that Brian Robinson received a call from hospital: it was unlikely his father would survive the night. Yet he was just about to do some of his best work:

> I drove there through atrocious weather, and found Ray pale
> and very weak. On the bedside table was a piece of paper with
> a few words pencilled, barely legible. I asked what he had

written. He'd had an idea for a new book … 'Tell me more,'
I said. We talked for the next two hours, and life just flowed
back into that frail body. Soon he was home, and writing.

The result, *The Wildest Tests*, was published by Pelham in
1972: a wholly original survey of those games of international
cricket marred by crowd unrest. Robinson then successfully sought a
six-month Commonwealth Literary Fund Fellowship—worth all of
$85 a week—in order to undertake preliminary research for a book
of profiles of Australia's Test captains. He later recounted some of
his windfalls, beginning with a telephone call from Mr Justice Rae
Else-Mitchell:

> The name Else-Mitchell concealed the identity of pioneer
> captain Dave Gregory's grandson, who had given time to
> researching the Gregorys' lives for the *Australian Dictionary
> of Biography*. The judge gave me the privilege of meeting his
> mother, only survivor of Dave Gregory's sixteen children.
> Though nearing ninety, she still had much of the charm she
> had possessed as Pearl Gregory, a brunette nurse who married
> a pharmacist … 'The Gregorys were too honest really,' she
> said. 'After walking a mile from Turramurra station with my
> schoolbag I told father I'd found a shilling on the train. He said
> to me: "My dear, take that straight back to the railway and give
> it to the stationmaster."'
>
> More luck came from my having been assigned to write
> about jumbo jets for the *Sydney Morning Herald*'s educational
> feature. That article made safe-enough landing for me to be
> entrusted with a broadsheet full page about cricket before the
> arrival of Ray Illingworth's English XI. In this expanse a woman
> noticed that WG Grace had scored 152 against Australia. The
> woman, Ruth Murdoch, left a message for me that her great-
> uncle WL Murdoch topped Grace by one run. A couple of
> years later, writing about Murdoch, I found her phone number
> and went to interview her twice at Burwood. She trusted me
> with relics of her great uncle, including letters he wrote to his

brother, her grandfather, telling of court cases in which he was a Cootamundra solicitor. How would a state react today to a player missing a day against Victoria to appear in a country court, then returning by milk train to resume wicket-keeping the next day? Murdoch was one of the most colourful captains. Newcastle solicitor Paul Trisley lent me an English magazine hinting he jilted a Derbyshire girl to marry a Bendigo gold magnate's heiress.

The merits of what became *On Top Down Under* were recognised at once: it swiftly sold 17000 in hardback. Thirty years after *Between Wickets*, Robinson again enjoyed critical acclaim in England, where the Cricket Society awarded him its Silver Jubilee Literary Award. 'This is characteristic Robinson prose,' said John Arlott in *Wisden*: 'informed, open-minded, perceptive, concentrated and readable; a blend of hard facts, character studies, illuminating anecdotes, criticism, evaluation and relation to background.' He was right about the blend, for not once does Robinson's scholarship stifle the zest of his storytelling. As David Frith notes, Robinson was ever the journalist, interested primarily in his readers, never the historian, conscious chiefly of his peers: 'Robbie's sacred attitude to facts and figures did not lead him—as it has led many another—to regard himself as the perfect scholar. Far from it. He laid his foundation and then built a house of fun.' The building metaphor is a good one; Robinson's is the prose of the craftsman with sweat on his brow. It doesn't flow like Cardus, or wink like Crusoe, or crackle like the arch controversialist Fingleton. Contemporaries like the *Sydney Morning Herald*'s Phil Wilkins have described Robinson toiling for hours in search of the arresting phrase:

> Long after the last ball was bowled each day, Robbie would be intently studying his notes, the information squeezed into little, incomprehensible cells in his notebook, his shorthand never failing him, tapping quietly away at his typewriter. He was invariably the last of the correspondents to abandon the

press box, his love of the game being as great as his love of the mother tongue. The Queen's English was always a lady to Robbie, one never to be abused or rushed off her feet.

No, there's nothing effortless about *On Top Down Under*, or any of its five predecessors. Robinson is like a batsman who, by dint of dedication and perseverance, manages to craft a cover-drive as attractive and effective as that of a natural strokemaker: you can tell the difference, but the ball streaks for four regardless. Cardus is peerless for expansive, poetic flourishes: ('Trumper was the bird in flight, Bradman the aeroplane'); Robinson is the master miniaturist ('Chewing gum, Bradman's jaw would stop soon after a bowler began his run-up; Hassett would munch on calmly until the ball was in the air'). To most observers, Richie Benaud has presented a cool, even a bland exterior—but not to Robinson:

> The surest pointer to any arousal was a drier tone of voice, uttered over a bottom lip like Maurice Chevalier or Mel Torme's—supposed in theatrical circles to indicate success. Benaud would shoot straight from the lip. If events demanded firm correction, Richie's lower lip jutted out, like a tramcar's step. You could measure how well correctives were working by the way it retracted until a dragonfly could no longer have alighted on it.

It's a vernacular style: racy, accessible and informed. For Robinson was still a popular visitor to the Australian dressing room, where players knew even of his crook stomach: Rod Marsh would take the top off a bottle of beer every tea time so it was flat by the time the writer called. When Kerry O'Keeffe was called on to briefly captain Australia against Minor Counties in 1977 due to an injury suffered by Doug Walters, teammates told him to advise Robinson immediately and seek inclusion in the updated *On Top Down Under*. Ian Chappell echoed Lindsay Hassett's long-before tribute:

'Bertie, you said ...' and with that Ray Robinson would search through his coat pockets and drag out several crumpled bits of newspaper which all looked as though a chook with ink-stained feet had walked across the margins. After peering at his scribbling through fast-fading eyes he'd produce from one particular scrap of paper a quotation of yours which could easily date back to schooldays. That sums up Australia's best cricket writer. Ray was meticulous when it came to quotations and consequently was a trusted member of the profession. So well trusted that players didn't baulk when he occasionally used a nickname that was considered for teammates' use only.

Australia's Ashes tour of 1977 was Robinson's last. He was incapacitated on his return by two heavy falls, and eked out a meagre freelance existence in his last few years, getting round to Test matches on buses and trains because he could not afford to fly. 'It grieved his friends to see him struggling through his last year,' wrote David Frith. 'The major and most ironic disability was his sight. You wanted, more than ever, to help him identify players and to read the distant scoreboard. You wanted to thank him again for *Between Wickets*, *From the Boundary* and most of all *On Top Down Under*.' He worked up to the very end. There was an obituary for Ken Mackay still in his typewriter when he was admitted to Royal North Shore Hospital in July 1982 suffering a host of complaints—he had burned himself on a heater, broken two ribs and punctured a lung in a fall, and was also diagnosed as suffering an intestinal blockage. To Robinson, no circumstance was so severe as to exclude the possibility of broadening his mind: he checked in holding a copy of *Martin Chuzzlewit*, the only Dickens novel he had not read. But his condition deteriorated quickly and he died a few days later, the memorial service in the North Chapel of the Northern Suburbs Crematorium being attended by a remarkable array of Test cricketers: Bill O'Reilly, Arthur Morris, Alan Davidson,

Norm O'Neill, Peter Philpott, Bill Hunt, Brian Taber and even 87-year-old Stork Hendry.

Republishing *On Top Down Under* two decades after its first edition, one wonders how Robinson is viewing the scene from his Elysian deckchair. The growing professionalism of cricket and the congestion of its calendar have affected how our captains evolve; the next appointee to the position will in all likelihood have done no more than play cricket their whole life. *On Top Down Under* reminds us of how the Australian Test captaincy reflected the country. 'The skippers in *On Top Down Under* have shared the qualities and frailties of the race,' Robinson argues. 'They have lived, laughed and loved, sweated and sworn, bled, wed and bred.' Future captains will reflect nothing but professional sport. Perhaps that enhances the book's value; it certainly evokes those values Robinson held dear. 'A dedicated cricket lover and writer fit to compare with the best,' was Bradman's considered opinion:

> I think his book *On Top Down Under* ... was his finest work and no cricket library could be complete without it. Ray lived as he wrote: honestly, modestly, sincerely respected a confidence. It was a privilege to have known him.

Right again, Sir Donald.

Foreword to *On Top Down Under*, 1996

The Continuing Crisis

What's often forgotten about Jack Fingleton's *Cricket Crisis* (1946) is that it was not so much a book as a counterblast. In 1942, Sir Pelham Warner published his self-serving, self-glorifying *Cricket between the Two Wars*, repeating the canard that Fingleton, then a journalist at Sydney's *Sun*, leaked the story of Warner's famous dressing room contretemps with Bill Woodfull. Fed up with the insinuation, Fingleton decided to write his own account 'of the war in cricket between the two other Wars'. It is by no means definitive or even sequential, and the second half of the book is composed of more conventional reminiscences. But it is trenchant, disarmingly fair-minded and informed by bitter experience. As Pliny's account of the eruption of Vesuvius has the whiff of sulphur, so *Cricket Crisis* has the scent of leather.

The tone is not so much anger as gravest melancholy. When Fingleton scored a century against the early form of Bodyline, for New South Wales, he experienced no 'wild thrill'. This, he explained, was not 'because of the physical pummelling I had taken' but because of 'the consciousness of a crashed ideal'. Bodyline hurt his attachment to cricket, and 'Test cricket lost something that it never regained'. What was worse was that, such was Bradman's omnipotence at the time, Fingleton could see the argument for it. Indeed, Fingleton felt 'positive that had Bradman been an Englishman and whipped the Australians as did he the English, the Australians would have been tempted to use some such drastic theory against Bradman'. All the same, he doubted its efficacy against Douglas Jardine: 'Jardine himself could have been battered black and blue and never cried "enough". He was chockful of courage.'

Fingleton was possessed of an unlikely admiration for England's iron duke:

> Never once ... did Jardine deviate from what he considered his path of duty. He was convinced he had been given a certain task to carry out. That task came within the laws of the game and, by the beard of Grace, he would carry out that job and all the barracking in and out of Australia would not deter him.

He was actually more impressed with Jardine than his own skipper: 'If any dignity was left to Test cricket at the end of that 1932–33 season it was due entirely to Mr WM Woodfull, but Bodyline was a grim and ruthless battle into which a leader of mild gentility came somewhat poorly equipped.'

Fingleton's sympathies came firmly on the side of players whom he felt had been misused by the authorities. Warner, for example, got a right old kicking:

> Cricket to him was life and religion, but when the MCC committee recanted on him and suggested that he should accept or do nothing about the dogma of bodyline creed, Warner became an apostate from his convictions and sought solace for his cricket soul in what he was pleased to call loyalty.

Harold Larwood, meanwhile, was described with genuine appreciation and skill:

> I, for one, will never cease to sing Larwood's praises as a bowler ... One could tell his art by his run to the wickets. It was a poem of athletic grace, as each muscle gave over to the other with perfect balance and the utmost power. He began

his long run slowly, this splendidly proportioned athlete, like a sprinter unleashed for a hundred yards dash. His legs and arms pistoned up his speed, and as he neared the wickets he was in very truth like the Flying Scotsman thundering through an east coast station ...

The first time I was in runs with Larwood bowling I was watching, naturally, the batsman at the other end as Larwood ran up. Just as Larwood approached the crease I heard a loud scraping sound and the thought flashed across my mind that Larwood had fallen. He had not. A few yards from the crease he gathered himself up and hurled all his force down onto a stiff right leg which skidded along the ground for some feet. How his muscles and bones stood this terrific test over the years is a mystery to me ...

I had this interesting experience from batting against Larwood. The first dorsal interosseous muscle between the thumb and the index finger ached for a week after batting against Larwood, so severe was the concussion of the ball hitting the bat. I experienced this against no other fast bowler.

The star of *Cricket Crisis*, of course, is Bradman, who is written of with clarity, insight and acute candour. 'His colleagues,' Fingleton admits, 'frequently felt that they were mere lay figures or items of scenery to be arranged to provide a background for the principal actor.' There is also some asperity, for Fingleton breaks the dressing room omerta to reveal that Woodfull and others were annoyed at the 'capers' that Bradman cut in trying to combat Larwood. The counterblast duly provoked its own, Johnnie Moyes setting to work at once on the apologia that became *Bradman* (1948). Thus did arguments begin that haven't finished yet.

Cricinfo, August 2007

The World of Twenty to Nine

In his own words, RC Robertson-Glasgow was 'doomed to affront those to whom cricket is a quasi-religion'. No highfalutin' claims about the game for him while he was correspondent of the *Morning Post* and *Observer*. Press box colleagues knew him for his blithe spirit, torrential eloquence and reverberating laugh; all three pervade his writing, beginning with *The Brighter Side of Cricket* (1933).

There was sadness, too, albeit well concealed. A sufferer from bipolar disorder, Robertson-Glasgow had his first breakdown in 1921, a second in 1924 and a third in 1931, when he attempted suicide. He lost hope again when his father died in 1938, and found the austerity of postwar England an acute hardship. His autobiography *46 Not Out* (1948), written as a form of therapy, begins with his learning cricket 'in the stable-yard, far away from the house, with a tennis ball, against a broom, under the gilt-handed clock, which had stopped at twenty to nine'. He wished for a world where time could be similarly stilled: in objection to a modern world 'emasculated by crooning and filed to nothing by wisecracks', *46 Not Out* evokes a lost world of grace and ease.

The result is a life story as fond and funny as any in the game's literature, filled with lines any writer would envy. Charlie Macartney is nowhere better summed up: 'He made slaves of bowlers.' Lionel Tennyson comes to life in Robertson-Glasgow's simile: 'He received the fast bowlers as the oak receives the storm.' What a compound of whimsy is suggested simply by the idea of Robertson-Glasgow writing about Arthur Mailey:

Arthur was a great bowler, with a teasing flight and acute power of spin. He was witty, quiet and easy-natured, and the seriousness required for Test cricket didn't rise naturally in him. He loved casual matches, where he could appear in old sandshoes and give away please-yourself runs to some local mayor or notable.

I believe his early days had been something of a struggle; anyhow, he had a fondness for dead-end kids, and would sign their autograph books with running questions about their private lives and ideas, and draw them comic and simian pictures of himself, with button nose and wide space between it and the mouth. I never saw Arthur bustled or bothered. If he got no wickets or plenty, why, there was another innings or match coming along. If he missed a train, well, someone would find a timetable with another one in it. He had a soft and quizzical way of speech. Of all the Australians I have known, he had the surest understanding of the English outlook and temperament, and the keenest awareness of Australian foibles.

There will often be argument as to whether Mailey or Grimmett was the great bowler. Grimmett, with his persistent length and lower flight, was the more economical. Mailey liked, and was blessed with, more runs to play with. He would seem to have been collared, then suddenly win with an unplayable leg break. Of the two, both cricketers of genius, Mailey was the more likely to defeat the great batsman who was well set. Grimmett caused Mailey deep and quiet delight; and Mailey used to relate how Grimmett, a New Zealander, came to him soon after his entry into Australian cricket and asked questions about their gyratory art. Mailey told him all he knew.

Years later, when Grimmett had won fame, there was some banquet or reunion at which both were present. Grimmett, probably elated by unaccustomed good cheer, for he was a man of abstinence, came up to Mailey and said in that voice like a ventriloquist speaking through a watering-can: 'Arthur, you told me wrong about the Bowzie.' Rather as if Virgil had been accused by Horace of giving misleading information on the number of feet in the Hexameter!

Robertson-Glasgow's weakness as a journalist, it is said, was deadlines, such were his toils in pursuit of the right word and the arresting metaphor. In *46 Not Out*, we have the care, the lapidary descriptions, the vivid vignettes, without the angst. He grew up around vivid women like Splendo-smoking, confectionery-coveting Auntie Bug, dabbler in theosophy and spiritualism; and taciturn men, particularly his father, who communicated mainly by correspondence of severe economy: 'I see you got a few wickets at Weston-Super-Mare. I lost two fish yesterday.' Figures from the writer's education come to rumbustious life, from his suffragette teacher Miss Mona, who 'would have made a kindergarten suck up Irregular Verbs like barley-sugar', to his classics master Frank Dames-Longworth, with his perfect trouser creases and caustic tongue. Danes-Longworth once disposed of an incompetent student with a long-suffering sigh: 'Sit down, boy, for heaven's sake, till you can get your sexes right. Women don't beget; they *bear*; a fact of which you may one day become cognisant, to your cost.'

'Stupid figures,' Robertson-Glasgow laments at one point, apropos arithmetic. 'How I loathed them, and loathe them still. What a mess mathematics make of man, damming his generous currents, frowning on joyous fallibility, pursing the dry lip at admirable error.' In fact, Robertson-Glasgow took 464 wickets at 26 bowling brisk medium pace for Oxford University and Somerset between 1920 and 1937. But statistics were to him a mean measure; he described a spell of 0 for 97 from 43 overs, well nigh perfectly, as 'much ado about nothing'. Cricket was for fun—and if it wasn't fun, it held no purpose. Five years after publication of *46 Not Out*, he stood up in the press box, announced tersely that he was finished, and retreated to the cottage where in March 1965 he took the overdose of barbiturates that finally killed him.

Cricinfo, February 2008

RONALD MASON'S 'OF THE LATE FREDERICK J. HYLAND'

My Heart's in the Hylands

Ronald Mason is not the greatest cricket writer who ever lived, nor perhaps is 'Of the Late Frederick J. Hyland' the finest example of the game's literature, yet it remains to me as fresh, charming and enticing as when I first encountered it. My copy of *Sing All a Green Willow*—in which this essay appears—was found in a second-hand bookshop perhaps twenty years ago. It still has what I imagine to be the previous owner's name inscribed: 'Timothy J. C. Grimshaw.' If you're out there, Tim, many thanks; I've read your cast-off again and again.

Mason's subject is a Hampshire cricketer of the most prosaic description imaginable: he played a solitary game for his county in 1924 that, thanks to rain, lasted only two overs. But as a first-class player, however briefly, Hyland earned the right to an obituary in the 1965 *Wisden*, causing Mason to ponder, rather than the game's chief luminaries, the greater cosmos of cricketers who are inevitably their backdrop. This theme captivated me, and still does. Cricket is still wedded to its own version of the Great Man Theory of History. Yet I feel an instinctive and abiding affinity for the teeming multitudes of Frederick Hyland; now, perhaps more than ever, as publishing houses annually spew forth such book substitutes as *Sir Vivian* and *The Don*.

I know little more of Mason than he knew of Hyland. He was a civil servant, a university tutor in literature, a novelist and the author of a critical study of Herman Melville; a sign of distinction in a cricket writer, one might think, given CLR James's *Mariners, Renegades and Castaways*. He wrote an enchanting sort-of-autobiography in 1955 called *Batsman's Paradise* and two enjoyable if rather dated biographies of Sir Jack Hobbs and Walter Hammond; three works of cricket history that, although they have their moments, rather fail to satisfy. I suspect that his metier was the form he found in the book of which this essay forms part, where he lets his wide-ranging mind wander freely. There's a touch about 'Hyland' of two of my favourite biographical experiments: AJA Symons's *The Quest for Corvo* and Jan Morris's *Fisher's Face*. It's a reminder, too, of a time when cricket books had something to say; so unlike today when you're surprised if they have anything to say.

To Sir, with Thanks

Still one of the chief regrets in my writer's life was occasioned by opening a 2001 edition of *Wisden Cricket Monthly*. This was the number fit to burst with eulogies for the dear departed Sir Donald Bradman. For me, however, the pang was at the far less conspicuous notification of the passing of Alan Ross.

Until that moment, I had nourished the vague thought that our paths would somehow cross, or else I'd find the nerve to write to him—then would there be the opportunity, at last, to express my gratitude for the pleasure I had derived from his cricket and other writings. First among these would have been *Australia 55*, an account of the MCC's 1954–55 Ashes triumph and a travelogue of his antipodean peregrinations, written in and around his duties as the cricket correspondent of the *Observer*. This forum will now have to suffice.

Ross is sometimes categorised as a cricket belletrist, such is his erudition and elegance; indeed, he began reading modern languages at St John's College, Oxford, in 1940, a contemporary of Kingsley Amis and Philip Larkin. But he lasted only a year, preferring a distinctly dangerous war in the Royal Navy. In particular, he was rescued at the Battle of the Barents Sea in December 1942 from the flooding hold of the HMS *Onslow*, lead destroyer in a flotilla warding off a powerful detachment of German capital ships intent on annihilating arctic convoy JW51B. *Onslow*'s commanding officer during that engagement, Robert St Vincent Sherbrooke, was awarded the Victoria Cross for coolly continuing to give orders after shrapnel had knocked an eye from his head. It was more than an airy martial allusion when Ross wrote in *Australia 55*: 'A good [cricket] captain needs ... to be something like a destroyer captain, a father confessor as well as an object of fear and inspiration.'

Ross approached Australia with undisguised ambition. 'I am as much interested in Australia as I am in cricket,' he explained— noting also that 'it would need be a dull fellow who was not'. En route he read not Cardus but *Kangaroo*, the novel of Australia dashed off by DH Lawrence during a few months in the New South Wales country hamlet of Thirroul that is nonetheless one of the sharpest fictional visions of the country and its people. And when Ross came to assessing his surrounds, it was in passages of Lawrentian astringency:

> Australians are ascetics, however, their civilisation is in its earliest adolescence, and they have the ascetic's lack of interest in, if not contempt for, the civilising indulgences: food, clothes, comfort, the appearance of things. This might argue an overworked technocratic society, with no time for the frivolities of style. On the contrary, Australians have all the time in the world: but they belong by nature, or rather accident, to an age that does not look at things, that is democratic to the extent of admiring the ordinary and fearing the excellent, for excellence, besides making demands of its own which require imagination and discipline, creates inequalities. It is not that Australians dislike inequality: despite their often reiterated belief that every man is as good as another (with which they half-wish you to quarrel), there are quite distinct social levels in every city. But they approve of the illusion of equality, which is only fair, for otherwise they are a genial race who allow themselves few deceptions.

In the main, the impressions were fair and fond, far and wide. Ross wrote prettily of the Great Barrier Reef, plausibly of surfing, appreciatively of Indigenous art, amusingly of the Melbourne Club: 'The Melbourne Club has a cloakroom of such delicacy that mirrors placed obliquely allow one to observe whether the various compartments, partly screened in anyway, are occupied, without need to approach and thereby risk disturbing members.' He warmed to the gregariousness of Australians, while also intuiting their tendency to authoritarianism, noting the large, censorious notices at The Oasis, a swimming centre in Brisbane: 'Wrestling and all forms of undue familiarity between couples are not permitted.'

The cricket, too, came off rather better, I suspect, than Ross anticipated. The massive fluctuations of the series—England, overwhelmed in Brisbane, won in Sydney, Melbourne and Adelaide to retain the Ashes—engaged his interest; his fascination with Hutton, a 'lonely figure struck down by as many disasters as any overworked hero in Greek mythology', deepened; and his excitement with the youth and elan of Tyson, May and Cowdrey grew by the day. 'May is a player of the Renaissance, lean, hungry, adventurous,' Ross decided. 'Cowdrey is a Georgian, discreet, handsome, and of substance.'

A capable enough medium pacer himself to have once opened the bowling with Alec Bedser, Ross's technical assessments of players were always better than mere impressionism, and his word pictures hard to fault. Two batsmen uneasily not out at tea were 'poised as precariously as curates on a dowager's Regency chairs', while a pair scampering smart singles exhibited 'the effrontery of urchins outwitting an old, blindfolded aunt'. No passage better conveyed Tom Graveney's mixture of fluency and frailty than this:

> A player of yacht-like character, beautiful in calm seas yet at the mercy of every change of weather. There are no obvious faults in construction but the barometer has only to fall away a point or two from fair for way to be completely lost and the boat broached to, if not turned for harbour.

For some years, I was without a copy of *Australia 55*—vexingly so, for I had lent it to someone, to this day I know not whom. One year when I was asked by a newspaper which book I would most like for Christmas, I replied: 'I would like my copy of *Australia 55* back!' Not even that did the trick, and I finally replaced it—the book is mentally marked 'never to be lent again'. I have a large enough stock of regret about my admiration for Alan Ross without wishing to add to it.

Cricinfo, July 2008

42

PETER ROEBUCK'S *IT NEVER RAINS*

Hello and Goodbye

PM Roebuck had a respectable season for Somerset in 1983, making 1235 first-class runs at 37.43. But it was what he got up to between times that mattered. An aspiring writer who had taken a First in Law at Cambridge University, he had already assembled a book, *Slices of Cricket* (1982), from his short pieces. That season he was recording his day-by-day impressions in a diary.

The result, *It Never Rains* (1984), was rightly judged a classic of the genre. Although Roebuck was never your average county pro, he managed to create something that had a touch of the 'everycricketer': a journal humdrum, hilarious and harrowing by turns. The experience of having to 'sleep, dine, drink, play and travel with the same fellows, always sharing the same dressing room and always relying on each other on the field' is a mix of the companionable and the claustrophobic; the almost daily measure of capability on the scoresheet provides a steady drumbeat, sometimes inspiriting, occasionally dirge-like.

'God how I hate getting out,' he muses sardonically after a mere handful of innings. 'I poked around again. Edged a single somewhere and then had my off stump knocked back. It was a good ball, at least I think it was. I say it left me and kept low. My partner Richards says it kept low and nipped back. It was probably straight.' Wry humour leavens the experience: '*The Times* says I was uncharacteristic in the first innings, the *Guardian* unsympathetically says I failed twice in the day and the *Telegraph* reckons I was out to a cruel shooter in the second innings. Luckily it's the *Telegraph* most cricketers read ...' But on occasion, the self-interrogation is so acute that it's almost a wonder normal cricket was possible:

> As [Somerset captain Brian] Rose and I sat in the warmth of the dressing room wondering how long we could desert our cold troops practising their fielding, he asked me if I wanted to open this year. My first sustained experience as an opener was last year and it was only a partial success. I started opening partly because it secured my place in the Somerset team—there were no other people willing and able to open in Championship cricket except some youngsters—and partly because there are hardly any openers in England and it was my only chance of representing my country.
>
> Mind you, I'm not certain that deep down I want to represent my country. Not everyone does. It is obvious to me that I either want to play for England too much or not at all. How else can I explain several total collapses of form when people begin to speculate that my chance is bound to come soon? Am I too excited or too fearful? I can remember a benefit game last year when, as I was walking out to bat, I heard a spectator say to his son, 'There goes England's next opener.' I remember thinking 'Oh no, don't say that.' Because it was something I desperately wanted? Or because I didn't relish the harsh exposure of a Test match?

Strangely, Roebuck's autobiography, *Sometimes I Forgot to Laugh* (2004), is a far less personal book—nor is it remotely as funny. The events are described from a self-protecting distance; the highs and lows are missing. The low of *It Never Rains* is very low indeed: at the nadir of the author's fortunes, the entry is blank. Roebuck has decided that cricket is a 'worthless existence' and that it is 'time to admit defeat and to give myself something to have a go at'. The next day, after talking to his favourite teammates, he reasons that cricket is not the problem, and feels his 'competitive instincts aroused' again. The season ends with a trophy for Somerset, and a fluent century that makes him wonder whether he hasn't been 'too intense' all along.

Roebuck later described the diary as a form of self-therapy: 'To me it was a way of saying Goodbye to All That. Once written, it was no longer true about my life, though it remains true about others.' Quite so. It's a rare cricketer of any level who will not recognise him or herself in some or even all of the attitudes on show in *It Never Rains*.

Cricinfo, January 2008

Through the Covers

The cover of Sujit Mukherjee's *Autobiography of an Unknown Cricketer* shows an everyday game in progress, the particular instant chosen being between deliveries. The anonymous striker is gathering his thoughts while the unknown bowler returns head-down to the end of his mark. The unidentified umpire has his hands in his pockets while the nameless fielders may be wondering about whether the goat at mid-off should move a little deeper.

Well ... yeah: as surely everyone knows, it is the first law of passing by any low-level game of cricket that nothing will be happening. You tense as you approach to see a flashing drive or a flying stump ... and, when you're close enough to see, the batsman's fiddling with his protector, or they're having drinks. As, indeed, it should be. For cricket doesn't surrender easily to the wandering eye: it needs some time, some attention and a little moral seriousness to get to the bottom of. Plus—and it's a big plus—it's a game to be played, rather than simply to be watched or pontificated over.

Okay, so that's the cover—and it sets the tone. For this unprepossessing 168-page memoir punches way above its apparently insubstantial weight. Mukherjee justifies his book with the first of many memorable aperçus: that cricket involves a 'heady mix of memory and desire', and that 'no memory can be more vivid, no desire more enduring, than those embodying the cricket one has

seen and known and played oneself'. This is not, however, a larkish
Rain Men or even *Yakking Around the World*: Mukherjee was an
earnest cricketer with *some* talent but not a great deal, who *wanted*
to be better but perhaps not quite enough. Attending state trials at
twenty-one 'certainly cured me permanently of any higher ambitions
in the game, because it taught me beyond doubt that this was about
the most I was meant to achieve, hence I should have no regrets that
I did not go further'. His loss became cricket's gain, for the great can
miss of the game what the ordinary discover.

Autobiography undersells Mukherjee's book, because it is
endlessly companionable, filled with characters like the cricket
coach Father Cleary whom the narrator convinced himself must
be India's premier all-rounder: 'Happily, this belief has never been
tested and, since it was never disproved, I may as well hold it till my
dying day. More than actuality, it was the imagination that he filled
for me, and there is no place in such realms for judgement.' Growing
up in the Raj's last days, he brushes past the departing English
while playing cricket against the 'sahebs' of the 'wholly reactionary
and imperial' Patna Cricket Club: 'In later life, whenever I met an
Englishman not interested in cricket, it has caused unreasonable
disappointment with the man.' His experience of playing with
Hemu Adhikari while at the National Defence Academy is still
more vivid, and deliciously evoked:

> Somebody pointed him out to me at a squadron party and I
> couldn't believe that this short, average-looking man sitting
> quietly in a corner could be a cricketer who had toured
> Australia with the India team and only a couple of years
> ago was vice-captain of India's tour of England. I sometimes
> thought Test cricketers could be identified off-field by a halo
> around their heads or some other kind of effulgence and would
> certainly be the centre of conversation at a party. Later, when I
> got to know Hemu, I realised that no matter how many Tests
> he played or cricket tours he made, he never sought or would

seek any social limelight. His wife Kamal was a perfect match for him in modesty and friendliness. Had she ever taken to playing cricket, I am sure her batting and bowling would have been the same as Hemu's. Maybe her fielding would have been less spectacular.

That it takes all sorts is later verified by the likes of Scotty, the cricketer-as-misanthrope, with whom Mukherjee plays for Fairmount CC in Pennsylvania while on a Fulbright Scholarship:

> Scotty did not get along either with his fellow countrymen or with us—which was a pity, because he was obviously crazy about cricket. This made him simply hog the batting and bowling whenever he got an opportunity to do so, and this naturally did not win him any friends. Now that I am older I can understand his situation better. He must have been fifty years old then and, in return for a day's labour in the field, sought to make the best of whatever was available, dreading perhaps that day in the future when he would no longer be able to play. As a bowler he didn't get many wickets but neither did he give away many runs. Whenever an opposing pair of batsmen looking like settling down, Scotty would practically demand to be put on—and once put on wouldn't easily let go. An inveterate smoker, he chain-smoked even while fielding. When his turn to bowl came, he would hand over a half-burnt cigarette to the umpire and take it back after completing his over. The only time he did not smoke was while batting, for which he employed a very effective range of prods and pushes which produced a single off the fifth or sixth ball of the over, which enabled him to retain the strike for several overs at a stretch.

At the time, Mukherjee was completing his PhD dissertation on the fluctuating literary reputation of Rabindrinath Tagore, the first significant work in a career that would make him India's most formidable literary critic and scholarly publisher. And in the last chapter, Mukherjee reveals the breadth and sweep that paradoxically makes him such a convincing interpreter of the small and local with an expansive meditation on cricket's various directions—including a view of cricket on television as severe as it is perceptive:

> Unavoidably a sense of loss persists. The telecast shows me only what the cameraman wants to show; the telecommentary tells me only what the commentator is capable of telling, much of it pointless. Large chunks of the match, and not only of play, are left out completely; small chips of play are shown magnified beyond proportion of their significance. Neither seems acceptable to me. I belong to a generation for whom going to a Test match was a pilgrimage. You paid homage to and appeased your white-clad gods, and at the same time acquired some redemption for yourself.

Stylish and thoughtful cricket writing is pouring out of India at present, but the country's literature has long been distinctive, and *Autobiography of an Unknown Cricketer* was one of the standard setters when published fifteen years ago. They say you can't judge a book by its cover—but look hard enough at this cover and you can.

Cricinfo, March 2008

Stranger than Fiction

'I know a man who knows a man who knows a man who once batted for four hours in a Test match with Vijay Hazare,' begins one of the essays in Ramachandra Guha's wide-ranging collection *An Anthropologist among the Marxists* (2001). A similar sense of connectedness is integral to the view of cricket of this fine historian: that in a country as populous, dispersed, stratified and religiously and culturally diverse as India, the attachment to the game is so deep and personal.

Thus the range and richness of Guha's longest and most satisfying excursion into cricket, *A Corner of a Foreign Field* (2003). It began as a biography of Palwankar Baloo, a Dalit who emancipated himself by his feats on India's inaugural tour of England, and later a pivotal figure in the Gandhian ascendancy. Investigating how Baloo's cricket abetted his social mobility led Guha to interrogate cricket from the angles of race, religion and nation as well as caste; to see the cricket field as 'both a theatre of imperial power and of Indian resistance'. The result is not so much a history of Indian cricket as a cricket history of India. 'To the dismay of some of my friends, this has become a book on cricket which does not focus exclusively on runs, wickets and catches, on epic innings and exciting matches,' he admits. 'The making of modern

India is its theme, with cricket serving merely as a vehicle, as my chief source of illustrative example.'

A Corner of a Foreign Field never loses its spirit as a personal journey, being animated by the same zest and zeal as Guha's earlier books *Wickets in the East* (1992) and *Spin and Other Turns* (1994). Guha's revisitation of the origins of the Bombay Quadrangular, for example, commences with him browsing in the shelves of the Marylebone Cricket Club Library at Lord's and being spellbound by an incomparably rare source: Shaporjee Sorabjee's *A Chronicle of Cricket Among Parsees and the Struggle: European Polo versus Native Cricket* (1897).

> Remarkably the battle of European polo versus Indian cricket has escaped the notice of previous historians. It would have escaped me too, had I not chanced upon a contemporary account in the library of the Lord's Cricket Ground. The book lay in an unused corner of that great library—away from the glass cases containing works on cricket at Home and the favoured Dominions (Australia and South Africa), and in the bottom of an open shelf marked 'other countries', a dull green binding concealing its original cover.

Nonetheless, this is very obviously the work of a cool and cultivated mind. Guha wears his learning lightly but he does wear it, and he pursues his subject untiringly and unsentimentally. The folksy image of Lord Harris as Indian cricket's indulgent uncle is utterly dispelled; Bal Thackery's past as a cricket cartoonist is wryly revisited; and CK Nayudu is so powerfully re-imagined that he almost walks out of the text and shakes you by the hand. For myth, there is patience but no tolerance. At one point, for instance, Guha quotes Vijay Merchant attesting the fellow feeling that characterised the 1936 Quadrangular, played in spite of unrest between Hindus and Muslims in Bombay thanks to the majestic figure of PJ Hindu Gymkhana president LR Tairsee. Too scrupulous a historian not to, Guha checks, finds otherwise, and is honest enough to express a tinge of disappointment:

> This is a compelling story, and it is embarrassing to have to dispute it. However, the riots of 1936 actually took place in the month of October; a calm, albeit an uneasy calm, had returned to the city well before the cricket began ... Perhaps the Hindus, drawn to play the Muslims in the first match, were nervous that violence might recur, and perhaps Tairsee assured them that it would not. But the cricket did not stop the riots. The old cricketer's recollections were flawed by the romance with which he remembered the now long-dead tournament.

This is cricket history on the grand scale, ambitious, provocative and also timely, for it hove into view six years ago as international cricket's Indian ascendancy was embedding itself, and became a key text in its interpretation, complemented more recently by Boria Majumdar's splendid *Twenty-Two Yards to Freedom* (2004). A few of Guha's judgements might be ripe for revisitation, such as his reflections on how cricketers from the subcontinent have ennobled the game: 'One must not forget, either, the essential decency and civility of these cricketers, their readiness to make friends with the opposition and the complete absence in their vocabulary of the words of abuse that come so easily to cricketers of other countries.' Indian cricketers have learned a few tricks since then! The edge in India's fan base, however, is abiding and unassailable.

The case can be made that as a *national sport* Indian cricket has no parallel. There may be more money in American basketball and as much passion in Brazilian soccer. It is the weight of numbers that makes Indian cricket bigger still, with money and passion being multiplied by the 500 million who partake of it.

Ray of Light

The elder statesman of English cricket photography, Dennis Oulds, once had trouble persuading Fred Trueman to participate in a team photograph. So he appealed to the Yorkshireman's sense of perpetuity. 'But Fred,' Oulds said. 'Just think about all those days when people won't ask.' Trueman paused, then softened. 'Aye,' he said. 'You're reet. Make it a good 'un.'

Mark Ray, a well-travelled cricket journalist, has been placing himself in the Oulds position since he started reporting on the game eleven years ago after a handy first-class career with NSW and Tasmania. Salting away a portfolio of candid and impromptu angles on cricket touring, Ray has sought the essence of the game rather than its surface spectacle. The result is a book about the game in which hardly a bat or ball is lifted in anger, yet does its subjects and sport proud, from David Boon smiling in his socks on the cover to umpires Randell and Bailache stripped to their Y-fronts within. This is the game in repose, incognito, and a reminder that members of the Australian team this season will spend more time in their own company boarding airliners, checking in and out of hotels, and loitering round dressing rooms than batting, bowling and chasing.

Judging and presenting this sort of material can be harder than it seems—it can easily become a sort of *Cricket's Naughtiest Home Videos* or *Censored Bloopers*—and Ray's *Cricket* has few precedents. Cricket might be regarded as a game full of long pauses for writerly reflection, and it might be relentlessly photographed and filmed, but most image making is of the action rather than of its relief. Crowds are anonymous, where they are in focus at all.

Ray's photographs delve beneath this public tip of the private world to reveal cricket in moments of regimentation and of abandon. His treatment of Steve Waugh is a good example. First we find the all-rounder looking grizzled in close-up beneath his baggy green. Then, still in his cap, we see him immersed in rehearsing the grip for his slower ball in the Nursery nets. Ray then positions Waugh beside his twin brother Mark in symmetry with the famously indistinguishable Bedser twins. The cap hasn't moved. Finally there is a glimpse of Waugh's kit—he is acknowledged as the team's messpot—and it is a truly crumpled ruin. It is Waugh as tough guy, as technician, in public history and private existence.

Crucially, Ray does nothing to deprive his subjects and the game of dignity, for this is a book by a cricketer as well as a photo journalist. The captions are plain and the design unadorned, with simple black framing lending the impression that one is actually peeping into a secret world. There is one glimpse of Ray in button-pushing action—reflected in a looking glass as part of a huddle around Viv Richards—but otherwise one is conscious only of the people and of posterity.

Australian, December 1994

Behind Closed Doors

Official histories have a bad name, being identified with vanity publishing and corporate brochures. An official history of a sporting body would seem to have still less recommending it, like a history of the Rolling Stones from the perspective of their road crew. What matters, surely, are the heroes: their acts, their art, their fame. Who else wants to know more?

In April 2006, the principals of Cricket Australia asked David Frith and myself to consider just this question, inviting us to research and write their organisation's history. What became *Inside Story* was a task first contemplated in the 1930s, and re-contemplated at intervals since, although always deferred because official histories are often not very good, because organisations are loath to give up their secrets and because the authorisation of one version of history challenges the polite fictions by which many individuals live.

Cricket Australia assured us that this no longer applied, and that they sought a 'warts and all' publication constrained only by the laws of defamation and considerations of commercial confidentiality. To a commendable degree they kept this bargain, imposing no limits on where we looked or to whom we spoke, and only a few on what we said. For the two of us, it became an unprecedented opportunity to examine the biggest existing collection of primary source documents on Australian cricket.

These were both compendious and a total mess, but they included priceless antiques: Bill Woodfull's woebegone reflections on Bodyline ('I am of the opinion that Mr Warner is against the theory ... but that the professional players are too strong in their influence') and his unvarnished view of Bradman ('the sooner he realised he could not captain an Australian team the better'); and Bradman himself on his Catholic contemporaries ('I don't think there is any doubt at all that there was a group of people, O'Reilly would have been one and Fingleton could have been another for certain, who wanted Stan McCabe to be captain') and on Kerry Packer ('Boy, have we got a problem'). There was freedom to examine in detail and interview the antagonists in a host of recent dramas, not least those involving Shane Warne, Australian cricket's number-one management challenge.

Most fascinating was Clem Jones's aide-mémoire proving that Sir Donald Bradman recommended the cancellation of South Africa's 1971–72 tour of Australia after consultation with the prime ministers of both countries, but pledged colleagues to keep this sub rosa lest they be seen as susceptible to political pressure. Jones gave this to me with great solemnity: the last survivor of the relevant meeting in September 1971, he thought it was time the truth be known. 'If I don't tell you now,' he said, 'I'll probably never tell anyone.' He died seven months later. Under no circumstance other than an official history would such a disclosure have come to light: it came close to justifying the whole exercise at a stroke.

Wisden Cricketers' Almanack, 2008

Odd Men Out

Cricket is a funny game that partakes of its fun seriously. Only a game so traditional, so formal and so ritualised could find so much scope for the odd, the unexpected and the ridiculous. For 'unusual occurrences' to be noted, there must be a firmly understood sense of the usual. So it is perhaps not surprising to find such a wealth of the bizarre in the sporting world's most po-faced and pedantically exact pages: the 144 editions of *Wisden Cricketers' Almanack*.

Lately, with its 'Chronicle' and its 'Index of Unusual Occurrences', *Wisden* has drawn attention to the quaint and the quirky concealed in its bulk. But it's a custom that stretches back to its earliest editions, when the almanack's compilers showed uncommon relish for contests like One Leg v One Arm, Bats v Broomsticks, and Sixteen of Sheffield v Sixteen of the Country Around Sheffield, where the cumulative age of the participants was 2036 years. Even when snorting the snuff of Victorian respectability, *Wisden* did not cease its surveillances with what took place on the field. In reports of Oxford v Cambridge, Eton v Harrow and Canterbury Week during the nineteenth century, the cricket vies for importance and is sometimes decidedly secondary to the social whirl, whether it is the university fixture of June 1877 brought to a halt by slowly promenading society belles ('Truly said a 20-years' regular attendant at Lord's, "It is a sight that never had an equal on a cricket-ground"') or the programme performed by the 'Old Stagers' during their theatrics at Canterbury four years later ('The Charming Woman', 'Out of Light', 'Tit for Tat', 'A Thumping Legacy' and 'Hester's Mystery').

Thus *Parachutist at Fine Leg*: a personal selection of episodes, irruptions, vignettes, digressions, detours and more than a few debacles, all reported in the classic *Wisden* vein. The title story pertains to one Anthony Adams Jnr, a Chilean cricketer-cum-parachutist who combined his two great interests by arriving for a 2004 game with his club La Dehesa from above, 'landing at fine leg, peeling off his gear and taking his place in the field at the very spot where he landed'. What gives this story the authentic *Wisden* stamp is neither the parachute nor Chile—it is the insistent exactitude of the fielding position, fine leg.

Unusual occurrences in cricket might be divided between those that are endogenous, occurring within the game, and exogenous, transpiring when there is some visitation from or reminder of the world outside. The first category here is represented principally by extraordinary feats of batting, bowling, fielding and umpiring; curious games and curious players; and, a hardy perennial, instances of ethical elasticity. *Wisden* had an eye and ear for this even in the days of *Rule Britannia* and *Vitai Lampada*, and wasn't always as censorious as might be imagined. The brothers Grace, happy enough to 'play the game' but keener on winning it, were especially beloved. Abducting prospective teammates, appealing for everything including hit the ball twice, WG strides majestically through these pages; there's also the superbly adamant EM, telling an umpire who had just called over: 'Shut up, I am going to have another.'

High dudgeon and high-handedness are complementary influences in this period. *Wisden* reported Derbyshire's John Hulme's refusal to take the field in June 1894 because of 'personal grievance against one of the players' arising from some 'unpleasantness', Somerset's HT Hewett retirement from a match at Scarborough in September 1895 after 'insulting remarks' from the crowd, Neville Cardus's tirelessly tactless hero Archie MacLaren dogmatically ending a game because of a heel print in the pitch, and the quintessential English amateur CB Fry casually disdaining to return to a ground after rain he judged too heavy. In a time of firmer social hierarchies and a more tactful and deferential press, players arguably got away with more than they do in these days of referees, codes, omniscient television cameras and omnipotent pundits.

In a technical sense, the unusual is not guaranteed to remain so. One of this book's most illuminating historical curios is a report from June 1896 of what sounds very like a reverse sweep, Yorkshire's John Brown losing his wicket after scoring a century by 'foolishly hitting back-handed at a lob'. The stroke is next glimpsed, very specifically, sixty-nine years later, in a Single Wicket Competition, with Mushtaq Mohammed changing 'in a flash from a right-handed batsman to a left-handed player to deal with a ball pitched well outside what was originally his off stump'. On the other hand, Bernard Anderson's 'overhead tennis smash' in 1934 and Dermot Reeve's hands-free exploits against Hants in 1996 have attracted no notable adherents. And if anyone parallels Mark Pettini's twenty-seven-ball hundred last season at Leicester and the 77 runs in an over from Robert Vance in 1989–90, it will only be regrettable.

The range of exogenous variation in cricket, meanwhile, is embodied chiefly in a catalogue of meteorological and other phenomena, including the astounding season of ice cricket in the winter of 1878–79, and the veritable menagerie of animals that have gambolled and frolicked across *Wisden*'s pages: sparrows, swallows, partridges, dogs, foxes, rabbits, deer, elk, sheep, boar, bees, wasps and even a few indolent snakes. Scope for the latter has increased since the almanack began to survey off-piste cricket more closely: the elk popped up in Finland, for instance, while the boar laid waste a ground in France. But a subtle reminder of cricket's rural origins has long been threaded through *Wisden*'s pages, as well as borne on its cover since 1938 in Eric Ravilious's famous fir-fringed woodcut.

Even when the intrusions from the non-cricket realm are of the most momentous kind, *Wisden* has shown a wonderful capacity for deadpan non-surprise. Its reporting of matches in wartime—like those here disturbed by 'the Battle of Britain', 'the liberation of Europe', 'the flying bombs' and the 'prolonged wait for "all clear"' (which did not prevent a result)—is some of its most flavoursome. When a public schools game was disturbed by the detonation of a V1 200 yards from Lord's in August 1944, for instance, *Wisden* was there, timing the interruption at 'little more than half a minute' and reporting that spectators 'showed their appreciation of the boys' pluck with hearty hand-claps'. The almanack has nodded to survivors of Ladysmith, victors at Alamein, commanders at Jutland and a host of crowned heads. There are hints here of the Cold War, too, such as Eisenhower at a Test in Pakistan, and Harold Wilson at an impromptu 'Test' in Moscow, shadowed by a suspicious NKVD.

Then again, who needs war when one considers some of the exquisite tortures that have lain in wait for cricketers down the years? Here will be found batsmen dismissed by consecutive balls in different innings, dismissed by the first ball of each innings, dismissed for a 'king pair' in hat-trick, dismissed for a pair inside an hour and a quarter, and dismissed for a pair spanning a painful 54 balls; look out, too, for bowlers conceding 34 in their maiden first-class over, 38 in a six-ball over or 250 from a single hit; seeing a ball they bowled vanish in the back of a long-distance lorry; and feeling 9 kilograms of their body weight vanish in a single day's play. Cricket, as they say, tests character—if, of course, it doesn't break it first.

In its own way, *Parachutist at Fine Leg* marks an unusual occurrence seldom recognised as such: the annual publication of *Wisden*. Who today would initiate a yearly book of 1700 pages containing more than any sane person need know about the twelve months of cricket just past? Yet it lands each April with a thud of reassuring familiarity, to be pored over by the cognoscenti and obsessed over by completists. One is not merely mentioned by *Wisden*; one is incorporated in it, never to escape. The ASI Berry involved in the madcap idea of a 24-hour game of cricket on Parker's Piece in June 1973 has made the best of this, recently becoming the almanack's editor.

In the age of abundant real-time information and a culture of instant gratification, *Wisden*'s abiding popularity is deeply mysterious. It exists as a kind of statistical Stonehenge—a sentinel whose use by past generations is only dimly understood, but which somehow visibly incarnates cricket's continuity, autonomous within while also inseparable from the game it is dedicated to documenting. If cricket is a funny game, then *Wisden* is assuredly a funny book—albeit, of course, that it is imbued with the deep seriousness of cricket itself.

Introduction to *The Parachutist at Fine Leg and Other Unusual Events from Wisden*, 2007

The Long Stop

In TS Eliot's poem, it is Webster, seeing 'the skull beneath the skin', who is 'very much possessed by death'. The same might be said of *Wisden*, publisher since 1892 of more than 10 000 obituaries, a custom begun with a notice in honour of its first distinguished editor, Charles Pardon, and now pursued with a certain vigour in a section more than twice the size of twenty years ago.

This makes a grim sort of sense, in a game whose most prestigious trophy sprang from a jest about cremation. The sample you might take to fill a book, however, isn't so obvious. Not much point is served by a pageant of Bradman and Graces, so amply served by the rest of the almanack; but little purpose lies in a mere parade of the quaint or queer either. While *Peter the Lord's Cat and Other Unexpected Obituaries from Wisden* is essentially an excuse for a stroll around this most lavish mausoleum, it's also a survey of its habits of memorialising.

Wisden's obituaries today enjoy a just fame for being elegant, discursive, accurate and often whimsical. The almanack's interest is pricked by cricket, but as *Peter the Lord's Cat* suggests it has always paid regard to a life well lived, with particular affection for all-round sportsmen (CW Alcock, CN Bruce, Max Woosnam), writers (JM Barrie, Samuel Beckett, Sir Arthur Conan Doyle, PG Wodehouse, Terrence Rattigan, Rupert Brooke, John Fowles, EW Hornung,

Peter Tinniswood) and generally heroes and notables (Douglas Bader, Lord Alexander, Lord Birkett, sundry kings, miscellaneous prime ministers). 'It may seem a little strange to include Cardinal Manning's name in a cricket obituary,' admitted the compilers of the 1893 edition, 'but inasmuch as he played for Harrow against Winchester ... his claim cannot be disputed.' One wonders if it brought comfort to Captain Oates as he faced his fatal blizzard that he would in due course be memorialised by *Wisden* on the basis of having 'played cricket for his House as a lower boy at Eton'.

'But it's more than a game,' said Tom Brown famously, 'it's an institution.' *Wisden*'s obituaries have preserved that sense of cricket as concerning more than on-field feats; a preparation for life when it did not remain in the main part of it. Prime Minister Lord Home, the almanack proposed, was in politics 'always at his best on a sticky wicket'; while the formative influence on the renowned pacifist Baron Soper was killing a boy with a bouncer in a junior game. It is sometimes complained that *Wisden* grants disproportionate and anachronistic attention to public schoolboy cricket. It has, nonetheless, guaranteed a steady stream of quirky death notices. Thanks to Kenneth Gandar-Dower's appearance for Harrow against Winchester in 1927, readers were enriched by tales of his exploits in six other sports, as an aviator, big-game hunter and trainer of a team of cheetahs racing on London greyhound tracks. Occasionally, in fact, the attention might be a little unwanted. Poor Victor Eberle, who died at 'about 90' in Bristol in 1974, was of interest to *Wisden* for dropping Albert Collins at 20 en route to 628 not out at Clifton College in 1899. Nothing more is reported of the hapless Eberle—he might have discovered a life-saving surgical treatment or broken the world land-speed record in a Stutz Bearcat. Yet in *Wisden*'s judgement, and therefore cricket's, he remained, even unto death, a butter-fingered boy.

Another strand that emerges is *Wisden*'s strong martial tradition, perhaps instilled in the world wars when the almanack strove to keep faith with collectors by continuing publication. Entries with a military flavour could easily fill their own book; *Peter the Lord's Cat* takes a cross-section of lives cut short, including Brig-Gen Roland Bradford, the British Army's youngest general, and Admiral Horace Hood, who died a fighting sailor's death at Jutland, but also survivors, such as Major George McCubbin, who shot down the German ace Max Immelman in June 1916, and Arthur Evans, an incorrigible POW camp escapologist before his Test debut. Despite this, *Wisden* is not an especially belligerent book. It gave more space to benighted Private Percy Hardy, a promising Surrey Colt who slit his own throat rather than go to war, than Lieutenant Sidney Woodroffe, winner of the Victoria Cross; it admired Brigadier Michael Harbottle, scorer of 156 in his only first-class innings and organiser of Generals for Peace and Disarmament; and it liked, above all, a man who took war in his stride, like Col William Wilkinson, whose wounds almost cost him his right hand, but did not prevent his scoring a hundred hundreds mainly with his left.

Certain entries in *Peter the Lord's Cat* are there, I am bound to admit, mainly because the individuals are personal favourites: Bob Crockett, Home Gordon, the gilded brotherhoods of Ashton and Crawley, the circumspect Arthur Clark who thought he should return to driving trains after failing to score in nine innings for Gloucestershire, and the salty Cec Pepper who 'could talk, spit, chew, belch and pass wind simultaneously'. I've a weakness, too, for improbable feats of endurance, from Harry Coxon's fifty-four years of scoring for Notts and Jimmy Cannon's sixty-five years in service at Lord's to Baron Walsingham's 1070 grouse in a day and David Halfyard's campervan with 400 000 kilometres on the clock.

Wisden, of course, revels in a record, however obscure, whether it's the 250 winners trained for the Queen Mother by Major Peter Cazalet or the 624 000 weeds that Charles Millar plucked for Marylebone. The almanack also seems to have retained a sneaking regard for feats of pedestrianism, from Gerald Lewis ('a fanatical walker' who patrolled Queen's Park Oval 'at a ferocious pace') to Bob Crisp (who 'told he had incurable cancer' promptly 'spent a year walking around Crete'), and from George Lacy ('one of the very few men who could claim to have walked across Africa from East to West before the Boer War') to Frank Harris ('he walked from Bidborough to London on his 70th birthday because his father did the same thing and told him that he would not be able to do so when he was 70').

Then, of course, there's the book's eponymous hero, 'a well-known cricket watcher at Lord's,' described by MCC's secretary as 'a cat of great character' who 'loved publicity'—the kind of cat, it seems, who would probably have appealed to TS Eliot in his guise as Old Possum. Coincidentally, both cat and cat fancier died in the same year, and they'd have made a pleasant pairing; alas, the poet hadn't done quite enough to endear himself to the almanack to engage its interest.

Wisden Cricketer, May 2006

Through the Looking Glass

A story is told of the young Tom Stoppard applying for a job in Fleet Street. 'It says here you're interested in politics,' said the interviewer. 'Okay. Who's the Home Secretary?' Stoppard blandly returned his gaze. 'I said I was interested,' he answered. 'Not obsessed.'

For the past six or so years, I have been interested in, rather than obsessed by, a former Lord Mayor of Sydney, William P McElhone. Once, I would scarcely have recognised his name. Then I began researching the early history of Australian cricket administration, and this tough, smart, insouciant Sydney lawyer stood out from all the other fob-watched, massively moustached men of means influential in such circles a century ago.

In the pioneering days of Australian cricket, the star players were at the centre, aided and abetted by the Melbourne Cricket Club, whose role was very similar to that occupied in England by the Marylebone Cricket Club. Australian cricket might have developed along lines quite similar to England's but for McElhone, then only in his early thirties. In debate, it was said, McElhone 'pranced like a warhorse'. Pursuing a line of enquiry, he was 'as tenacious as a terrier after a rat'. As the inaugural secretary of the Australian Board of Control, he more or less invented the federal governance structure of Australian cricket that survives to this day, marginalising both the Melbourne Club and the players.

Yet, when McElhone disappeared into the shadows of municipal politics, he left little to remember him by, dying without issue in 1933. All that survives at Cricket Australia are the minute books he kept, in a superb copperplate hand; when I searched high and low six years ago, I could find just one small portrait of him on his own. Otherwise, he stared out of a handful of group shots, wearing an inscrutable half-smile and his trademark round spectacles, looking for all the world like a Dickensian beadle.

Like I said, this wasn't an obsession; just an interest. I moved on. But it ate at me. Australia is full of such figures: hugely important in ways now only dimly understood, yet perplexingly difficult to research. So, from time to time, I'd go back to him. One day, I decided to order his birth and death certificates; another, I trawled through newspapers to locate as many obituaries as possible. Then last year, on the spur of the moment, I rang the Sydney law firm that still bears his name. As I suspected, the receptionist apologised: 'I'm sorry. We've no connection with the family. In fact, I'm not even sure there *is* a family.' Oh well ... But a couple of days later, she rang back. She'd been talking to some people in the office. There was this old partner who'd retired some years back: he might be able to help. I'll call him Mr Smith.

Mr Smith was quite difficult to reach. I rang him weekly for a couple of months; no answer. I checked that I had the right number; it was, so I persisted. Then one day, he answered. Sorry, he'd been overseas. Billy McElhone? Why, yes. Yes, indeed. About thirty years ago, when the firm had been moving premises, various of Billy McElhone's effects had been earmarked for disposal. Hmm, Mr Smith had thought: 'One day, somebody may want these.' He had put them in a trunk. He had put the trunk ... well, somewhere. He promised to look.

Frabjous day—if not quite calloo callay. Patience was needed. Months passed, then more months. In my diary, I pencilled 'Mr Smith' at eight-weekly intervals. Had he had a chance to look? No, he'd been away. No, he would need to search his farm. Mr

Smith's manners were always impeccable—he always called me 'Mr Haigh'—but I didn't want it to seem like I was importuning him. I beat down my expectations. The trunk would be lost. The contents would be junk. It didn't matter anyway. Because, just to reiterate, this was only an interest; not an obsession. Finally, nearly a year after our first contact, Mr Smith advised that he had found the trunk, and retrieved it. We arranged to meet next time I was in Sydney.

So it was that in May this year I knocked at an apartment in a big Sydney block. Mr Smith, a softly spoken, silver-haired gentleman in his seventies, admitted me to rooms accoutred in immaculate taste. The furniture and ornamentation bore their expense lightly; the walls were lined with Old Masters, his lifetime passion. What were they worth? Hundreds of thousands? Easily. Millions? Very probably. But I wasn't there for art. My consuming interest lay in the kitchen.

The trunk wasn't big, nor was it full. But what had survived was more than enough to gratify any interest. Letters, postcards, diaries, legal files, newspaper clippings, invitations and menus for official dinners of the kind popular at the time, featuring such exotic marvels as 'Les Cotelettes d'Agneau aux Petit Pots' and old favourites like 'Assorted Wine Jellies'. There were his little books of spiritual solace, 'Catholic Piety' and 'Garden of the Soul': one of nine children, McElhone was a rock-ribbed Roman Catholic.

Suddenly there were more pictures of McElhone than anyone could need, including a framed photograph in full mayoral regalia, which apparently hung in the reception of his chambers. There was a signed photograph, too, of a young soldier. He was, Mr Smith explained, McElhone's articled clerk, who had enlisted in the AIF and been killed in France: the picture had reposed on his boss's desk ever after. Finally, from a book of old cricket scores, slid a small, hard, rectangular case in age-stiffened leather. I opened it. There they were: the spectacles, ownership corroborated by the handwritten inscription inside the lid, 'W. P. McElhone'.

Glasses are the most intimate of items: they suit only the wearer, and not merely their eyesight but the frame of their face. McElhone's have arms of the sort that hook round the ears; putting them on would have been quite a deliberate act. They are small, flat, not quite symmetrical and might almost have been designed for staring through severely, or glancing over dubiously; removed, they would naturally conduce to thoughtful fiddling or animated gesturing. And through these glasses, it was heady to realise, were overseen the decisive meetings in the management of this country's most popular game. They're sitting uppermost on my desk right now, Mr Smith having been kind enough to pass the trunk's contents on in the name of research. And you're right. I confess it. This *was* an interest; *now* it's an obsession.

Monthly, September 2007